THE SPICE COMPANION

THE SPICE COMPANION

A GUIDE TO THE WORLD OF SPICES

LIOR LEV SERCARZ
founder of LA BOÎTE

with
JAIME GOTTLIEB

Photographs by
THOMAS SCHAUER

Illustrations by
NADINE BERNARD WESTCOTT

Design by
CHRISTINE FISCHER

CLARKSON POTTER/PUBLISHERS
New York

Published in the United States by Clarkson Potter/Publishers,
an imprint of the Crown Publishing Group, a division of
Penguin Random House LLC, New York.
crownpublishing.com
clarksonpotter.com

CLARKSON POTTER is a trademark and POTTER with colophon
is a registered trademark of Penguin Random House LLC.

Library of Congress Cataloging-in-Publication Data
Names: Sercarz, Lior Lev, author. | Gottlieb, Jaime, author. | Schauer,
    Thomas, 1969- photographer (expression) | Westcott, Nadine Bernard,
    illustrator.
Title: The spice companion : a guide to the world of spices / Lior Lev Sercarz, founder of La Boîte
    with Jaime Gottlieb ; photography by Thomas Schauer ; illustrations by Nadine Bernard Westcott.
Description: First edition. | New York : Clarkson/Potter Publishers, [2016] | Includes index.
Identifiers: LCCN 2016004584 (print) | LCCN 2016014614 (ebook) |
    ISBN 9781101905463 (hardcover) | ISBN 9781101905470 (eISBN) | ISBN 9781101905470 (ebook)
Subjects: LCSH: Spices.
Classification: LCC TX406 .S47 2016 (print) | LCC TX406 (ebook) |
    DDC 641.3/383—dc23
LC record available at http://lccn.loc.gov/2016004584

ISBN 978-1-101-90546-3
eBook ISBN 978-1-101-90547-0

Printed in China

Book and cover design by
CHRISTINE FISCHER

10 9 8 7 6 5

First Edition

To my parents,
Ayala and Moshe Lev Sercarz,
for letting me sail into the horizon

To Lisa, Luca, and Lennon,
for the daily inspiration

CONTENTS

FOREWORD BY OLIVIER ROELLINGER *9*

INTRODUCTION *11*

MY SPICE PHILOSOPHY *15*

HISTORY & ORIGIN *19*

SOURCING SPICES *23*

HOW TO BLEND SPICES *29*

STORING SPICES *35*

→

THE SPICES *39*

THE CLASSICS *296*

ACKNOWLEDGMENTS *299*

INDEX *300*

ICON KEY *303*

CONTRIBUTORS *304*

FOREWORD

I started cooking in 1982, and from that moment I began developing what I call "the French Art of Spices." Much like a nose in perfumery, I consider myself a palate in the creation of flavors. In 1998, Lior Lev Sercarz joined us as part of his internship with the Institut Paul Bocuse. He began his training at Les Maisons de Bricourt by learning bread baking in our wood oven, pastry, as well as working in the kitchen. In time, we started sharing our ideas and thoughts about spices and the stories they told about his personal narrative in Israel and mine inspired by the French East India Company. Lior was able to witness the creation of our brand Épices-Roellinger and became involved in our first communications with small producers and farmers around the world, of which we now work with about 1,200.

This book is a marvelous guide to what we call spices—the universe of fruits, grains, stems, flowers, and roots that grow in faraway places. It offers unique insights into the very things that enhance the flavors of everything we eat, providing home cooks and chefs alike access to something they don't always consider in their daily lives.

Spices create a richness and complexity, delivering a mouthful of tastes and aromas; they speak of our relationship with the unknown and unfamiliar, and of our encounters with other places in the world. They allow us to consume the vast horizons, capturing the sensations of every country and the cuisines of every place without ever leaving home. With this book, Lior enables each and every one of us to access this Garden of Eden.

OLIVIER ROELLINGER,
chef-owner, LES MAISONS DE BRICOURT,
Brittany, France

INTRODUCTION

I was born and raised on Kibbutz Dan in northern Israel. Although it was a great place to grow up as a child, food was the least exciting thing about it. The generation of Jews who escaped Europe before the war, or came after, built this country on the idea that food was purely a means of survival. Unfortunately, my kibbutz was also founded by these same eastern Europeans, who left behind many of the culinary traditions of their native homes; all I can remember from my early days is boiled, flavorless dishes —too often oversweetened or way too vinegary.

Luckily, we took trips to Kiryat Shmona, the nearest town, and Tel Aviv, where street food offered a variety of new flavors and ingredients. Keep in mind that until the early '90s, the culinary scene in Israel, generally speaking, was as interesting as hummus in a can! The best meals were at home, and if you were lucky enough, you had a Moroccan or Persian friend who would invite you over for dinner.

There were also interesting culinary influences from our neighbors just over the Lebanese border, only a half mile away. We shopped and ate in areas that are now part of Palestine, and there were a few Druze villages just twenty minutes north where we could enjoy freshly made falafel, grilled meats, and sweets, as well as a delicious Arabic coffee spiced with cardamom. These cultures greatly impacted our meals at home, bringing new ingredients and dishes into our limited repertoire. Today, Israel has close to seventy different ethnic groups and, in turn, access to each of their uniquely authentic cuisines. We are finally seeing a culinary revolution that is as exciting as anywhere else on the planet. Israeli cuisine has certainly come a long way.

Growing up in the Galilee did have its advantages: we were surrounded by nature. The Dan River, which flows into the Jordan, brought schools of rainbow trout, which we'd catch, stuff to the gills with wild herbs, and cook whole, simply, on the grill. Within reach were sprawling apple orchards, cornfields, and citrus groves. As kids we would venture out and fill up on everything we could pick ourselves, especially since we knew what was waiting for us back at the communal dining room for dinner.

Still, not every dish in the kibbutz was worth avoiding. One highlight from those days was the flatbreads my friends and I would bake in makeshift dirt ovens and eat with sour labneh cheese and fragrant za'atar, a mix of sesame, sumac, thyme, and other herbs. Picking fresh thyme, oregano, or rosemary was a matter of going out into the garden or into the nearby fields where they grew wild. (To this day, I have a hard time paying for herbs packed in plastic clamshells at the supermarket.)

After we left the kibbutz, I started cooking because my mother worked late and my sisters and I needed to eat. It was that simple. She would leave ingredients and directions out on the counter, and we were on our own. Often the recipes would hail from one of my family's different cultures—my mother's father was Tunisian and his wife was Transylvanian.

When I was seven, my father's work brought us to Belgium for four years, and we would venture to nearby Paris or Holland sometimes on the weekend. We all brought a little something back from that experience—I'm just glad my mother returned to Israel with a new love of cooking and the exposure to what we considered exotic ingredients at the time. Seafood, which was not readily available in Israel—mussels and clams simply don't thrive in the Mediterranean Sea—and pork were introduced to our dinner table. Even though kosher laws did not permit either, it was certainly a nice break from mashed chickpeas and tahini. (Was my family kosher? It depends who you ask.)

As teenagers my sisters and I had to work one day a week and half of our summer vacations at the kibbutz. For a while, I did my part by picking apples and avocados, but I mainly worked in our fish farms harvesting trout, carp, and tilapia. I think that my first spice blend was made on the banks of a large dirt fishpond. After a long day of harvesting fish, we started a small fire and cleaned a few tilapias. I remember grabbing some chile flakes, salt, paprika, garlic, and fresh za'atar leaves from our cooler and coating the fish with this impromptu mixture before grilling them. This was to become our signature fish rub for the next few years.

When I turned nineteen, I became a sergeant in the Israeli Army to complete my mandatory military service. It was the first time I was officially in charge of a kitchen—one of my many duties during that time. After my service ended, my older sister convinced me to do some traveling. I spent the next year venturing through South America, eagerly exploring every open-air market and bazaar I came across. Seeing endless mounds of chiles, merkén spice (a blend of smoked pepper and coriander), and Chilean Chiloé berry, none of which I had encountered before, sent me on a quest to learn about their origins and how they grew. I visited family-run farms in Peru and Ecuador to watch the chile harvests and ventured to Colombia to see firsthand how cardamom was grown.

Upon returning to Israel, I began seeing markets in an entirely new light. I loved the interaction with the vendors and the bargaining, particularly that Persian guy at Levinsky Spice Market in Tel Aviv. Each bag of spices at the market was a journey to a faraway place. Even now, I can't begin to count how many times I walked the three-block-long spice market looking for a new treasure.

CULINARY SCHOOL & OLIVIER ROELLINGER

My newfound passion for spices brought me to search for a job in a professional kitchen. But without any culinary school training, I couldn't even land a job as a dishwasher. After many attempts, I was lucky to meet chef Gil Frank, who owned the Menta catering company and who loved the fact that I hadn't been jaded by the culinary industry yet. He hired me as a sous chef and taught me some basic kitchen skills, and we spent three fantastic years working together. He encouraged me to attend culinary school, and I owe him a lot for having faith in me and for his support.

On his suggestion, I enrolled at the Institut Paul Bocuse in Lyon, France, where I would learn the techniques needed to make these ingredients come to life. During my first and second years, I had to do externships lasting six to seven months. When it was time for my second externship, one of the chefs at school who knew how fascinated I was with spices lent me a book by Olivier Roellinger. I knew nothing about him or his restaurant. I read that book twenty times in the next few days, and I couldn't understand how this worked: a French chef

in Brittany was seasoning local ingredients with exotic spices from all over the world. I always thought the French were satisfied with salt, pepper, and a sprig of fresh thyme.

I immediately sent him an application letter. It came back denied, saying they did not accept interns. So I sent a second one. To my surprise, I was accepted. I arrived there on a spring afternoon and was greeted by Olivier's wife, Jane, who told me to place my things in the attic, where I would sleep, and to be downstairs for dinner service at five p.m. A few hours later, I found myself in a small kitchen surrounded by many types of fish, seafood, vegetables, and bags of turmeric, galangal, and curry leaves. Seeing these spices in a French kitchen was certainly a first; it took me a few days to understand what Chef Roellinger was doing.

Cancale is located twenty minutes or so from the port of Saint-Malo on the Atlantic Ocean, once an important harbor for ships trading coffee, vanilla, and other spices from the Far East. Olivier was reviving this forgotten cultural exchange using modern-day techniques and seasonal ingredients.

I wanted to learn everything from him—the history and trade routes, the larger story. But Olivier, the consummate mentor, pushed me to do my own research and develop my own style. I needed to connect with spices by creating my own path, not by simply following his. I didn't understand it at the time, but now, years later, I can only thank him for doing so.

When I moved back to Lyon, I worked in a small restaurant where, for the first time, I was able to create my own dishes and use spices as I saw fit. The city had a large Lebanese and Armenian community, so I was fortunate enough to have access to mahlab seeds (page 178) and sumac (page 260). After three great years there, I moved to New York City in 2002, ready for change.

NEW YORK CITY & DANIEL BOULUD

I joined Chef Daniel Boulud's flagship restaurant, Daniel, in September 2002. I began by working in the private dining room and soon established a great relationship with him. He was always fond of spices and fascinated by Middle Eastern cuisine, and when he found out about our shared passions, he had a spice shelf built at the restaurant so I could create blends for his kitchen. Or, more than likely, so I would stop bothering him.

While I was there, Daniel asked me to be part of a team that would create a line of spice blends to be sold in stores. This was the first time I had to think beyond the flavors, scents, and creative aspects of blending and consider costs and budgets. It was a great exercise that helped me when I founded La Boîte.

During my five and a half years with Daniel, I started understanding that, although I had been cooking professionally for nearly fifteen years by then, I was losing the desire to work in a restaurant. My days felt repetitive, and I could not step out of the kitchen to see the diners coming in to eat the dishes I had worked so hard to prepare. I needed to try something else, and what kept coming to mind was what I enjoyed most: using spices and baking cookies.

In 2007 I was offered a sous chef position in the private dining room of a large bank. For me, it was the perfect opportunity to step aside from the traditional restaurant world and have some time to think about the future. I was able to combine a trip for a wedding in the United Kingdom with a twenty-four-hour visit to see Olivier in Cancale. After a fantastic dinner together, I met with Olivier the next day and told him about my plans: to start a cookie and spice business. He quickly stopped me, assuring me that I already knew what I wanted to do. He was incredibly supportive, and before we parted he was kind enough to suggest I call my new company "La Boîte à Biscuits," which I did.

LA BOÎTE

In 2007, with Olivier's wisdom and too much free time in the evenings and on weekends while working as a corporate chef, I started baking cookies in my apartment, experimenting with adding sweet or savory spices to them. Through a referral, I got a call from Laurent Tourondel, a French chef in New York, who was about to open a few places and asked me to create some unique spice blends for him. I jumped at the opportunity and created some blends and special packaging for him. The next thing I knew, I had my first client and seven products on the market. Within a couple of years, my dream really started to take shape, and I began to believe that I could make it happen.

I spent six months writing a lengthy, well-thought-out plan for a cookie and spice shop, but could not find a soul to invest in my concept. Following the good advice of a friend, I realized I might be able to pull it off on my own. And so there I was, looking for a commercial space and affordable equipment. In New York City. After visiting more than thirty places and having countless meetings with real estate brokers, I found the perfect space in Hell's Kitchen. I signed the lease in June 2009 and opened the doors of La Boîte that October.

My new space would become the home of La Boîte à Biscuits and La Boîte à Epice. Though the spices have somewhat taken over the cookies, even now I bake two biscuit collections every year, each featuring a different artist and blend of spices. Today, I make more than sixty spice blends and have clients across the world—from the United States, Puerto Rico, and Canada to France, Singapore, Israel, and Dubai.

I am constantly striving to perfect my sourcing and blending. The growing demand for spices and interest in global fare pushes me to keep innovating and learning. It took twenty years of cooking, baking, and working in professional restaurants to prepare me for what I do today. And I love doing it every day.

I wrote this book because I have found that most people know relatively little about spices: where they are from, how they grow, what they look like in their natural environment, how labor-intensive it is to harvest many of them, and, ultimately, how to use them and be inspired by them in the kitchen. The selection of spices in this book is intentional. It's not just about the exotic and unknown, but about what people already have in their pantries. Here is a collection of spices that 1) can be found anywhere and 2) are essential in certain parts of the world. I could've written about hundreds more, but some are impossible to get and others I simply don't use. This is not a spice encyclopedia in the traditional sense; this is a comprehensive guide of the 102 spices I think you should know about and use. My hope is that this book will be something people will find helpful in their kitchens every day. Or perhaps they will at least sit down and read to learn about world cuisines and the flavors of distant lands. My goal is to encourage everyone to try something new, to take their cooking to the next level, and to find new inspiration in the kitchen.

LIOR LEV SERCARZ

MY SPICE PHILOSOPHY

I believe that cooking is based mainly on three things: ingredients, seasoning, and technique. When I say "seasoning," I mean spices. I consider everything in a dry form that can be ground and used to add flavor to be a spice, even if the dictionary says differently. For most people, spices are cayenne, black pepper, and the like, but for me, they are also herbs, roots, bark, berries, rhizomes, and nearly any part of a plant that enhances the taste of food. Any dried ingredient that elevates food or drink is a spice.

Although pure ingredients are tasty on their own, they still need a touch of spice to reveal their layers of flavor and really bring them to life. Seasoning can be done before and during cooking, or just before serving. You can even season raw ingredients and eat them, as in beef tartare or a salad. This is the beauty of spices: they can be used and enjoyed even without cooking.

The problem with most recipes is that they end with "season with salt and pepper," when what they really should say is "season with sodium and heat." Each recipe should have at least the three basic flavors: acidity, saltiness, and heat. But it's really up to you how you are going to deliver them. If all you use are salt and pepper, at least make an effort to buy the best-quality salt and pepper. Instead of using generic table salt, you might want to try fleur de sel or Maldon sea salt. The same goes for pepper: try white or green peppercorns instead of your typical black peppercorns and explore their unique attributes. Not all salts and peppers are created equal.

Spices are important to every meal and even beverage throughout the day. Why wouldn't you want your coffee, tea, water, or even your breakfast cereal to taste better? Spices not only enrich dishes and ingredients, but also serve as substitutes for sugar and sodium in some cases. The sensation you get after eating certain spices creates the perception of sweetness or saltiness without actually adding those elements to a dish—take Sichuan pepper (page 254) or celery seed (page 86), for example. It has also been proven that consuming well-seasoned food satisfies your hunger faster, giving you better control over how much you eat. We don't use spices solely for the purpose of healthy eating, but it is an added bonus.

I am a big fan of using what you have on hand. Take cinnamon, for example—particularly if you don't usually like it. It offers a natural sweetness without adding sugar. You can add it to tomato sauce for pasta; it works perfectly well in Sicily, where North African influences shine through on the plate. Reverse your thinking by substituting the spices you typically associate with sweet dishes for those you would only consider using in savory ones.

Or go one step further and base your next meal on a spice or spice blend you already have. Rather than buying a rack of lamb and then trying to figure out what to do with it, use spices, whether a great jar of Aleppo chile powder or whole coriander seeds, to drive a recipe. Spices should be as important as everything else in a dish.

And don't be afraid to expand your horizons beyond the familiar. The next time you go out to eat, evaluate the flavors, textures, and scents that make a dish authentic to its place of origin and its people. What makes a sambal taste like a sambal, or a shakshuka unleash its rich, tomatoey heat? Think about how rattling cascabel chiles are used in Mexico, or how Australians favor local lemon verbena leaves over citrus fruits to impart bright, fresh notes. They know what works with their indigenous ingredients because they have been using them for centuries. You don't have to use them in the exact same way, but it's a good place to start. Transform your favorite recipes by incorporating techniques you've read about in other recipes. Or prepare something you make all the time, and add a little bit of spice to see what happens. It can be as simple as sprinkling ground ginger on your morning toast. Maybe it doesn't work, but maybe it does. Imagine the upside of trying.

In the twenty or so years that I have cooked in professional kitchens, I have noticed a serious lack of knowledge about spices. We are not all born in a culture where they are essential to the cuisine. More than likely, we actually use very few at all. Spices have long been thought of as something only found in exotic, ethnic cuisines, not straying far from their countries of origin. When most people eat Indian food, they don't imagine using those flavors and spices in other types of cuisines.

I often meet people at my shop who are surprised and delighted when I tell them they can use spices they associate with Spanish paella, Vietnamese phở, or even Thai curry in the dishes they make and eat every day at home. The notion that they can use unfamiliar flavors in familiar recipes is enlightening; it frees them of the preconceived idea that they can only use spices in the foods they are found in traditionally. People start to think of using spices as a way to accessorize what they eat with something new, rather than replacing it entirely. It's a first step.

Today, we are traveling more and farther away than we ever did in the past, discovering new foods and ways of cooking that were never accessible before. And with these new culinary discoveries come spices, some of the best tools in your kitchen. They tell the story of a place, stirring up the emotions and memories of your journeys without you ever leaving your kitchen. They transport you to faraway places and can transform your everyday cooking into something exciting and ever-changing.

SPICE BLENDS

I realized over the years that most people, both at home and in professional kitchens, do not have the time or patience to deal with whole spices or make their own blends. The result is that they use very few, if any, or only add whole spices to a dish and then discard them before serving. It is perfectly fine to buy spices already ground if you're confident in their quality, but you'll get much better flavor and scent from whole spices. And if you are going to try blending your own, starting with whole spices gives you one option preground spices don't: variety in texture.

But before you turn on your spice grinder, consider the blends you are already familiar with. If you've ever bought a spice blend at your grocery store, you probably noticed the label specifying a predetermined usage: maybe it was a Smoky BBQ Rub, or a Fish or Steak Seasoning. As a teenager, I remember asking my mom if I could use the Chicken Spice for fish. She immediately replied that since the label says to use it with chicken, it should not be used for fish—or anything but chicken. Why limit a spice or a blend to just one preparation? What if every blend were used in different dishes, in every meal throughout the day?

That thought led to one of the first decisions I made when I founded La Boîte: to create blends that have no specific usage or purpose. Each mixture has the ability to be good with whatever you choose to put it on, and you can elevate and customize your food and drinks with the flavors you love. You can also say good-bye to the many jars of old, random spices that you will never use anyway.

MAKING YOUR OWN BLENDS

There are many reasons you should make your own blends: one thoughtfully mixed blend is the sum of many good spices, which creates a unique flavor profile; blends are ready to use when you are ready to cook; to give you control of the quality and freshness of each spice (you never know how long a blend has been sitting on a grocery store shelf); and you can make something you truly enjoy, that suits your style of cooking, and that you will use again and again.

My approach to blending is very similar to my approach to cooking:

1. Keep it simple.

2. Have a good idea of what you want to achieve before you get started.

3. Tell a story.

4. Create a complex, layered, and balanced combination.

5. Deliver an exciting flavor profile that makes you think.

PIERRE POIVRE AND
LA COMPAGNIE DES INDES

During my spice research, I came across the name Pierre Poivre, a French missionary. When I first read about him, I was blown away by his story. He's the sole person responsible for putting spices on the supermarket shelf; he is *the* reason La Boîte exists today. Poivre was part of La Compagnie des Indes, the French East India Company, one of many trading companies established by European countries in hope of getting into the spice business. They set out to exploit spice trade to Asia, India, and the East Indies. Poivre was one of the company's many agents hired and sent to distant countries to establish work relationships, while also bringing with them the word of Christianity.

Pierre Poivre ("Peter Pepper" in English) was destined for this. His evangelical work sent him to China and Indochina, where, through a miscommunication, he was imprisoned. After talking his way out from behind bars, he left his mission and headed home to France. During his journey in the South China Seas, he was injured in a run-in with a British naval ship—France and Britain were rumored to be at war at the time. The British left him in Dutch-claimed Djakarta (then Batavia), where he was first introduced to the spice trade. He was particularly spellbound by the cloves, nutmeg, and cinnamon he found there.

Upon stopping over in Pondicherry en route to France, he met an officer of the French East India Company whom he would later follow to the island of Mauritius. It was in Mauritius that his devotion to agriculture, something I admire, led him to plant a beautiful garden that still exists today. When he realized that the climate in Mauritius was comparable to that of the Spice Islands, he knew he could disrupt the Dutch monopoly.

So despite the Dutch attempts to sterilize seeds—nutmeg, in particular—Poivre smuggled out a number of plants and fertile seeds and planted them in Mauritius, where his efforts began the slow demise of the spice-monopoly era. It is because of him that we can buy a jar of nutmeg for much less than a brick of gold. I named a pepper blend after him to honor and celebrate this spice rebel who allowed free trade. He made spices accessible to everyone. If I had to explain what I am trying to achieve at La Boîte, it has everything to do with this guy.

HISTORY & ORIGIN

When I started La Boîte, one of my first exercises was to read (or reread) the history of the spice trade and educate myself on how we got to where we are today. The stories most people take for granted influence my cooking every day; they transport me to another time and place and inform how I buy and blend spices—even how I name my blends. The way people used spices centuries ago, the factors that determine costs, and much of how they are grown and harvested haven't really changed. So the history of spices, for me, is very much the present. It's part of my daily life and every decision I make for my business. If you want to blend or use spices, you have to start at the beginning.

Spices have always been desired, particularly by those who could not easily access them. They were darlings of the wealthy, who threw lavish feasts to show off dishes seasoned with rare and expensive saffron, nutmeg, and cloves. To manage the growing demand, the spice trade and the Age of Discovery were born.

Following the early Asian, Indian, and Greco-Roman trades, Arabs caravanned desert landscapes to connect the Middle East and southern Asia as early as 900 BC. They held a monopoly on the trade route with fairy tales about cassia and cinnamon being guarded by dangerous creatures. To find alternate routes, lengthy, dangerous crusades set off by sea—the Romans sailed from Egypt to India in search of coveted pepper, cinnamon, nutmeg, cloves, and ginger, and the Europeans sought exclusive trade routes to India, China, and the islands of Indonesia, including the Moluccas (Spice Islands).

Marco Polo's exploration of Asia in the thirteenth century established Venice as a major port city, and later, Vasco da Gama's journey around the Cape of Good Hope connected him with Calcutta, India, and its bounty of exotic flavors. Spain and Portugal were no longer going to pay full price for spices if they could get them directly. This was the same reason Christopher Columbus was sent out on his fabled voyage to the New World: he was meant to find a new route to China, India, and the spice islands of Asia, but instead landed on what would become the Americas. His voyage was fruitful nonetheless: he brought back chiles, allspice, and vanilla, which disseminated across Europe.

Simply by being along the route, ports developed into important trade centers. Convoys would stop off on their way to some other destination, sharing what they had collected with the locals before traveling to the New World, or wherever else. This influenced trade but also unintentionally blended food cultures and traditions; it is the reason ginger (page 134) flavors Yemenite coffee and that saffron (page 238) stains Italian risotto red.

Because the Portuguese, English, and Dutch wanted to control these foreign lands in order to trade the spices and crops growing there, they built European colonies to occupy spice-rich places all over the world. Wars were fought, laws were put into place, and drastic measures were taken to maintain strict monopolies on spices.

The Dutch even went to the extent of destroying any clove plant not owned by them and punishing anyone caught growing the plants or harvesting seeds. They limited export by dumping any excess into the sea—the very definition of supply and demand in the seventeenth and eighteenth centuries. The Dutch conquered the islands surrounding the Malay Peninsula and the city of Malacca and put exclusive trading rights in place for pepper along the Malabar Coast. They had taken over the spice trade in Asia, for a time.

With the onset of the Industrial Revolution in the late 1700s and early 1800s, spices slowly began to lose their glory. The encroaching colonies disappeared and the areas where they formerly reigned gained independence. European, and in particular French, cuisines, which did not use many spices, became increasingly popular. Spices became easier to transport, culinary trends changed, and the mass production of foods required fewer spices for preservation. The cost of spices dropped, making them more accessible to everyone and less of a sign of wealth. Spices became reserved for Asian or Middle Eastern street foods and perceived as common and inexpensive. This would remain the case for a long time.

In the 1900s, with the introduction of cheaper mass-produced items, people began relying more on prepared, canned, and frozen foods. Consumers seeking efficiencies in the kitchen embraced modern stabilizers and preserving agents, as well as new inventions like the all-important freezer.

For years we rejected the traditional recipes of our grandmothers; we wanted to be different, sophisticated, and "modern." In my opinion, this decision to eschew our past became the downfall of food quality and, thus, our overall health and well-being. Foods are now overly processed, and we are feeding steroids and hormones to the animals we eat. And because of this, we are seeing the most obese generation in our history with more preventable illnesses than we know what to do with. Mass production may have created efficiencies in the kitchen, but it certainly hasn't made us happier.

In the last fifteen years or so, I've noticed a new generation of young chefs and food influencers finally embracing their heritage. We now understand that eating healthier means living better, and in order to do so we look back at our history to seek pure, clean ingredients. We scour food traditions to create a food culture that is full of flavor. And nothing creates more flavor than spices.

Fortunately, most spice-growing countries never stopped producing them, and farmers still use the same methods they have for thousands of years, continuing to cultivate what is essential to their cuisines. And while their methods haven't changed, they have a better understanding of modern irrigation, which creates better crop yield and higher sanitation standards, which result in safer products for everyone. I regularly contact growers, traders, and local cooks to learn how they work and how best to use their spices. This is my commitment to our clients, so that I can be better at what I do and so that we all eat better.

Interest in spices is finally seeing resurgence—but a higher demand for spices can also mean shortages. In the same way that we learned how to cultivate better coffee, wine grapes, meat, and dairy products, people are now going back to the spice plantation to see how it can be improved. Where traditional agricultural methods can't keep up, modern techniques can deliver—though even the most tech-savvy equipment can't replace the traditional production of spices that simply can't grow any other way (take vanilla, page 282, for example).

Just as in history, wars and conflicts also affect the ability for regions to grow and supply their spice crops. Look what is happening with Iranian saffron (page 238). There's also the uncontrollable issue of weather. Back in 2004, Hurricane Ivan swept through Grenada, completely devastating the nutmeg supply.

What matters is that new chefs are creating more dishes that look deeper into the world of spices as a source of inspiration. Traveling has never been easier, and the Internet offers a world without boundaries where you can order an ounce of spice from any country and have it delivered to your doorstep.

Things are looking good for spices. The people coming into my shop are expressing a growing interest. They want to be better cooks, and they see spices as an easy way to make a big impact at the table. This ever-growing interest pushes us all to do a better job, and the result is tastier food and a better, healthier lifestyle for everyone. Our history is finally catching up with us, and it's in the form of unassuming powders in simple jars.

SPICES AS MEDICINE

Apart from their inherent ability to enhance aromas and flavors in dishes, spices have been used for millennia for their medicinal qualities. Whether they were prized for their mystical powers or for their actual health benefits is up for some debate. Archaeologists discovered that King Tut's tomb was adorned with spices: black nigella seeds, six cloves of garlic, Mediterranean thyme, and a garland made with wild celery were all said to be found joining him in his journey to the afterlife. Alexander the Great was said to soak in a bath steeped with saffron threads to heal his battle wounds during the Asian campaigns, and in the seventeenth century, herbs like hyssop (also noted in the Bible) were strewn around sickrooms to quash the spread of infection. Ancient Indian medical writings like the *Suśrutasamhitā*, which was foundational to the traditional Ayurvedic texts, included a number of references to spices and their healing properties—cinnamon, cardamom, ginger, turmeric, and pepper among them. Greek physician Hippocrates noted several hundred medicines that had spices to thank for their curative properties.

Cilantro and coriander have anti-inflammatory properties; cardamom and cubeb (Java pepper) have natural antiseptic qualities; bergamot, anise seed, and chocolate, not surprisingly, have sedative virtues; and eucalyptus, ginger, and onion help those with colds to recover.

Today, we are seeing a resurgence of ancient traditions, from a renewed interest in Chinese medicine, built primarily on herbs and spices, to an interest in exotic cuisines such as Indian, which relies on turmeric, fenugreek, garlic, onion, and ginger, all of which benefit overall health. While we may no longer need to rely on bathing in expensive saffron-steeped waters, we can enjoy a better, healthier lifestyle as a welcome side effect of savoring well-seasoned food.

MYTH: SPICES WERE USED TO ENHANCE POOR-QUALITY FOOD

You will often hear that, long ago, spices were used to cover up the bad odors of spoiled food. I would argue, along with some historians, that since the cost of spices was so high, only a man of means could afford them. But, of course, if you had the money, you could afford good-quality food that wouldn't need any covering up to begin with. I have a hard time believing that the poor farmer who barely had enough money to survive could afford a few ounces of nutmeg (page 192) or zedoary (page 292) to season his piece of rotten meat.

The opposite is true with beer and wine: there was a time when adding spices to either of these would mask less-than-savory aromas and flavors. On the plus side, we enjoy spiced or mulled wine today because of this.

It is also true that spices, particularly salt (page 242), were (and still are) used to preserve food for long sea journeys, such as during the Crusades, or through winter months when meat would otherwise be unavailable. It doesn't make poor-quality food palatable, but rather prevents its decomposition to begin with.

SOURCING SPICES

In the spice aisle at the grocery store, one can't possibly imagine the journeys and trials each ground powder traversed to find its way into an expensive yet nondescript glass jar. Used for medicinal, religious, preservative, and culinary purposes, spices can be traced nearly to the beginning of humanity. The "salt and pepper" called for in a recipe may not seem like a big deal, but the former is actually the origin of the word *salary,* used to pay Roman soldiers in ancient times, and the latter was once worth its weight in gold—you could literally pay your way in peppercorns. The use of ancient exotic spices in recent food trends and this sudden excitement for world cuisines are just a revival of one of the oldest trades ever known. Spices are one of the only commodities that have always been a part of everyday life, nearly everywhere.

Each region of the world offers unique spices that lay the foundation for the local cuisine, but no one place grows them all. This may mean more work for me, but there's a reason things are the way they are. Crops that grow in more than one place take on different characteristics according to their *terroir*; Indian and Turkish cumin just don't taste the same. The good news is, when weather has a negative impact on the crops in one place, the other can step in to fill demand. While throughout history spices have traveled to new lands for cultivation in newer, more modern ways, there's something to be said about getting them from their native source. However, the important thing is that you get them at all.

Just like fruits and vegetables, spices grow in fields, orchards, and plantations; have designated harvesting seasons; and are equally affected by bad weather and climate change. Where they really differ from your standard grocery store produce is that they are largely still grown via old methods where the usage of modern mechanical equipment is limited. Also, each spice requires a particular climate and *terroir* to thrive.

Even though there is an increasing demand for spices worldwide, many farmers still grow only small quantities. They rely on cattle and donkeys to access otherwise insurmountable terrain in order to harvest the spices. This labor-intensive process leaves them seeking alternative sources of income. They have to diversify their offerings to offset risk. Some spices, including chiles, mustard, and coriander, have been successfully modified for modern agriculture. This does not necessarily guarantee better quality but, for the most part, does mean better pricing and a consistent supply.

Weather and geopolitical variations can determine whether a crop is readily available or on the verge of extinction. I doubt most people ever consider the quality of this year's peppers over those from last year. I do. In years with more rainfall, hot peppers become very soft, are less pungent, and can be lost to spoilage. Where I notice this most is with the Espelette chile. The color and sweetness depend entirely on the amount of rainfall during the growing period. In drier seasons, some spices tend to be smaller but more intense because of their lower water content.

In times of geopolitical strife, spices suffer too. The side effect of the ongoing battle in Syria is a prime example. The village in which eponymous Aleppo chiles (page 42) are grown is in the very heart of the military confrontation. Farmers who have been forced to leave their homes have also left their farms, and those who remain have virtually no one to sell to. These chiles are fast becoming a coveted rare spice that was once much more easily attainable. They are now being grown in safer lands just over the border in Turkey (where they are called Maraş chiles), though many would say the *terroir* has altered them slightly.

In some countries, such as India, the government has put spice quotas in place. These quotas are amounts that first need to be sold domestically for local consumption. Anything produced beyond that can be exported. Because India is the largest consumer of spices worldwide, the government wants to ensure its population has what it needs before selling anything to the rest of the world.

FROM SEED TO JAR

Spices can be dried seeds, fruits or parts of fruits, herbs (some will argue this point), rhizomes, roots, shoots, or even tree bark. In most cases, they have specific harvest seasons—some, like cardamom, have more than one. There are spices that are harvested when fully ripe and others that are picked well before that (think green chiles). All of them are sorted and cleaned.

The crucial part in the process is drying spices properly to preserve them over time and avoid spoilage—though some are freeze-dried or brined, as green peppercorns are. Drying is often still done by exposure to sun and wind where the spices are vulnerable to insects and other "friends," but more and more we are seeing large oven-like dehydrators used to speed the process and provide better, cleaner results.

Although the goal is to dry them, you do not want to remove all of their moisture; that would adversely affect their taste and scent. The idea is to dry them to the point where they are shelf stable but still retain their natural oils. Whereas in the past, this point was determined by a farmer's knowledge and experience, modern techniques and labs offer a simple test for that. Once dried, the spices are packed in large fabric bags and prepared for shipping to their next destination: the packing facility.

Since most farmers grow only a small quantity of spices, a broker will gather harvests from each farm until he has a bulk amount. In some instances, the farmers will sell the fresh spice to a large company and that company will handle the cleaning and drying. The broker, or the company he works for, will sort the various spices and weigh, label, and package them, as well as handle all the lab tests. Because of labor and production costs, most ground spices are processed in their country of origin.

Spices are mostly, but not always, sanitized in their countries of origin prior to exportation. Once they arrive at their destination, they are then repackaged in small jars or bags, or mixed with other spices to create blends. Some countries—the United States included—require proof that a spice has been treated before it can be imported or proof that it was treated domestically before being released to the market. At home you are probably not washing your spices before using them, especially not if they're ground, so it is important to know that they arrived at your home already safe to eat. If I don't buy treated spices, I need to know my source personally; my Espelette pepper farmer in France is immaculate and particular about his methods, so I trust him.

SANITIZING SPICES

Spices are sanitized in three primary ways:

1. **STEAM** Whole spices are placed in a large-scale steamer for a few minutes to kill bacteria and other harmful agents. It is a very natural process, but it takes away some of the spice's flavor and color.

2. **IRRADIATION** This method treats spices with electricity or radiation to eliminate all foodborne hazards. It is fast and does not affect the quality or characteristics of the spices. Though it has been criticized as carrying a potential risk to humans, more and more research shows that it is not harmful. The FDA mandates that foods that have been directly irradiated include specific statements indicating this on their packaging.

3. **ETHYLENE OXIDE (ETO) AND PROPYLENE OXIDE (PPO)** These methods expose spices to fumigants at low temperatures to eliminate harmful pathogens. The fumigants then evaporate, leaving no trace behind. This practice is one of the most common, particularly because it is said to ensure food safety while protecting the characteristics of each spice. Though some would argue their safety merits, both of these fumigants have been used by the food and pharmaceutical industries for years.

At La Boîte, I buy some of our products directly from growers. This is my preferred method since I have a great dialogue with them. However, most growers are in remote areas and do not sell their products directly to consumers. In the United States, I rely on importers to source spices because they have long-term relationships with growers and brokers. I give them clear instructions on quantities needed, as well as the quality and pricing I am looking for. In some cases I even plan ahead for what will be needed in coming years.

Even though the climate is favorable for it, the United States grows hardly any of its own spices. My hope is that there will be more crops grown domestically. This will ensure that I have a better, more direct connection with the growers, as well as faster access to the product.

What we are seeing in some places is the use of spice cultivation as a solution for unemployment and to combat the growth of illegal drugs. In Afghanistan, the government is encouraging, and forcing, farmers to replace their opium poppy crops with saffron. Making the switch means more money for local farmers, a legal way of life, and less money going into the pockets of the Taliban. Since the climate is stable for it, a change in crop offers a lucrative opportunity to shift focus onto straighter paths. Growing spices is just good business, and it's even better for us as consumers.

HOW TO BUY SPICES (AND HOW NOT TO)

Most people know what to consider when buying a good wine or a truly vine-ripened tomato, but they rarely take into account the fact that spices should be purchased (or homegrown and dried) thoughtfully. Most grocery stores, markets, and specialty stores carry a variety of spices to choose from, and you can find them whole or ground in jars, bags, or in bulk. There are maxims to consider when buying spices, things to look for in terms of quality, and ways to evaluate what you already have.

I love a good sale as much as the next person, but not when it comes to spices (make that spices *and* fish). My advice would be to stay away from clearance items. Due to large global demand and climate change, prices have dramatically increased in the last few years. I am not saying that an expensive store is better than a discount grocer, but in many cases more expensive spice packaging is a sign of better quality. Also, keep in mind that you will need to use less of a high-quality and pungent spice, so you are actually paying the same amount in the end anyway.

Find a source or a store (physical or online) that you trust, and start by buying small quantities to evaluate the quality. Ethnic stores are also a great place to find things you may not see at your local grocer. To determine quality, the immediate test is the visual. Singular spices should have a uniform color. If you notice both dark and light particles or different shades, it could mean the spice was harvested before maturation, the selection wasn't the best, or the sorting wasn't done properly. If you buy black pepper and it's gray, you know something is not right.

Spices should also have the most vibrant, intense color possible. If they look grayish or faded, that might be a tell that they have been sitting on the store's shelf for way too long. Also, if you notice a lot of powder on the bottom of a package of whole spices, this can mean they are old and have started breaking down. This is especially true with dried herbs.

It is important to note that by the time you see a jar or bag of spices at the store, they are probably already five to seven months old. There is nothing wrong with them; that's just the way spice production works. Actually, most brands don't even mention any "best before" or expiration dates on their packaging; the FDA just doesn't require this information on spices. I wish they did. Unlike some wines, spices do not become better with time.

In terms of quantity, buy only what you need and intend to use up within a few months. Spices are not the kinds of things we need to be passing down to our children;

they should be used, not saved. People are often tempted to buy in bulk because of the cost savings, but will never use it all before the quality fades. Unless you really think you are going to consume three pounds of cubeb in a matter of months, buy spices in small quantities and refresh your stock often.

After you bring home a new spice, open the packaging and evaluate the scent. Spices should smell—and the more intense the smell, the better. Do note that not all spices will have a very *pleasant* scent. Asafoetida (page 58) will have an overpowering smell like fermented onion and garlic, but that is what you want from this particular spice.

The next step is to taste the spice. Again, not all spices will taste good on their own, but if you know what to look for, you'll know if you've found it. Some might be a bit bitter, hot, or sour, but this may be just right. The point is that spices should taste like *something*; otherwise, why add them to your dish?

Keep in mind that the flavor, taste, and smell will change a lot in contact with raw or cooked foods, or when infused into a liquid. The easiest way to evaluate the quality is to sprinkle some on part of a raw or already cooked dish. You do not want to ruin a whole meal with an experiment gone wrong. Sometimes I test spices on popcorn, in a little broth, or on a small piece of chicken. Take notes to remember what you smell and taste, and then rate the spice in some way so that if you buy it from another source, you can easily compare them. You will have to compare a few sources to become better at buying spices. Unfortunately, most of us are not taught to evaluate them at all, not even in the world of professional chefs. But thanks to online and specialty stores, we now have convenient, regular access to a variety of spices, so you can buy small quantities to try without having to stock up on things you don't end up liking enough to use. It is a good habit to check on your stock every once in a while. I actually love to see what I have left and often create a dish or a meal based on what I find or want to use up.

WHOLE OR GROUND?

This is a million-dollar question to which there is no definite answer. If you think that you will have the energy to deal with grinding whole spices, then you definitely should. If you don't have the time and want to use what little you have on actually cooking a meal, buying ground spices is the way to go. Not everyone wants to come home after a full day of work and grind spices. That's okay. Some spices—such as turmeric, paprika, and ginger—can rarely be found whole anyway. These require heavy-duty hammer mill grinders and are usually ground in their respective countries of origin.

However, I would highly recommend that you buy certain spices whole because of the risk of adulteration. Sadly, the spice industry is not spared from people trying to make an extra dollar at your expense by adding fillers to bulk up weight. I've heard of instances in which olive pits are ground and blended into black pepper, the skins and roots of onions and garlic included in their respective powders, and beet powder mixed with sumac to perk up the color. It's foul play.

In any case, you should trust your judgment and knowledge of the way you cook and shop. There is nothing wrong with buying ground spices if they come from a reputable source. They can save you a lot of time. In my experience, people usually cook more if they have ground spices and blends on hand versus having to start from scratch every time. What matters is that you use them.

HOW TO BLEND SPICES

Blending your own spices is not complicated. Of course you can buy premade blends, but for those of us who would rather have control of the ingredients and an outlet for our creative ideas, there really is nothing better than doing it yourself. It also provides the opportunity to fully discover and appreciate each individual spice that goes into a blend, smell its unique aroma, choose how coarsely you want to grind it, and decide what each one brings to the table. It is what I would consider the most important step in making food that tastes good.

To start making your own spice blends, there are some important steps to consider:

1. DEFINE A CONCEPT

The key to a good blend is a good idea. There is no point in throwing various spices together and hoping for magic to happen. Consider these four guiding principles before you begin:

Inspiration → Is this blend motivated by a specific dish you want to use it for? Is it inspired by something you've recently eaten? Does it need to be versatile enough to use for many different kinds of dishes? Ask yourself why you want to make this blend. Is it to sprinkle on pizza, stir into soup, add heat to grilled fish, or impart a different sweet element to your morning coffee? This is your starting point and the answer you will go back to throughout the process to stay focused on your original goal.

Flavor Profile → Consider how you like your steak. Do you prefer your steak rubs to be a bit salty or acidic, or to have a coarse texture? Or would you rather use brown sugar to caramelize and make a sweet crust on the outside? Decide what tastes good to you, and then consider if your blend is meant for just one use or if it can flavor many dishes—you may find it works in more ways than one after all. Think of at least three other things you can use it for (maybe in addition to steak, it works great on roasted potatoes and in Caesar salad dressing). Then, try three more. Every blend you create, so long as it tastes good to you, can become versatile.

Be mindful of how aggressive you are when adding certain spices to a blend—even your favorites. Some are not meant for the spotlight. For instance, I'm a huge fan of coriander, but for others it just tastes like soap. Chile peppers can be overpowering, so use a little at a time and taste as you go. You can always add more. Also, it's a misconception that sugar and salt cut heat. If you find yourself with a blend that's just too hot, it is best start again. You won't be able to cover it up.

Texture → The texture, or mouthfeel, of what we eat is one of the most important components in food, or we'd all be drinking soup. When you chew on coarser spices, they will release natural oils and really come to life, developing as you eat them. Aside from what spices do visually for the blend, the texture will contribute to a complex recipe that lasts longer while eating. Some spices are just better left the way they are. On the other hand, some are better when ground finer than others. Whole dried lemongrass, for example, is just inedible. Powders dissolve more quickly in the mouth, and thus have the first impact and then fade away.

Appearance → What looks good tastes good. There's a reason you get hungry when you see beautifully presented food. It is a matter of balancing variety, color, and texture, and of considering when you'll be using it during the cooking process. Since you might use a blend to finish a dish or to sprinkle on a raw ingredient as a garnish, you want to have a great visual. Spices are beautiful to begin with, but when making a blend, you want to make sure the end result still looks appealing. A dark brown blend may still taste good, but you might be encouraged to use a more attractive one more often.

2. WRITE DOWN THE INGREDIENTS

Write down the ingredients before you begin blending to help identify if you are going in the right direction. Have you chosen ingredients that follow your concept? Try to limit yourself to five to seven ingredients until you get proficient, and start with the main components. This will also become your future recipe, so make sure it is clearly documented. Like writing any concept, while working on it you often figure out some things turn out to be better or worse than you'd expected. That's not a bad thing. It is also like writing a shopping list: you have an idea of what you need before you go to the store—maybe acidity from sumac or lemon peel, and salty notes from cumin, celery seeds, or seaweed—or you end up with a cart full of things you didn't really need.

3. MEASURE THE INGREDIENTS

Let me emphasize this: when measuring, always use a *scale* and always write down the *exact* quantities. Both of these steps are absolutely necessary for efficiency and accuracy. Your blend will hopefully become a recipe you make again and again, so it needs to be exact and easy to reproduce consistently. Don't worry; writing a recipe down does not take away any of the creative aspect of it. Change it all you like, but keep track so you are creating a blend that works. You will never remember everything.

A scale never lies. Other measuring devices might yield different quantities for different people. I recommend using a food scale that has the smallest increments possible. I prefer a digital scale that goes up to 5 to 10 pounds with a 1-gram precision.

Also, keep all the ingredients in separate containers. This will allow you to easily make changes during the process. Take note of any adjustments along the way and, once you've approved the recipe, create a clean version of it. You might also want to add a few columns for larger batches so you can easily multiply yields and have those numbers handy.

4. TOAST OR DRY ROAST THE SPICES

I toast spices for three reasons: sanitation (they travel in bags or boxes all over the world, and it doesn't hurt to make them safer); to release the aromatic essential oils that would otherwise remain dormant; and to allow the spices to get better acquainted. It also makes them easier to grind and drives off excess moisture, which can be a problem in storage. When creating a blend, you want to achieve as many layers of taste, flavor, and texture as possible. Toasting or roasting your spices will allow you to get there.

In some places, such as India, the toasting process is essential to every dish. Spices are first fried in ghee, oil, or a dry pan, and then other ingredients such as vegetables and proteins are added. In this case, spices will not be ground; they will be left whole in the dish. There are also cases in which, after frying the spices and letting them cool, they will be ground and made into paste. Frying in oil is a great technique, but it does require that you use the blends within a short period of time. For the purposes of this section, I am specifically addressing dry roasting or toasting.

First, decide what spices will need to be toasted; not all of them can or should be—I have noted my recommendation for each spice on its respective page. Some, like herbs and powders, will burn, and others just don't get any better when toasted—black and white pepper are good examples of this. It's trial and error. Whatever you decide works best, note the details in your recipe.

5. GRIND THE SPICES

Once you've decided which spices to grind, please avoid using your beautiful mortar and pestle to do so. Most of the spices end up on the floor, there's no uniform result, and it takes an incredible amount of strength and technique. Try grinding some cardamom seeds and you'll see what I mean.

What you need is a coffee grinder, which gives fast, consistent results; is affordable; and is easy to use. The option to do quick pulses or run it longer helps to achieve varying degrees of grind to give you the layers, textures, and appearance you want. A blender works well, too, but not for small quantities.

Grind each spice separately. This will help you avoid mistakes and make sure each one gets the proper attention. There is nothing wrong with grinding all of them together once you get better at it and you're sure your recipe works.

HOW TO TOAST OR ROAST SPICES

You can toast spices in a pan on the stove or dry roast them in the oven. Both are good methods; it's a matter of preference.

PAN TOASTING
PROS: You can see what's happening and smell when the spices are ready.
CONS: You have to keep an eye on the pan and stir continuously, because heat is only delivered from the bottom. Not everyone has time for that.
METHOD: Put the spices in a skillet and toast over medium heat, stirring with a wooden spoon. Once you get a nice scent, transfer the spices to a cold container to stop the cooking process. For first-timers, start by toasting the spices individually. When you get better at it, go all in. There are no specific cooking times. It's up to your personal preference and the fragrance. You'll know if you've gone too far.

OVEN OR DRY ROASTING
PROS: You get uniform results; it's easy to do and very efficient. It's also great for multitasking; you don't have to worry about stirring or burning.
CONS: Not everyone wants to heat up the oven or has time to wait for that. And you really have to open the oven to smell for doneness. Do try roasting in a convection oven, but be sure to cover the spices with a second baking sheet—everything will blow away if left uncovered.
METHOD: Preheat the oven to 325°F. Pour the spices onto a rimmed baking sheet, cover with a second baking sheet, and transfer to the oven. (Covering the spices keeps them from spilling out and ensures they get heated from the bottom and the top.) Set the timer: start with 2 to 3 minutes and add more time until you get there. On average it takes 5 to 8 minutes. To assess doneness, open the oven to take a whiff.

6. BLEND AND STORE

Once all the spices are ready (toasted, roasted, ground, or whole), combine them in a bowl and stir together until well blended. Allow the mixture to cool, if necessary, and store in an airtight container out of direct sunlight and far away from your stove; the heat will ruin them. (For more on storing, see page 35.)

7. WALK AWAY

By the end of this process you might not have the best judgment. Smelling and tasting so many things can give you sensory overload. I always recommend stepping away and waiting a while before analyzing a blend. This will allow you to have a better perspective of what you have created. It's a bit like making art: sometimes it is better to take a break and come back to it. You'll see it, and smell it, in a fresh way.

8. EVALUATE

Start by analyzing your new blend visually. It should look appealing. Now, taste your new blend. Try to identify the flavors and notes. Do you like it? Does it deliver on the initial idea or concept? Did you get salty and acidic or bitter and tangy notes? Most important, remember that this is not a dish; it may taste a bit bitter, sour, or hot. You are not going to consume it as is with a spoon. Some of those harsh notes will disappear when the blend is used with food.

You also want to evaluate the texture by rubbing it between your fingers to see how it feels and whether the color rubs off. Try to infuse some of the blend in separate bowls or glasses of cold and hot water to see what would happen visually and texturally if you were to add it to a cocktail or broth. Does it release a lot of color? If you want to make a white rice dish and the blend stains everything red, it won't work. If you want to use it in a silky soup and it's coarsely ground, it won't work. Go back and grind it further, or just use it in another dish. It's okay to make adjustments; start by adding a little more of something or by trying something else entirely.

9. NAME YOUR BLEND

Congratulations, you just created a blend! Now is a good time to give it a name or a number. I usually name my blends after the source of inspiration, often a person or place. You can also name it after the preparation it was made for—such as barbecue, pizza, or salad—or the cuisine it's founded in. It can be whatever you want. It's your blend. You are free to be creative.

10. START COOKING

This is where the real testing begins. After all, this blend was destined for food. I recommend that you try it first in simple dishes like salads, vegetables, seared meat, or fish. Experiment with familiar recipes; you do not want to start by trying unfamiliar dishes and then adding an unfamiliar spice. Chances are it will not work. Once you get to know your blend, you can start exploring new dishes.

Try adding your blend before or after you cook. Would it have been better if you roasted the chicken with the spice already on it? Try it in as many ways as possible, including breakfast, snacks, sweet or savory dishes, cocktails, or soups. Then, share it with others—you may get some helpful feedback.

BUYING FROM THE OPEN MARKET

There was a time, long ago, when certain cultures were using so many spices that vendors only had to open large bags and create beautiful, colorful pyramids of them to attract clients. Within a few days the bags would be empty. Today, these market spice pyramids remain as beautiful as they have always been, but since they don't sell the way they used to, they mainly collect dust and urban pollutants.

As a rule, these precious spices should be kept in sealed containers out of the sun's heat (see page 35) in order to preserve their great scents and flavors. Exposing them to air and light just deteriorates their best attributes. What you smell is gone. So, do take pictures of these beautiful bags in the markets on your travels, but try to buy spices that are properly packaged.

CONSIDERING ORGANIC SPICES

As much as I love organic products, it's important to mention that, because they are not subject to any treatments, they can sometimes be at high risk for containing bugs. Having the organic designation doesn't mean that a spice is of better quality or tastes better, just that it may be cleaner or may not have any residual pesticides. To be fair, there are a handful of reputable organic purveyors out there. You really just have to check your sources and test the quality before committing to any big purchases. Organic or not, the choice is entirely up to you.

DRYING HERBS & SPICES AT HOME

In as long as it takes you to go out and buy dried herbs, it's just as easy (and often more cost-effective) to dry your own at home. Drying gives a second life to what would otherwise be waste, whether it's a large bunch of fresh dill in your refrigerator or an overabundance of rosemary in your garden.

Nearly any herb can be dried on parchment paper on your kitchen counter by a window within a few days; most herbs take only one to two days, while wetter, thicker-stemmed herbs may take a few days more. In either case, they can be completely dried and packed in a jar fairly quickly. You can also keep stems in the freezer or use them up while fresh as part of a bouquet garni to flavor soups and stocks. A word of advice on hanging herbs to dry: it's nice, but it'll leave a mess on your counter.

If you are up to the challenge, you can use up citrus peels—organic and untreated, or very clean and wax-free—by leaving them out in the open to dry. Then, either keep the peels whole or grind them before storing in an airtight jar. This way you'll have full control of the process and the end result.

Some spices, on the other hand, are not worth the effort, and in these cases, it's better to just go out and buy them. Here are my recommendations, but feel free to experiment:

DRY YOUR OWN: herbs, citrus peels, chiles, leaves, lemongrass

DON'T BOTHER: garlic, galangal, turmeric, ginger, lavender

STORING SPICES

Whether you have whole spices, ground spices, or spice blends, storing them properly ensures their longevity. Keeping them forever won't make you sick—they rarely ferment or spoil—but old spices aren't worth holding on to; they just don't retain their fresh aromas and flavors. I often get asked about the best way to keep spices. The simple answer is that spices should be kept in the same places you would want to be: no place with extreme heat or cold, and away from humidity. This means out of a sunny window, away from the oven, and not usually in the freezer.

If you are going to go through the effort to blend spices or purchase good-quality ones, you should also know how to preserve them. Besides, keeping them out on display will make you more likely to use them regularly as an important part of your cooking routine.

Here are some things to consider when choosing the right storage for your spices:

1. THE CONTAINER

Spices should be kept in a sealed container that keeps out humidity, does not conduct heat or react to the spice, has little or no exposure to light, and is easy to clean. Any change in heat will cause a loss in scent and flavor; humidity will create lumps or big chunks and can also develop mold on chile flakes or cause garlic and onion to ferment. Of course, containers should also look good in your kitchen and fit your cooking style and needs.

Here are some tips that can help you choose the right container for you:

Glass
PROS: Glass is very good since it does not react to the ingredients, unlike some plastics or woods. It does not conduct a lot of heat; you can easily see what is inside to keep track of inventory; it is easy to clean; and, quite simply, it's nice to look at.
CONS: There is a risk of breakage and exposure to light.

Plastic
PROS: There is a low risk of breakage in the kitchen, and if it's opaque, there's no concern of light exposure.
CONS: A lot of plastic containers can react to the acidity found in spices, which can actually eat away at or dissolve the material. Not all plastic materials are BPA-free. Unless it is clear, you'll have to open it to see what's left in the jar.

Metal
PROS: It is easy to clean and does not react to spices or retain odors. There's no risk of breakage or light exposure.
CONS: It conducts heat and offers no ability to keep track of inventory without opening the container to look inside.

Wood
PROS: There is no risk of breakage or light exposure, and there is little risk of heat conductivity.

CONS: The material could react to spices, which makes it difficult to clean. It is also a breathing material that might allow humidity to seep through, and there is no way to see the inventory inside without opening the container.

Plastic Bags
PROS: They take up very little storage space because they can be laid flat and stacked.
CONS: They do not seal very well; they risk exposure to light; and because they do not stand on their own, they are not practical in the kitchen.

2. REFRIGERATION & FREEZING

While keeping spices at low temperatures can help expand their shelf life, if stored incorrectly there is a risk of humidity sneaking in. Also, storing spices with other food products increases the chances that they will impart their scent to your food, or the other way around. While I do not recommend storing spices in the refrigerator or freezer, if you must, storing them in an airtight container is best.

3. LABELING

You should always label your containers. Spices (and spice blends in particular) can often look the same, and you can't always rely on your memory to know what you have. You could even go one step further and add the purchase date so you know when it is time to start using up that nearly vintage cumin—it will not get better with time. You might even add the country of origin and where the spice was purchased. Spices that grow in more than one place, like oregano and cumin, should be kept separated based on place of origin—they taste different and shouldn't be lumped together.

4. SPICE RACKS & DISPLAYS

There is not one answer as to what you should have in terms of a rack or storage system, but there are some things to consider. Prefilled spice racks should be avoided at all costs. You'll never know when they were packaged or how old the spices are. Buy an empty one and fill it with the newly dried or freshly purchased spices you need. Spices should be out on the counter or mounted on the wall of your kitchen so you can see them. If they are not accessible to where you are cooking or are hidden in a cabinet somewhere, you'll use them less often and might even completely forget what you have.

THE
SPICES

→

AJOWAN

TRACHYSPERMUM AMMI

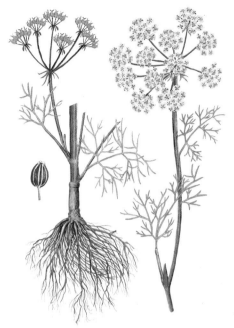

Dried herbaceous fruits essential to Gujarati Indian cuisine

———

FLAVOR & AROMA When I want to introduce complex herbal notes with a slight bitterness—particularly when raw—ajowan is my go-to spice. The bitter element, which I actually love, mellows when cooked or baked, resulting in a nice nutty taste. Its additional notes of thyme, oregano, fennel, cumin, and even celery work well in breads and baked goods, especially since the spice adds a textural element when left whole.

Ajowan, like many other spices, benefits from being fried in fat until lightly brown to develop its flavor. This results in the added bonus of an aromatic, infused cooking fat, which you can—and should—use later.

ORIGIN ☞ Native to South India ☞ Cultivated in India, Iran, Egypt, Pakistan, and Afghanistan

HARVEST SEASON Ajowan is an annual herb in the parsley (Apiaceae) family that grows 1 to 2 feet in height and bears small, red-speckled white flowers and fleshy round leaves. Because it is frost tender, it is mainly grown as a winter crop in subtropical climates and as a summer crop in temperate climates. When the seeds fully ripen, in 120 to 140 days, the stems are cut, dried, and threshed.

PARTS USED Seeds, essential oils, and roots

ABOUT Often referred to as ajwain or carum, ajowan seeds are grayish-green and oval shaped with stripes, similar to caraway or cumin. They are predominantly found in Indian cuisine in baked goods and,

in particular, in Gujarati vegetarian fare, including batters for *bhajias* (fritters). In Gujarat, they also mix whole or crushed seeds with cilantro and chile peppers to give *pudlas* (chickpea pancakes) a wonderful aromatic flavor. Because ajowan is mainly used in these cuisines, most people outside of India and southwest Asia—including myself at first—have hardly heard of it. It is well worth seeking out.

Ajowan is also incredibly perfumy. Its seeds contain about 5% essential oil, of which half is the widely used medicinal element thymol. Its essential oils are used for treating everything from arthritis and asthma to indigestion and sore throats. The root is also said to help with digestion.

TRADITIONAL USES

Baghaar (method of seasoning by
frying spices in oil)—India
Chaat masala (spice blend)—India and Pakistan
Berbere (spice blend)—Ethiopia and Eritrea
Parathas (flatbread)—Southwestern Asia
Pakoras (fritters)—Southwestern Asia and Gujarat

NOTE
Toasting recommended

RECOMMENDED PAIRINGS
Spinach salad
Sautéed artichokes
Baked bass
Split peas
Roast turkey

SPICE PAIRINGS
caraway, chile flakes, cumin, fennel, turmeric

RECIPE IDEAS
1. Add whole ajowan seeds to your favorite pancake recipe
and serve with whipped feta cheese for brunch.
2. Season thinly sliced cucumber with whole ajowan seeds,
white wine vinegar, and coarse salt for a quick pickle.
3. Simmer peeled garlic cloves in milk until tender, season with
whole ajowan seeds, and purée until smooth for a condiment.

QUICK BLEND
Gujarat

Use this slightly bitter, herbaceous blend to season cooked potato purée,
which you can then shape into small patties and pan-fry in olive oil until
golden brown. It is also great on fried eggplant served with yogurt.

Makes about ⅓ cup/26 grams

2½ tablespoons/5 grams dried dill
1½ tablespoons/3 grams crushed dried cilantro
1 tablespoon/15 grams ajowan seeds, toasted
2 teaspoons/2 grams crushed dried mint
½ teaspoon/1 gram pepperoncino chile flakes, or other chile flakes

ALEPPO

CAPSICUM ANNUUM

A fruity, pleasantly hot chile native to the village of Aleppo, Syria

---

FLAVOR & AROMA It's as if one day Aleppo chiles were introduced to the world and there was no going back. For years I didn't know a thing about them, until my friend Ana Sortun, chef-owner of Oleana in Cambridge, Massachusetts, brought me some. Life was never going to be the same. These magical chile flakes have citrus and sun-dried tomato notes and a mild, pleasant heat. They are robust with fruitiness and earthy cumin and cayenne undertones with just a touch of salt. They're a good example of how chiles can offer so much more than heat; they can deliver sweet, acidic notes as well.

The coarsely ground large flakes add texture and complexity to dishes, and because they don't dissolve right away, you can use the spice in cold dishes or longer-cooked ones. Needless to say, it is one of my favorite spices.

ORIGIN ☞ Native to South and Central America and later the northern Syrian town of Aleppo ☞ Cultivated in Syria and Turkey

HARVEST SEASON Aleppo pepper plants, which can reach 4 feet high, thrive in warm, dry climates. Each offers an abundance of peppers that ripen from green to deep burgundy-red and are ready to be harvested around September (75 to 85 days from sowing). Growing several inches in length and just under 2 inches wide, pods are laid out in the sun to dry naturally, though not fully, to preserve their natural oils. Then they are seeded and coarsely ground. Often, salt will be added to the flakes for flavor and to avoid clumping.

PARTS USED Whole chiles

ABOUT Also known as Halaby pepper, true Aleppo is a deep red, complex pepper in the nightshade (Solanaceae) family that traditionally grows in one of the world's oldest and continuously inhabited cities. Rich in Islamic history and architecture, this Syrian town just south of the Turkish border was said to be one of the last stops on the storied Silk Road.

The Aleppo chile has long been an essential ingredient in Mediterranean and Middle Eastern cuisine, only gaining popularity around the world at the end of the twentieth century. Traditionally, it's used as a table condiment, not unlike salt and pepper, and for seasoning grilled meats. Today, it's used as a more complex substitute for any dish where crushed pepper is called for, like pizza, chili, and a variety of sauces.

Syria's current geopolitical climate and a lingering drought have made this coveted pepper a near endangered species. Aleppo's farmers either can't grow it or can't sell it. What grows on the other side of the border in Turkey, though considered a sibling pepper, just isn't the same. Some are opting for—or being baited-and-switched with—Maraş, a pepper grown in the Turkish province of Kahramanmaraş. While we hold on tight to our stash of the authentic Syrian spice, we'll have to wait patiently and hope the heritage of Aleppo—the town, its people, and the chile—makes a revival.

TRADITIONAL USES

Koftes (minced meat kebabs)—Turkey
Acuka (walnut-pepper spread)—Turkey
Muhammara (hot pepper dip)—Middle East
Kebabs—Middle East
Ful medames (mashed fava bean dish)—Egypt

NOTE
Toasting not recommended

RECOMMENDED PAIRINGS
Grilled fish
Aglio e olio spaghetti
Scallopini
Guacamole
Chocolate chip cookies

SPICE PAIRINGS
cumin, oregano, rose, sesame, sumac

HEAT INDEX
Light to medium heat

RECIPE IDEAS
1. Combine Aleppo chile flakes with fresh lemon juice, brown sugar, fresh mint, and sparkling water for a spicy, refreshing lemonade.
2. Season sliced mango with Aleppo chile flakes, lime juice, and sea salt for a snack.
3. Marinate calamari slices with Aleppo chile flakes, chopped fresh ginger, and orange juice before quickly searing in a pan.

QUICK BLEND
Biber

Sprinkle a few pinches of this blend over ground lamb and use to make fiery grilled kebabs. It's also a great match for a red bell pepper and bean stew.

Makes about ¼ cup/25 grams

2 tablespoons/15 grams Aleppo chile flakes
½ tablespoon/5 grams cumin seeds, toasted and ground
½ tablespoon/3 grams dried garlic slices, ground
1 teaspoon/1 gram dried oregano
Scant ½ teaspoon/1 gram ground sumac

ALLSPICE

PIMENTA DIOICA

A warm, versatile spice that pairs equally well with sweet and savory dishes

---

FLAVOR & AROMA I like to compare allspice to the percussion section of an orchestra; it is the heart and soul of spices. Because of its complexity, it somehow harmonizes with all the other spices in a blend or the ingredients in a dish. It's what we call a warm spice. Its flavor and aromatic notes of clove, nutmeg, and cinnamon with peppery overtones give every dish a comforting feeling. Plus, it's incredibly versatile. It is used in almost every continent and ethnic food, and it complements both sweet and savory dishes as well as beverages and cocktails.

Although most people use whole or ground berries, I prefer to crush them and use the larger pieces in long-cooked dishes for a great complex taste.

ORIGIN ☞ Native to the West Indies and Central America ☞ Cultivated mainly in Jamaica but also in Tonga, Honduras, Mexico, Guatemala, and Hawaii

HARVEST SEASON Allspice berries are handpicked when they reach full size but are still unripe and green; their aromatic essential oils are lost when the berries ripen fully.

As soon as they are ready to harvest (around July and August) small twigs bearing bunches of berries are broken off and spread out under the hot sun for several days to dry, turning them a deep brown color. The berries are later separated from the stalks and packaged. Never buy faded or dusty-looking allspice.

PARTS USED Berries and leaves (known as Indian bay leaves)

ABOUT Allspice, which resembles a fat peppercorn, is the berry of the evergreen pimiento tree in the myrtle (Myrtaceae) family. It was discovered in Jamaica by Christopher Columbus during his second voyage to the New World and named by his physician and companion, Dr. Diego Álvarez Chanca. During the sixteenth century, it made its way into European and Mediterranean cuisines, and during the Napoleonic war of 1812, it is said that Russian soldiers put it in their boots for warmth and

as a deodorizer. Its essential oils are still used today in men's cosmetics.

But even with its travels across the globe, allspice is still grown primarily in Jamaica. A few other countries in Central America produce smaller quantities—I get mine from Guatemala. Over the centuries, allspice has collected a number of monikers; it's known as *poivre de la Jamaïque* ("Jamaican pepper") and *bois d'inde* ("Indian wood") in French, English pepper in Hebrew, and pimento in Jamaica. (My guess is the British occupation of Israel in the '20s and '30s had something to do with the Hebrew name.)

Whatever you call it, allspice earned its names because it tastes like an amalgam of so many spices, including juniper berries, nutmeg, clove, pepper, and cinnamon. It's no surprise that it can be found in a number of cuisines. The Spanish use it in escabeche. It is essential to Jamaican jerk seasoning. It's used to season roasted meats in the Middle East. It adds warmth to European desserts and mulling spice (page 297). And it's one of the key elements of English "mixed spice," which is used in sweet baked goods. Even the leaves and wood are used for smoking meats.

TRADITIONAL USES

Pimento dram (allspice liqueur)—West Indies
Jerk seasoning—Jamaica
Pickled herring—Scandinavia
Berbere (spice blend)—Ethiopia
Meatballs—Sweden

NOTE

Toasting recommended

RECOMMENDED PAIRINGS

Hot chocolate
Sweet potato purée
Gravy
Quinoa
Beef bourguignon

SPICE PAIRINGS

black pepper, cardamom, cinnamon, clove, vanilla

RECIPE IDEAS

1. Put whole allspice, cardamom pods, and whole cloves in a French press, fill with boiling water, and press for a spiced tea.
2. Season waffle batter with a little ground allspice.
3. For a warm, spiced salad dressing base, add ground allspice to simmering red wine and cook down until it becomes a thick syrup.

QUICK BLEND
Bahar

Use this blend as a rub for pork shoulder destined for low-and-slow cooking on a grill or in the oven. It works equally well in chocolate mousse or pudding.

Makes about ¼ cup/23 grams

1½ tablespoons/15 grams allspice berries, toasted and ground
1 teaspoon/3 grams cloves, ground
Scant ¾ teaspoon/2 grams black peppercorns, ground
Scant ¾ teaspoon/2 grams cubeb, ground
½ teaspoon/1 gram Sichuan pepper, ground

AMCHOOR

MANGIFERA INDICA

A tart, slightly sweet spice made from dried green mangoes

FLAVOR & AROMA Amchoor has a citrusy fresh smell and a sour, slightly sweet taste with some herbaceous notes. I often refer to amchoor as my secret weapon. Since I am a huge fan of acidity and sourness, amchoor allows me to introduce these elements into many blends. While some use it in place of tamarind or lemon, I like to add it to European-style blends in place of dried citrus peel, which tends to lose its sour trait over time. Citrus can also add bitter notes, and its brightness will fade during cooking. Amchoor, on the other hand, holds on to these elements even in dishes that are cooked over a longer time. It also makes a great meat tenderizer: when used in a marinade, its enzymes help break down even the toughest cuts of meat with ease.

ORIGIN ☞ Native to and cultivated in India

HARVEST SEASON Mangoes are biennial plants that bear fruit once every other year—and sometimes only every few years. Their cream or pink flowers are pollinated, giving way to medium-size oblong fruits, which are handpicked or plucked with a harvester while they're still unripe and green. Many of these trees still grow in the wild and produce more fruit the older they get.

PARTS USED Dried unripe mango slices

ABOUT As one of the oldest cultivated fruits, mango has been growing in India and Southeast Asia for thousands of years. *Amchoor* is a Hindi word that means "mango powder." I get all my amchoor from India, the only place where the dried spice is produced. It's actually one of only a few spices

I purchase already ground. A member of the Anacardiaceae, or sumac, family, amchoor is essential to Indian cuisine, where its natural acidic qualities shine through in curries, soups, marinades, chutneys, and pickles.

➥ TRADITIONAL USES

Authentic to India
Mango chutney
Chaat masala (spice blend)
Potato *pakora* (fritter)
Samosa (savory baked or fried pastry)
Chickpea soup

NOTE

Toasting not recommended

RECOMMENDED PAIRINGS

Yogurt parfait
Lentil salad
Cauliflower velouté
Steamed mussels
Apple pie

SPICE PAIRINGS

basil, dried garlic, ginger, orange peel, turmeric

RECIPE IDEAS

1. Peel and chop 1 ripe mango and purée in a blender with 2 pinches of amchoor and a splash of hot sauce. Use as a sauce for meats and fish.

2. Stir ground amchoor and shredded chicken into simmering coconut milk and chicken stock for a quick Asian-inspired soup.

3. Mix 2 pinches of amchoor with 2 chopped ripe avocados, chopped cilantro, and sliced scallions, season with salt, and serve as a dip or spread.

QUICK BLEND
Green to Red

See photograph, page 48.

Season corn with this blend and salt before grilling; its flavors wake up the sweet corn and complement the smoky notes the grill imparts. I also like to use it in squash soup.

Makes about 2 tablespoons/23 grams

1½ tablespoons/15 grams amchoor
½ tablespoon/5 grams sweet pimentón
1 teaspoon/2 grams ground cinnamon, preferably Vietnamese
Scant ½ teaspoon/1 gram ground Aleppo

ANCHO

CAPSICUM ANNUUM

*A mild chile with a vivid color
and plum flavor notes*

FLAVOR & AROMA There are an endless number of chiles, and each has its own particular notes. I use anchos since they offer complex notes of plum and raisin with mild heat. What I really enjoy is the dark, deep color they get from the drying process; it adds great visual richness to dishes and blends.

Where anchos really shine is when they are used in soups, stews, or grilled dishes. I often use them to bring paprika to life, particularly in seasons when that spice is lighter in color and the flavor fades. Since anchos never lose their bold taste, they really help to complement and correct any inconsistencies with paprika.

ORIGIN ☞ Native to Puebla, Mexico ☞ Cultivated mainly in Mexico and California

HARVEST SEASON Anchos are actually poblano peppers, a member of the nightshade (Solanaceae) family, that are left on the vine to ripen fully, changing from a fresh green color to a deep, reddish black. The first harvests of green chiles are sold as poblanos, while anchos stay in the field, where the flavors and sugars have more time to develop (about 6 months from sowing). These 3- to 6-inch-long fruits flourish in the hot summer temperatures of Mexico and are harvested late in the season by being cut from the stem. They are traditionally laid out in the sun on mats that allow air to flow underneath as they dry for a few weeks.

PARTS USED Dried whole pepper

HISTORY One of the most popular dried chile varieties in the world, the ancho originates in the Puebla Valley, just southeast of Mexico City. It was used as a main ingredient in Mexican cuisine long before the Spanish conquest and continues to grow and thrive there. Along with the mulato and pasilla chiles (the former is also a poblano, picked and dried at a different time), they form what is considered the holy trinity of chiles, those that are essential to traditional mole sauces.

Anchos are often toasted and ground to add just a little extra heat to sauces, or rehydrated and stuffed. You will very often find them on the ingredient list for red chili, enchiladas, salsa, and tamales.

TRADITIONAL USES

Authentic to Mexico
Chiles rellenos (stuffed peppers)
Tamales
Adobo marinade for lamb
Braised black beans
Red mole sauce

NOTE
Toasting not recommended

RECOMMENDED PAIRINGS
Squash soup
Roast duck
Barbecue sauce
Beef stew
Chocolate mousse

SPICE PAIRINGS
cumin, garlic, orange peel, oregano, paprika

HEAT INDEX
Light heat

RECIPE IDEAS
1. Mix cooked egg yolk with ancho chile powder, mayonnaise, lime juice, and chopped fresh cilantro to prepare Mexican-inspired deviled eggs.
2. Grate whole ripe tomatoes on the large holes of a box grater. Add ancho chile powder, lemon juice, olive oil, and chopped onions for a quick salsa.
3. In a blender, purée cooked red beans, ancho chile powder, and fresh garlic cloves. Season with salt for a pungent spread or side dish.

QUICK BLEND
Puebla
See photograph, page 53.

Season kabocha, or other squash varieties, with a bit of this blend and olive oil before roasting until tender. It also adds complexity and mild heat to a balsamic vinaigrette destined for pork belly or arugula salad.

Makes about 3 tablespoons/26 grams

1½ tablespoons/15 grams ancho chile powder
½ tablespoon/5 grams cumin, toasted and ground
1 teaspoon/3 grams unsweetened cocoa powder
Scant ¾ teaspoon/2 grams white sesame seeds, toasted
Scant ½ teaspoon/1 gram chipotle powder

ANISE

PIMPINELLA ANISUM

A sweet, fennel- and caraway-scented seed

—

FLAVOR & AROMA Anise, also known as green anise, has fennel, caraway, licorice, camphor, and even some acidic notes. Its flavors linger and its natural sweetness is a nice alternative to sugar in breads and dishes both savory and sweet. I love pairing it with fish and seafood as well as fruits and chocolate. The small seeds, when left whole, are also great in blends because, when you chew them, they release layers of taste and a refreshing, cooling sensation that adds complexity to dishes. I source all my anise seeds from Turkey and India.

ORIGIN ☞ Native to the Eastern Mediterranean, Egypt, and the Middle East ☞ Cultivated in Western Asia, Europe, and North America

HARVEST SEASON This annual plant of the parsley (Apiaceae) family reaches about 18 inches high and its white flowers bloom in July. After flowering, its seeds ripen August through September and are harvested by cutting the whole plant. They are laid out to dry for about a week, and then threshed to separate the seeds.

PARTS USED Seeds, leaves, and stems

ABOUT Anise (not to be confused with star anise) is related to cumin, dill, and caraway. Its use dates back to ancient Egypt as early as 1500 BC, and the Romans are said to have added it to a spiced cake called *mustacae* to aid digestion. For centuries, the sweet licorice-flavored seed has been featured in German spiced cakes and soups; the cordials of France, Spain, and Italy; and the raki and ouzo of Turkey and Greece, respectively. In addition to its seeds, its young leaves can also be eaten raw or cooked and are especially good in salads, teas, soups, and stews.

Today, most will instantly recognize artificial licorice flavoring in candies, chewing gum, and even cough syrups. Anise's essential oils have a long-held reputation of being an effective cough suppressant and treatment for bronchitis.

TRADITIONAL USES

Pastis (anise-flavored spirit)—France
Pain d'épices (spice bread)—France
Ouzo (anise-flavored aperitif)—Greece
Pizzelles (thin waffle cookies)—Italy
Biscotti (twice-baked cookies)—Italy

NOTE
Toasting recommended

RECOMMENDED PAIRINGS
Celery rémoulade
Fennel velouté
Roast leg of lamb
Shortbread cookies
Peach cobbler

SPICE PAIRINGS
caraway, clove, mace, pink pepperberries, tarragon

RECIPE IDEAS
1. Season sliced radishes with anise seeds, olive oil, coarse salt, and orange juice for a salad.
2. Incorporate anise seeds into piecrust dough for a surprising texture and great flavor.
3. Upgrade your tuna salad with anise seeds, black olives, and lemon juice.

QUICK BLEND
Anisette

Season a lentil salad with this crunchy blend and dress it with Dijon mustard and red wine vinegar, or sprinkle it on a bagel with lox and cream cheese for added flavor and texture.

Makes about 3 tablespoons/27 grams

2½ tablespoons/15 grams anise seeds, toasted
½ tablespoon/5 grams yellow mustard seeds
1 teaspoon/3 grams caraway seeds, toasted
Scant ¾ teaspoon/2 grams black mustard seeds
Scant ¾ teaspoon/2 grams poppy seeds

ANNATTO

BIXA ORELLANA

A peppery, starchy seed that delivers a bold, reddish hue

FLAVOR & AROMA I find that annatto both tastes and smells a little of tomato. It has a slight acidity and a sweet, peppery flavor. Its aroma also has a hint of nutmeg and a musky quality. I mainly use it for the color it imparts in marinades and as a secret weapon for a deeply hued tomato sauce or soup. But I also like annatto for its rich, starchy quality that thickens sauces and stews. It creates great rubs that really stick to meat.

The whole seeds are impossibly hard to grind, which is probably why people tend to buy them already ground. I only buy whole seeds, and I have to admit it is a nightmare to process them. They are rich in natural oils and can get the grinders stuck—I once spent two hours cleaning one of our larger grinders. If you choose to buy and keep them whole (and not break your grinder), know that the seeds become tender after longer cooking times. You can also infuse warm oil with the seeds to obtain a beautiful red seasoning oil. Unless you know and trust the source of your ground annatto, which is sometimes blended with salt, the other reason to buy whole seeds is that the potency holds up much better over time.

ORIGIN ☞ Native to tropical regions in Mexico, Central America, South America, and the Caribbean ☞ Cultivated mainly in Africa, Asia, Central America, and the Caribbean

HARVEST SEASON Annatto seeds come from the tropical *Bixa orellana* plant in the achiote (Bixaceae) family. The plants flower only in the second or third year after planting, beginning around August and continuing for about 7 months. Heart-shaped fruit pods, which are covered in red prickly spikes, ripen approximately 30 days after flowering and split open to reveal 10 to 50 seeds nestled in bright red pulp. The seeds have the appearance of tiny brick-red triangles.

Traditionally, ripe pod clusters are cut and laid out in the sun for 3 to 10 days or placed in a dryer to hasten the process. To collect the dye, which is often used to color cakes, ripe fruits are macerated in water, allowing the dye to settle. Dried pods are then beaten with sticks to remove the seeds, and carefully winnowed so as not to lose the colorful coating.

PARTS USED Dried seeds and pulp

ABOUT I discovered annatto seeds in the United States, where I learned they are traditionally used for their vibrant red-orange color. In ancient times they were used for Mayan war paint, dyeing fabrics, and later as a natural food coloring. Large manufacturers use it to give mustard, cheeses, and other dairy products their hues.

Also known in the Mexican, Caribbean, and Latin markets as achiote, annatto is featured in much of Yucatecan cuisine and can be purchased in paste or block form. It is an essential part of rubs, marinades, the *recado rojo* used as a basis for *pollo pibil* (marinated chicken wrapped in banana leaves), and especially *cochinita pibil* (a braised pork dish). Each dish benefits from the deep red color the annatto gives up during cooking. It is also one of the main ingredients in the Venezuelan spice blend *aliño criollo*. In the Philippines, where it's known as *atsuwete* or *achuete*, it can be found in *kare-kare* (vegetable and oxtail stew), *pipian* (chicken stew), and *ukoy* (shrimp and potato fritters).

TRADITIONAL USES

Achiote paste—Mexico
Tamales—Mexico
Gouda cheese—Europe
Adobo—Spain and Portugal
Mustard—Worldwide

NOTE

Toasting not recommended

RECOMMENDED PAIRINGS

🍝 Bolognese
🍳 Pomodoro
🥣 Squash velouté
🌿 Sweet potato purée
🌾 Paella

SPICE PAIRINGS

cumin, garlic, sumac, tomato powder, yellow mustard

RECIPE IDEAS

1. Steep whole annatto seeds in warm oil for about 10 minutes and then filter. Use the red oil in sauces and salad dressings.
2. Mix ground annatto seeds and cayenne powder with crushed dried oregano leaves and use as a marinade for fish.
3. In a mixer, blend annatto powder, yellow mustard seed, white wine vinegar, salt, and vegetable oil for a quick homemade mustard.

QUICK BLEND
Rojo

Rub this vibrant, musky blend on a piece of skirt steak and let it marinate for 2 to 3 hours before grilling or cooking it in a cast-iron pan.

Makes about ⅓ cup/38 grams

2 tablespoons/20 grams annatto seed, ground
1 tablespoon/10 grams yellow mustard seed, coarsely ground
1 tablespoon/5 grams dried garlic, ground (garlic powder)
½ tablespoon/3 grams ground ginger

ASAFOETIDA

FERULA ASAFOETIDA

Intensely aromatic resin that mellows wonderfully when cooked

FLAVOR & AROMA You will not like asafoetida the first time you smell it. It's kind of like fermented onion or garlic meeting sulfur or rotten eggs. This is why it is commonly referred to as stinking gum and devil's dung. Nothing about this sounds appealing, especially when you think about adding it to your food. But it is one of the few spices that smells bad on its own and does wonders to food when cooked and used with other ingredients.

When I started using it, I researched Indian, Afghan, and Iranian cuisines to see how they implemented it in their dishes. I discovered that it is often blended with other spices and that cooking it is essential. I also found that Brahmin and Jain sects use it as a replacement for onion and garlic, two things their diet forbids. So, those extreme garlic and onion notes are actually a good thing.

I have met a few people over the years who were all excited about a fish and spinach dish they had eaten in India that had what they considered a "magic" flavor. In most cases, what made it special was the asafoetida. I like to use it in curry-type blends, where it adds a savory element that's hard to pinpoint but would be greatly missed if left behind.

ORIGIN ☞ Native to Iran and Afghanistan ☞ Cultivated mainly in Iran and Afghanistan, but also in parts of India and Pakistan

HARVEST SEASON Asafoetida is a milky, resin-like substance drawn out of the large taproot of ferula (giant fennel) plants in the parsley (Apiaceae) family. Before the plants flower in the spring, the stem is cut off near the crown, and the resin is extracted. In the days that follow, and repeatedly over 3 months until the roots dry up, fresh cuts are made until all the resin has been extracted.

PARTS USED Dried resin from stems and rhizomes, or taproots

ABOUT Also known as hing, asafoetida has been used in Europe for at least two millennia and was a popular spice in the Middle Ages. Before the extinction of the North African silphion plant, it was used as a less expensive option in ancient Greek and Roman cuisines, and afterward it continued to be found in dishes like mutton in France. But beyond the sixteenth century, it all but disappeared from European cuisine.

Where you will find it today is in South India, Iran, and Afghanistan. Actually, very little is used outside of its native countries, apart from their communities of immigrants around the world. In Indian cuisine, particularly the vegetarian dishes of South India, asafoetida is used to flavor fish, curry powders, the *sambar podi* spice mixture, soups, sauces, and *chaat masala*. Anywhere garlic will work, asafoetida will too.

In stores you will find asafoetida mostly in a powder form and, even more often, mixed with rice flour. Asafoetida is expensive, so cutting it with rice flour lowers the price. The ground form is less intense than the resin and can be used without first being cooked, but it doesn't have the same shelf life. It'll last a few years but will lose its scent, while the resin seems nearly indestructible. The resin needs to be cooked to dissolve and be incorporated into a dish. It's also very strong, so a little goes a long way. Note that if you buy resin pearls, which you can only find in India, they will be hard to grind.

TRADITIONAL USES
Authentic to India
Chaat masala (spice blend)
Sambar (vegetable stew)
Pickles and chutneys
Lentil stews
Palak paneer (spinach and cheese)

NOTE
Toasting not recommended

RECOMMENDED PAIRINGS
Split pea soup
Roasted beets
Grilled octopus
Lamb stew
Soba noodles

SPICE PAIRINGS
amchoor, coriander, galangal, ginger, wasabi

RECIPE IDEAS
1. Stir ground asafoetida into full-fat Greek yogurt and use to marinate lamb chops before grilling or broiling them.
2. Season diced pineapple with ground asafoetida, rice wine vinegar, and hot sauce and simmer until tender for a spicy chutney.
3. Sprinkle ground asafoetida over diced cooked leeks, add bread crumbs, raw egg, and ricotta cheese, and form little patties to make leek fritters for frying.

QUICK BLEND
Ferula

Use this pungent, oniony blend to season sautéed spinach with crumbled feta cheese and lemon sauce. It also adds a garlicky flavor to crispy potato pancakes.

Makes about 2 tablespoons/18 grams

1 tablespoon/10 grams ground asafoetida
Scant ¾ teaspoon/2 grams ground amchoor
½ tablespoon/5 grams yellow mustard seeds, coarsely ground
Scant ½ teaspoon/1 gram ground chipotle

BARBERRY

BERBERIS VULGARIS

*Sweet-tart berries that are
surprisingly versatile*

—

FLAVOR & AROMA I discovered barberries as a child at a Persian friend's house. To this day, I remember his mother preparing some of the best rice dishes using these little tart-yet-sweet berries. I always thought they were sour raisins until I learned otherwise. Unlike many other dried fruits and berries, they have no added sugar or sulfur, so their great natural flavor can really shine through—they taste better than they smell. They are also rich in pectin, which makes them good for jams and jellies.

ORIGIN ☞ Native to central and southern Europe, northwest Africa, and Western Asia ☞ Cultivated in Iran (Khorasan), Northern Europe, Britain, and the New England region of the United States

HARVEST SEASON *Berberis vulgaris*, not to be confused with a number of other barberry varieties also in the barberry (Berberidaceae) family, is a dense perennial bush that grows in the wild. Yellow flowers bloom in late spring, giving way to oblong, sour red berries in late summer or early fall. Traditionally, they are harvested manually by cutting the branches, and then drying them.

PARTS USED Berries

ABOUT In the South Khorasan province of Iran, cultivated barberry has been traced back some two hundred years. It is said to have been brought onto United States soil around the seventeenth century in the hope that it would create nice thorn hedges and yellow dye, and that early settlers could use its flavorful sour berries for jam. What they didn't count on was that the plant would be a consummate host for wheat rust, obliterating crops all over the country. It wasn't until the early twentieth century that the plant was nearly eradicated. Barberry is very persistent. In the United States, it remains prominent in New England states, where it is used in pickles served with fish or meat.

Today, the spice remains an expensive berry compared to other more mainstream varieties. Persians, who call it *zereshk,* are fanatic about buying the best-quality bright red berries. Barberry can turn dark and brown very fast, so it's better to refrigerate it if you are not using it right away. I also recommend keeping the berries whole (grinding them will make a paste) and combining them with whole spices, though sometimes I'll coarsely chop them with a knife.

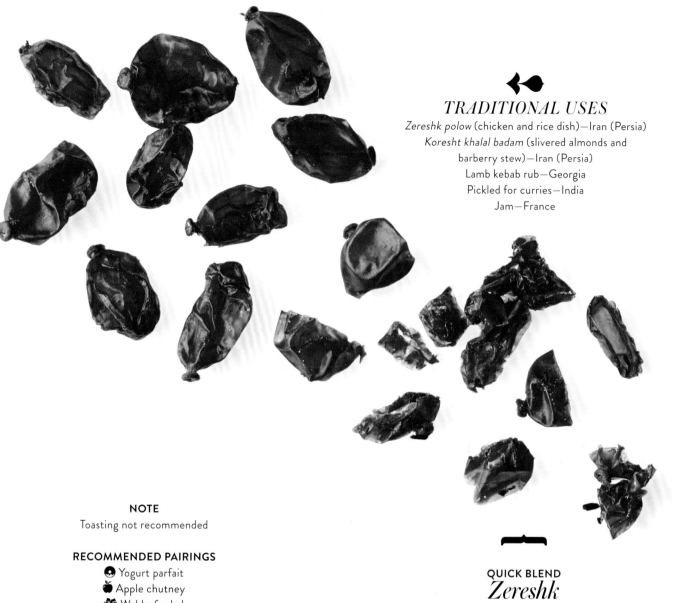

TRADITIONAL USES

Zereshk polow (chicken and rice dish)—Iran (Persia)
Koresht khalal badam (slivered almonds and
barberry stew)—Iran (Persia)
Lamb kebab rub—Georgia
Pickled for curries—India
Jam—France

NOTE
Toasting not recommended

RECOMMENDED PAIRINGS
Yogurt parfait
Apple chutney
Waldorf salad
Lamb sliders
Couscous

SPICE PAIRINGS
caraway, cardamom, dill, fennel, tarragon

RECIPE IDEAS
1. Mix whole barberries with Greek yogurt, olive oil, lemon juice,
salt, and pepper for a quick, tangy dressing.
2. Toss some cauliflower florets with whole barberries, olive oil,
and orange juice before roasting in the oven.
3. In a blender, purée barberries with apple cider, salt,
and hot sauce to make a thick marinade for pork chops.

QUICK BLEND
Zereshk

This is a sweet-tart nutty blend to season a thick halibut fillet before
broiling or baking. It also gives potato salad an added dimension of flavor.

Makes about ⅓ cup/30 grams

3 tablespoons/15 grams barberries, coarsely chopped with a knife
1 tablespoon/10 grams white sesame seeds, toasted
1 tablespoon/3 grams dried dill
Scant ½ teaspoon/2 grams coarse gray salt

BASIL

OCIMUM BASILICUM

One of a family of sweet, somewhat peppery, anise-scented leafy herbs

---

FLAVOR & AROMA Basil has peppery, clove-like notes that make it versatile. I buy my dried basil from Israel, and the quality is great. It has such a sweet, concentrated scent, and the leaves are crushed to a large size, allowing me to either leave them whole or grind them more finely if I want to. I love grilling or searing with dried basil, because even when it gets charred it still has a great flavor; fresh leaves would burn and become bitter.

The underutilized parts of the plant are the seeds. You can sprinkle them into salads or into doughs, or even soak them in liquids to make a thick, gelatinous mixture (think chia seeds). In Thailand, the seeds are used to make a popular summertime drink called *nam manglak*.

Sweet basil is the most used culinary variety of the many available. From the anise-like flavor of the deep purple Genovese variety, to tiny-leafed Greek bush basil and the licorice-scented green-purple Thai basil, there are well over one hundred types to choose from. Some are better for hedges than cuisine, so I'd recommend starting with sweet basil and expanding your culinary journey from there.

ORIGIN ☞ Native to tropical Asia and Africa ☞ Cultivated in many Asian and Mediterranean countries and the United States

HARVEST SEASON Sweet basil, the most common variety, is a tender annual that can reach up to 2 feet in height. Basil leaves can be harvested in early summer (if planted before the last spring frost) as soon as the plants reach about 6 inches, and small white flowers typically bloom from June through the frost.

PARTS USED Leaves and flower buds

ABOUT Basil belongs to the mint (Lamiaceae) family, and its name comes from the Greek word *basiliskos*, meaning "royal, kinglike." It is said that basil was once used to ward off offending insects and reptiles. That's not entirely a myth: this leafy herb, known mostly for adorning our pizzas and tomato sauces, is also a natural insect repellent.

Dried basil, as with many other dried herbs, does not replace fresh basil. They both serve different purposes. While fresh leaves are used for salads and as last-minute additions to soups and pastas, dried basil is great in dressings and marinades. In France, it is a major part of the famed herbes de Provence for grilling and roasting, and many countries add it to stuffing and cured meats because it doesn't oxidize from marinating or aging.

❧

TRADITIONAL USES

Dried pasta dough —Italy
Meatballs—Italy
Pistou—France
Herbes de Provence (spice blend)—France
Chutney—India

NOTE

Toasting not recommended

RECOMMENDED PAIRINGS

🍎 Strawberry jam
🥚 Mushroom omelet
🥄 Tomato salsa
🌿 Stuffed tomatoes
🐚 Braised octopus

SPICE PAIRINGS

cilantro, fennel, pink pepperberries, rosemary, white pepper

RECIPE IDEAS

1. Mix crushed dried basil leaves with grated Parmesan cheese and chopped pecans and use to season sautéed zucchini.
2. In a food processor, purée feta cheese with crushed dried basil leaves and green olives to make a cheese spread.
3. Infuse simmering milk with crushed dried basil leaves and use to prepare an herbaceous potato purée.

QUICK BLEND

Basilicum

See photograph, pages 64–65.

Season whole, cleaned branzino fish with this blend before roasting it in the oven with lemon wedges. It also adds a savory, herbaceous element to baked portobello mushrooms.

Makes about ½ cup/22 grams

¼ cup/10 grams crushed dried basil
1½ tablespoons/3 grams crushed dried marjoram
1 tablespoon/3 grams crushed dried mint
½ tablespoon/3 grams dried garlic flakes, coarsely ground
½ tablespoon/3 grams coriander, toasted and coarsely ground

BAY

LAURUS NOBILIS

An intensely aromatic leaf used to enhance dishes and then, sadly, discarded

FLAVOR & AROMA Dried bay leaves have a strong, pungent aroma that is as good as what you'll find in fresh leaves. They have fewer bitter and soapy notes than fresh when cooked for long periods, and they are more shelf stable, since there is no risk of spoiling. I would recommend buying leaves whole instead of ground. You can buy a large amount of fresh leaves and easily dry them yourself on a piece of parchment paper on the kitchen counter. Fresh leaves will also store very well in the freezer.

The dried leaves are great in brines, pickles, and marinades. In spice blends, they add a fresh, somewhat resinous note reminiscent of eucalyptus, which comes from the natural eugenol in the essential oils—and which mellows during cooking. Either way, you do not need much to make your point. I also love to throw some onto hot coals in the grill to get an aromatic smoke while grilling.

ORIGIN ☞ Native to the Eastern Mediterranean ☞ Cultivated mainly in Turkey but also in Northern Europe and the Americas

HARVEST SEASON Bay, or bay laurel, is a hardy evergreen shrub in the laurel (Lauraceae) family that can grow to nearly 60 feet high. Fresh leaves, which are shiny and dark green on top with a muted green underside, can be harvested at any time. This slow-growing shrub also produces yellow-white flowers in May and small purple-black berries in the fall.

PARTS USED Leaves

ABOUT When you think of bay laurel, the images of Olympic medalists or ancient Roman emperors donning wreaths may come to mind. What we now mostly use for culinary purposes has been considered a symbol of peace, honor, and triumph for poets, scholars, and athletes since the time of the Ancient Greeks, who ascribed it to Apollo in their myths. It also goes by the name Apollo's bay leaf, after all.

This aromatic herb, which grows predominantly in Turkey, is not to be confused with the California variety (*Umbellularia californica*), which is often sold as a substitute; it is not. That variety has larger leaves that are a bit oilier and more pungent. Some people have been known to have a bad reaction—sneezing, headaches, and sinus irritation—to its natural toxic umbellulone element.

Bay laurel is an essential ingredient in a number of longer-cooking dishes such as stews, stocks, and soups because its flavor seeps out slowly. Most people are familiar with fishing it out of soup broth and tossing it before serving—though you could chop it up and eat it too.

Growing up in Israel, I used to go out and pick a few laurel leaves as needed. Living in New York makes this more of a memory than a reality, which is perhaps why I somehow neglected this spice for many years and forgot how great it was. Now I always have a jar of dried leaves in my kitchen to add to nearly every soup or stew I make, and I even throw one or two into pans of roasting vegetables.

TRADITIONAL USES

Bouquet garni (herb bundle)—France
Béchamel sauce (white sauce)—France
Provençal daube (braised beef
and wine stew)—France
Court bouillon (cooking liquid)—France
Garam masala (spice mixture)—India

NOTE
Toasting not recommended

RECOMMENDED PAIRINGS
🦀 Crab boil
🥣 Chicken noodle soup
🌱 Roasted potatoes
🍳 Mushroom gravy
🐖 Brine for pork loin

SPICE PAIRINGS
anise, lemon peel, onion, oregano, white pepper

RECIPE IDEAS
1. Sprinkle ground bay leaf into salted boiling water when cooking pastas or blanching vegetables for an aromatic element.
2. While searing fish in a pan, ignite 1 or 2 bay leafs, drop them into the pan, cover, and let them burn to get a smoky, wood-grilled flavor.
3. Whisk a few pinches of ground bay leaf into eggs to enhance a spinach omelet.

QUICK BLEND
Apollo

Use this blend to season bass and shallot kebabs and serve with tartar sauce. It also adds resinous notes to pickled pearl onions.

Makes about ⅓ cup/19 grams

1 cup/10 grams dried bay leaves, ground
2 tablespoons/2 grams crushed dried tarragon leaves
1 tablespoon/3 grams crushed dried mint leaves
2 teaspoons/2 grams crushed dried basil leaves
Scant ¾ teaspoon/2 grams ground sumac

BIRD'S EYE CHILE

CAPSICUM ANNUUM

An unassuming little chile that packs a lot of heat with a touch of acidity

FLAVOR & AROMA Many dishes need heat to elevate them and lend some complexity. Most recipes that call for "seasoning" are only referring to salt and pepper. Who says you can't use a bird's eye chile? This chile delivers punch, but also acidic and fruity notes. Many of us have access to dried red chiles only, but even dry they still add great color and flavor to dishes. Another advantage of using them dry is that you can create a powder without adding any humidity to an otherwise crisp dish. The less ripe yellow and green bird's eye chiles have light sour notes and are usually pickled or sold fresh rather than dried.

A member of the Solanaceae, or nightshade, family (just like tomatoes), bird's eye chiles have a very high capsaicin content, delivering a lot of heat and flavor with 100,000 to 225,000 Scoville heat units. Bird's eye chile is not to be confused with the African bird's eye chile called piri piri (page 224), which is a touch less hot.

ORIGIN ☞ Native to South and Central America and later Southeast Asia ☞ Cultivated in India, Thailand, Vietnam, and Malaysia

HARVEST SEASON Bird's eye chiles are a warm weather crop best planted 2 to 3 weeks after the last frost. If you want to harvest them when they are green or yellow, they can be cut at the stem about 100 or more days from transplant. These small 1- to 1½-inch chiles take on a vibrant red color when they reach full maturity (around 130 days from transplanting), when they are typically harvested and dried. Thai curries get their signature colors and flavors from the bird's eye's different stages of ripeness (yellow, green, and red).

PARTS USED Whole peppers

ABOUT Though commonly used in traditional Southeast Asian cuisines and one of a number of chiles that goes by the name "Thai chile," bird's eye chiles, like all capsicums, are descendants of American ancestors. Around five hundred years ago, Spanish conquistadors brought American chiles to Asia, where, over time, new cultivars like the bird's eye were born.

This chile is great chopped or used whole in both raw and longer-cooked dishes, and is commonly used as a garnish or added to soups and salads. You may recognize them in a number of sambals and as a staple of Kerala cuisine. Some cultures will even pickle them or grind them into a sauce. I like to add one or two whole chiles to a dish while it's cooking, and then remove them at the end to leave a subtle trace of heat behind (and to eat them later).

TRADITIONAL USES

Kochchi sambal (salad)—Thailand
Beef Penang curry—Malaysia
Khao kha moo (stewed pork served with
rice)—Thailand
Sambal oelek (chile paste)—Indonesia
Nasi goreng (stir-fried rice)—Indonesia

QUICK BLEND
Little Bird

This fiery blend is great for seasoning whole bok choy heads
before roasting them and serving with steamed rice. It also brings
warmth and acidity to beef broth and noodles.

Makes about 2 tablespoons/19 grams

3 pieces/6 grams whole star anise, ground
½ tablespoon/5 grams ground turmeric
2 teaspoons/6 grams dried bird's eye chile, stemmed and coarsely ground
Scant ½ teaspoon/2 grams fleur de sel

NOTE
Toasting not recommended

RECOMMENDED PAIRINGS
Coconut-shrimp soup
Sushi rice
Ceviche
Steamed clams
Spicy chicken wings

SPICE PAIRINGS
cilantro, cumin, garlic, ginger, lemon peel

HEAT INDEX
High heat

RECIPE IDEAS
1. Cook coarsely ground bird's eye chile in olive oil with
chopped garlic and rosemary for a quick pasta sauce.
2. Mix a little ground dried bird's eye chile with grated
pecorino cheese and use to season fried baby artichokes.
3. In a blender, purée fresh cantaloupe melon with a few pinches
of ground dried bird's eye chile, lime juice, and sour cream for
a chilled soup.

CALAMINT

CALAMINTHA NEPETA

The oregano- and mint-scented leaves and flowers of a wild Mediterranean herb

---

FLAVOR & AROMA A few years ago, an Italian chef gave me a small sample bag of calamint, calling it *nipitella*. I loved its oregano notes that also had a hint of mint, sage, and savory. It even reminded me of the za'atar herb mixture from Israel. The dried leaves are great in teas, but the fresh leaves are better when cooked. Its small flowers, which have a mellower flavor, can be used as a garnish or sprinkled onto salads.

ORIGIN ☞ Native to Italy ☞ Cultivated in the Mediterranean, Europe, and parts of the Americas

HARVEST SEASON This bushy perennial plant of the mint (Lamiaceae) family grows wild in the Mediterranean—in Tuscany and Umbria in particular. Small green leaves cover upright stems reaching up to 18 inches tall and can be harvested from late spring through the summer. Tiny lavender flowers, which attract butterflies, bloom for around 6 weeks starting in August before the plant goes dormant in the winter.

PARTS USED Leaves, stems, and flowers

ABOUT Once I was introduced to calamint, more commonly known as lesser calamint, I immediately wanted more. But because it mainly grows in Italy in small quantities and only as a seasonal ingredient, it isn't always easy to come by. Nobody was able to supply me with enough of it until I found a grower in Tuscany. In the United States, your best bet is finding it as a potted plant or at a farmers' market. In Italy, where it grows wild as an herb and an attractive landscape perennial, they don't have this problem.

It was used during medieval times for medicinal purposes and has been a staple of Mediterranean, specifically Italian, cuisine for centuries. If you are ever searching for it, it is known in Italy as *mentuccia, nipitella,* or *nepitella* and shouldn't be confused with its better-known relatives *Calamintha officinalis* and *Calamintha grandiflora* (they're similar, but not the same).

In Turkey, they sometimes use the leaves in place of mint, but I love adding it to a simple pasta dish or to just a bit of olive oil and lemon juice for a fresh dressing. It also works great on meat and seafood while grilling. Cooking it with artichokes is fantastic because it balances the strong flavors of the artichoke, addressing the long-held challenge of pairing artichokes with wine. And if it helps to enjoy wine, sign me up.

TRADITIONAL USES

Shrimp with calamint, garlic, and red
chiles—Sardinia
Braised artichokes—Tuscany, Italy
Wild mushrooms with calamint—Italy
Risotto—Italy
Grilled fish—Turkey

NOTE
Toasting not recommended

RECOMMENDED PAIRINGS
Cheese omelet
White bean soup
Pork meatballs
Mushroom lasagna
Lamb roast

SPICE PAIRINGS
anise, fennel, green peppercorn, lemon peel, sage

RECIPE IDEAS
1. Mix ground calamint with bread crumbs, olive oil, and
chopped garlic and sprinkle over steamed asparagus.
2. Coat slices of fresh goat cheese with olive oil and a little ground
calamint and broil quickly before serving on toast.
3. Season thick orange wedges with olive oil, a few pinches of
ground calamint, and salt. Grill and serve with grilled seafood.

QUICK BLEND
Siena

Season fresh ricotta cheese with this blend and serve with
garlic-rubbed toasted sourdough bread. It also brightens
up fettuccine pasta and porcini mushrooms.

Makes about ⅓ cup/19 grams

¼ cup/10 grams dried calamint
2 teaspoons/5 grams fennel seeds, toasted and ground
Scant ¾ teaspoon/2 grams granulated dried orange peel
½ teaspoon/1 gram dried green peppercorns, ground
Scant ½ teaspoon/1 gram anise seeds, ground

CARAWAY

CARUM CARVI

The anise-scented seeds that give rye bread its familiar crunch

---

FLAVOR & AROMA With a strong aroma and a lingering flavor, caraway seeds are a cross between cumin and fennel with hints of anise. Many people who do not care much for fennel-anise flavors do like caraway, because of its depth of flavor and milder notes. They add a fresh, sweet, and savory element to a variety of dishes, developing a layer of complexity in both taste and texture.

ORIGIN ☞ Native to Central Europe through Asia ☞ Cultivated mainly in Holland, but also Finland, Eastern Europe, Germany, Canada, the United States, and North Africa

HARVEST SEASON The seeds of this plant in the parsley (Apiaceae) family are harvested after the second year of growth, after they darken, between July and September and before the first frost. They are reaped with a binder or cut, dried (unripe seeds will also ripen as they dry), and then threshed. Leaves can be harvested throughout the growing period, and roots, which resemble a small parsnip, can be pulled in the second year.

PARTS USED Seeds

ABOUT You probably recognize caraway seeds from rye bread. I remember eating pumpernickel bread as a child at my grandparents' house and loving the anise-like sweet taste of the seeds in it. Later, I learned that many countries use caraway to add these complex notes to their dishes. (Just don't confuse caraway with Persian *sajira* or black cumin, these two have a similar appearance but stronger cumin notes.

Mostly popular in European cuisines, caraway can be found in British seed cake, caraway-flavored spirits like German Kümmel, Tunisian *tabil* (spice blend), cheeses, stews, sausages, cabbage dishes, and pickle brine. I especially love the North African methods of adding it to vegetable dishes and condiments. The size of the seed is also perfect for using whole in many recipes, and caraway works great with fruit and cheese.

TRADITIONAL USES

Aquavit—Scandinavia

Harissa—Tunisia

Jewish rye breads/German pumpernickel
breads—Europe and Israel

Pain d'épices (spice blend or gingerbread)—France

Cabbage borscht—Central Europe

NOTE
Toasting recommended

RECOMMENDED PAIRINGS
Pickled carrots

Leek soup

Wheat berries

Gravlax

Biscotti

SPICE PAIRINGS
clove, dill, Espelette chile, juniper berries, orange peel

RECIPE IDEAS
1. Season grated carrots with toasted caraway seeds and add
raisins, lemon juice, and cayenne for a fresh salad.

2. In a blender, purée cooked English peas, toasted caraway seeds,
garlic, and salted butter for a side dish.

3. Spread Dijon mustard on pork chops, season with caraway seeds
and coarse black pepper, and broil.

QUICK BLEND
Pumpernickel

Use this blend to season halved Brussels sprouts before sautéing
and again when deglazing with an anise-based spirit such as Aquavit.
It also adds a great color and texture to whitefish salad.

Makes about 3 tablespoons/25 grams

2 tablespoons/15 grams caraway seeds, toasted and coarsely ground
½ tablespoon/5 grams ground turmeric
1 teaspoon/3 grams ground sweet paprika
1 teaspoon/2 grams dried garlic flakes, ground

BLACK CARDAMOM

AMOMUM SUBULATUM/AMOMUM COSTATUM

The larger, smokier cousin of green cardamom, with a flavor and identity all its own

—

FLAVOR & AROMA Black cardamom has nothing much in common with green cardamom. It is larger, smokier, more savory, and has floral notes of ginger. This spice is traditionally used only in savory dishes, but I like to pair it with dark chocolate and fruit. It gives sweets and desserts a savory element. It is also a great source of smoky notes that mimic those of grilling and meat in vegetable or vegan dishes.

Pods are mainly sold whole, and it's important to look for ones without splits or cracks, as those tend to have lost some of their flavor. Wait until the last minute to grind the seeds for the best results.

ORIGIN ☞ Native to the Eastern Himalayas ☞ Cultivated in Eastern Nepal, India, and Bhutan

HARVEST SEASON Black cardamom pods are traditionally handpicked or cut with a knife before they fully ripen and crack open. Starting from the third year after planting, reddish-brown pods ripen from August through November. First, they are gathered in a bamboo *nanglo* (flat woven tray) and winnowed. Then—and this is essential to their flavor—they are dried and cured using an age-old method of direct heating in a *bhatty*. In this system, the pods spend nearly a full day drying by the smoke of an open fire, which gives them their characteristic dark brown color and smoky smell and taste.

PARTS USED Pods and seeds

ABOUT Black cardamom, or large cardamom, is a member of the ginger (Zingiberaceae) family and is a symbol of hospitality in Nepal. The Nepalese chew these leathery, dark brown wrinkled seeds to cleanse the palate and freshen the breath after a spicy meal.

If green cardamom is a stranger to most kitchens in the West, black cardamom is nearly unheard of. Yet in North Indian and South Asian cuisines, there just isn't another spice that can impart its bold, smoky, perfumy flavor. It is considered a warming spice that is essential to India's garam masala spice mixture (page 297), which you'll find as a main component of rice pilafs and curry dishes. In China's Sichuan province, it plays a starring role in long-cooking meat stews.

TRADITIONAL USES

Garam masala (spice mixture)—India
Pan masala (herb, nut, and seed mixture)—India
Basmati rice pilaf—India
Phở (soup)—Vietnam
Sichuan braised meats—China

NOTE
Toasting not recommended

RECOMMENDED PAIRINGS
Old-fashioned
Seafood gumbo
Mole sauce
Brisket
Chocolate truffles

SPICE PAIRINGS
basil, cumin, fennel, garlic, lemongrass

RECIPE IDEAS
1. Add black cardamom pods to boiling water with sliced peaches, sliced lemons, and honey and let chill for an iced tea.
2. Season ground lamb with ground black cardamom, salt, and chopped garlic. Stuff whole portobello mushrooms with the mixture and bake.
3. Sprinkle ground black cardamom into simmering chicken stock and use to poach halibut fillets.

QUICK BLEND
Nanglo

Sprinkle in this blend when caramelizing sliced red onions with sherry vinegar and serve as a condiment for meat or fish. It also gives a smoky, warming element to mole sauces.

Makes about 3 tablespoons/23 grams

2 tablespoons/10 grams black cardamom pods and seeds, ground
½ tablespoon/5 grams dried onion slices, ground
½ tablespoon/5 grams celery seeds
1 teaspoon/3 grams yellow mustard seeds

GREEN AND WHITE CARDAMOM

ELETTARIA CARDAMOMUM

An ancient spice that delivers complex, peppery notes from its seeds and pods

FLAVOR & AROMA Green cardamom has a pungent, dominating taste that is complex and flavorful with slightly sweet, spicy, resinous, floral, and citrus notes. The aftertaste is peppery with an almost herbal bitterness and warm with menthol properties like eucalyptus, staying on the tongue throughout the meal. White cardamom, on the other hand, doesn't have the same sharp notes, and its scent is much more floral and sweet. I even think it has some dairy, cheese-like notes.

While most of the cardamom in the world is sold ground, the quality of whole pods that you grind yourself is far superior. The seeds are delicious on their own when sprinkled on salads, but the pods are worth keeping for their floral, fresh notes.

ORIGIN ☞ Native to the Western Ghats of South India ☞ Cultivated mainly in Guatemala and India (specifically Kerala, Karnataka, and Tamil Nadu), but also in Colombia, Costa Rica, El Salvador, Vietnam, Nepal, Laos, Cambodia, Bengal, Java, Sri Lanka, and Tanzania

HARVEST SEASON The harvesting of just-ripened fruits occurs from the third year onward, once per month. Fully ripe or overripe fruits tend to split and do not have the coveted, premium-priced dark green hue. In Kerala, cardamom capsules are harvested October to February, but generally peak harvesting time is September to November.

PARTS USED Seeds and pods

ABOUT This ancient spice, also known as true cardamom, originates in the forests of the Western Ghats and is a perennial herb in the ginger (Zingiberaceae) family. Historically, Egyptians chewed the seeds to cleanse their teeth, and its natural oil was used as a perfume in ancient Rome and Greece. A thousand years ago the Vikings delivered it to Scandinavia, where it is common in cooking today. It was introduced to Guatemala in the 1920s, where it is now chiefly produced (of the output, 60% is exported to Saudi Arabia, due to its popularity in coffee). It is essential to many traditional dishes found in India, Africa, Nordic countries, the Middle East, and Asia. The seeds and pods have also been used for centuries medicinally to aid digestion and clear infection.

White cardamom is a blanched version of green cardamom that is better for storing; the quality of green cardamom tends to fade over time. The white pods are very expensive and used mainly in Persian and Scandinavian cuisines. My theory is that because the journey to Scandinavia took so long, the pods were blanched to better survive the trip.

At La Boîte, I source all my cardamom from Colombia, where it is organically grown by a couple of local families. A few years ago, one of these farmers came to me with what I considered at the time to be an average product. From then on, we worked together to help the growers achieve a higher-quality crop. It became so good that I now have to fight just to get my share of it. It's a good problem to have.

TRADITIONAL USES

Curries and curry powders—Asia and India
Masala chai (spiced black tea)—India
Pudding and desserts, such as *kulfi*—India
Coffee drinks—Turkey, Egypt, and Colombia
Zhoug (chile paste)—Yemen and Israel

NOTE
Toasting recommended

RECOMMENDED PAIRINGS
Iced tea
Chicken soup
Rice pilaf
Applesauce
Chocolate mousse

SPICE PAIRINGS
caraway, cinnamon, cumin, dill, juniper berries

RECIPE IDEAS

1. Season mango slices with ground green cardamom pods and
seeds, dark rum, and honey before grilling them.
2. Stir green cardamom seeds into simmering coconut milk,
and use as a poaching liquid for shrimp.
3. Combine ground white cardamom pods and seeds with
rice wine vinegar and sugar for a quick green bean pickling brine.

QUICK BLEND
Gravlax
See photograph, page 79.

Coat a piece of raw salmon with this blend and refrigerate it
overnight for a quick, simple, gravlax-style cured fish. Add it
to pickling liquid for beets for a layer of complexity.

Makes about ¼ cup/43 grams

1 tablespoon/10 grams juniper berries, ground
1 tablespoon/8 grams green cardamom pods, toasted and ground
½ tablespoon/25 grams coarse salt

CASCABEL

CAPSICUM ANNUUM

A mild- to medium-heat ball-shaped chile that, once dried, rattles when shaken

FLAVOR & AROMA I like using cascabels since they bring a touch of heat with a bit of sweetness, tomato notes, and acidity. They also have a nutty, slightly smoky element that pairs well with nearly any meat or fish. I usually coarsely grind them (with or without seeds) into medium flakes, which really adds to the texture of a spice blend and the dish it's used in. When rehydrating, I wouldn't recommend soaking them for longer than 20 minutes; they tend to get bitter.

ORIGIN ☞ Native to Central Mexico ☞ Cultivated in Mexico, specifically Jalisco, Durango, Coahuila, Guerrero, and San Luis Potosí

HARVESTING This perennial pepper plant in the nightshade (Solanaceae) family grows up to 2 feet tall over the warm summer months, when small, white flowers give way to round, cherry tomato–size chiles. They ripen from green to red and, when dried, turn a deep brownish-red, somewhat translucent color. Cascabels are harvested before the first frost by cutting at the stem. They are most commonly used after they have lain out to dry completely and wrinkle slightly.

PARTS USED Whole chiles

ABOUT The cascabel chile may be small, but what it lacks in size it makes up for in taste. Fresh chiles are commonly referred to as bola chile or *chile bola,* meaning "ball chile" in Spanish, a fitting name when you see one. When dried, the seeds inside become loose and rattle when shaken, earning cascabels another nickname, "rattle chile."

Unlike poblanos and jalapeños, which have different names when fresh or dried (ancho and chipotle, respectively), the name *cascabel* is used regardless of the state of the chile. In Mexico, where it grows and is mostly used, it is often toasted first on a *comal* (flat skillet) before being added to salsas, stews, soups, tamales, and rich sauces.

TRADITIONAL USES

Tomatillo-cascabel salsa—Mexico
Roasted pork cascabel sauce—Mexico
Beef and cascabel chili—Mexico
Pickled cascabel—Mexico
Cascabel romesco sauce—Spain

NOTE

Toasting not recommended

RECOMMENDED PAIRINGS

Minestrone soup
Baked beans
Chicken fajitas
Sausage and peppers
Salmon skewers

SPICE PAIRINGS

clove, cumin, garlic, oregano, tomato powder

HEAT INDEX

Light to medium heat

RECIPE IDEAS

1. Soak about a dozen whole, stemmed, dried cascabel peppers in warm water and then purée them in a blender with garlic, salt, and fresh cilantro leaves for a chile condiment.
2. Season shredded red cabbage with ground dried cascabel, lime juice, and sour cream for a salad.
3. Mix raw peanuts with ground cascabel, lightly beaten egg white, and salt and bake until toasted for spicy mixed nuts.

QUICK BLEND
Little Bell

Combine a few pinches of this blend with honey and cider vinegar and use to season chicken drumsticks before grilling or roasting them for a sticky, smoky finish.

Makes about ⅓ cup/28 grams

1½ tablespoons/15 grams coarsely ground dried cascabel
1½ tablespoons/7 grams allspice berries, ground
1½ tablespoons/3 grams dried marjoram
1 teaspoon/3 grams dried fenugreek seeds

CAYENNE PEPPER

CAPSICUM ANNUUM

The all-purpose hot chile commonly found in Western hot sauce

FLAVOR & AROMA Cayenne is a medium- to high-heat chile with sweet-and-sour notes, dusty overtones, and a great orangey color. When using cayenne, heat will not necessarily be the first thing you will taste, although it will hit you a few seconds after.

This chile is almost always sold ground into a powder. You want to look for a vibrant color and a pleasant scent. The advantage of using cayenne powder in cooking is that it incorporates well into liquids and other ingredients, so you get heat without texture. Because it is ground, it also releases its flavor, and of course heat, much faster. I highly recommend that every kitchen have a small jar of cayenne.

ORIGIN ☞ Native to French Guiana, Central and South America ☞ Cultivated in Mexico, Africa, India, and Louisiana

HARVEST SEASON These heat-loving peppers grow during the warm summer months and are ready to pick around 100 days after planting (typically August) and before the first frost. Chiles will turn from green to a bright red when they are full-flavored and ripe toward the end of the season, signaling that they are ready to harvest. They must be picked while still firm, waxy in appearance, and wrinkle-free, or they tend to rot. They are then hung or laid out in the sun when there is no chance of rain or humidity, until they are completely dry, in about a week or so.

PARTS USED Dried chiles

ABOUT Cayenne is part of the night-shade (Solanaceae) family, and the perfect example of a chile that can easily be used in nearly everything you cook or prepare. There's also a good chance you have this spice in a jar in your pantry. You might even use it

in the form of hot sauce on your scrambled eggs in the morning. Cayenne is a ubiquitous chile, used and loved all over the world as a bottled table condiment and, in its ground form, adding heat to anything from casseroles and beef chili to barbecue sauces and ketchup to fried fish and curry. Although it originated in French Guiana (it's actually named for the capital city), today good chiles grow all over the world.

TRADITIONAL USES

Hot sauce—Worldwide
Rouille sauce—France
Buffalo chicken wings—United States
Andouille sausage—Louisiana, United States
Gumbo—Louisiana, United States

NOTE

Toasting not recommended

RECOMMENDED PAIRINGS

Creole mustard sauce
Lobster salad
Aioli
Seared bass
Braised pork belly

SPICE PAIRINGS

coriander, garlic, ginger, lemon peel, sumac

HEAT INDEX

Medium to high heat

RECIPE IDEAS

1. Season pomegranate juice with cayenne powder and freeze in an ice cube tray to use in cocktails.
2. Flavor maple syrup with cayenne powder and soy sauce and use for glazing bacon slices for breakfast.
3. Mix cayenne powder with Dijon mustard, mayonnaise, lime juice, and ketchup for a quick, spicy cocktail sauce.

QUICK BLEND
Guiana

See photograph, page 84.

This hot, herbaceous blend is perfect for seasoning a whole head of blanched cauliflower before roasting it in the oven with olive oil until golden brown.

Makes about 2 tablespoons/13 grams

½ tablespoon/5 grams cayenne powder
2 teaspoons/2 grams crushed dried oregano
½ tablespoon/3 grams dried thyme leaves
Scant ¾ teaspoon/2 grams ground ginger
½ teaspoon/1 gram dried onion flakes, ground

CELERY

APIUM GRAVEOLENS

A fresh, herbaceous spice made from the seeds of the wild smallage plant

———

FLAVOR & AROMA Celery seeds suffer from bad PR. They are mainly known as a component of celery salt, but the irony is that celery seeds actually contain natural sodium and can be used to *reduce* salt in many recipes. Try adding some to your next soup or broth before adding regular salt, and you'll see what I mean. I like to leave them whole in many of my blends because they are very small and don't need much grinding. They bring great herbaceous and fresh notes to blends and dishes, and have a distinctively earthy, celery scent. I buy mine from India.

ORIGIN ☞ Native to the Mediterranean ☞ Cultivated mainly in India, but also France, England, the United States (particularly California and Arizona), and China

HARVEST SEASON Celery seeds (fruits) come from the smallage plant, a wild form of celery. Fruits are harvested year-round in California, the end of June in Arizona, and after the second year of planting in India, typically in the spring. The tiny oval fruits are harvested from flat-topped flowering umbels after they turn brown.

PARTS USED Though you can certainly use nearly all parts of the smallage plant, including the dry sliced stems, leaves, fresh stalks, and roots, I am specifically referring to the seeds here.

ABOUT Not to be confused with the celery stalks in your mirepoix, celery seeds (parsley family, Apiaceae) come from the wild-growing smallage plant. Cultivated in the Mediterranean for thousands of years, spreading to Europe, then the United States, and then much later to India, celery seeds

have been around long before debuting in your chicken salad. The flowers of the small-age plant are even said to have been part of the garlands on King Tut's tomb.

This small seed obviously made an impact, because it can be found in a variety of cuisines all over the world, including Indian curries, soup broths in France and Russia, and, of course, your mother's potato salad. It also adds a great flavor and texture to pickles, chicken dishes, egg salad, seafood poaching liquid, and meat loaf.

TRADITIONAL USES

Celery salt—Worldwide
Bloody Mary cocktail—United States
Crab boil—United States
Cured meats—France
Tomato and celery curry—India

NOTE

Toasting not recommended

RECOMMENDED PAIRINGS

- Potato salad
- Beef-barley soup
- Poached cod
- Poached crab claws
- Pickled beets

SPICE PAIRINGS

cubeb, fennel, mustard, onion, rosemary

RECIPE IDEAS

1. Stir celery seeds into mayonnaise, chopped cooked egg yolk, minced garlic, and lemon juice and use as a crudité dip.

2. Mix celery seeds into whipped butter with coarse salt and a pinch of cayenne and serve with boiled potatoes.

3. In a blender, purée cooked celery root, ground celery seeds, and a touch of heavy cream for a side dish.

QUICK BLEND
Apium

This blend adds great texture when used to season thinly sliced jicama drizzled with olive oil, lemon juice, and coarse salt and served as a snack or side dish. It also gives cold pasta salad a lightly salty crunch.

Makes about ¼ cup/25 grams

2 tablespoons/15 grams celery seeds
½ tablespoon/5 grams poppy seeds
1½ heaping teaspoons/3 grams caraway seeds, ground
Scant ¾ teaspoon/2 grams black sesame seeds

CHAMOMILE

CHAMAEMELUM NOBILE / MATRICARIA CHAMOMILLA

A sweet, apple-scented flower known for its calming properties

FLAVOR & AROMA Though mainly associated with teas and tea blends, chamomile flowers are also great in spice blends or in savory and sweet recipes. It is important to buy good-quality flowers. Always look for whole, not ground, flowers with intense color. The aroma, which is sweet, fruity, and herbaceous, should be strong and pleasant. If the flowers don't have a smell, they are too old. I like to add some to delicate broths and fish poaching liquid. They impart a honeysuckle- or apple-like flavor with a slight bitterness when infused into cream for making chocolate desserts.

ORIGIN ☞ Native to Western Europe and North Africa ☞ Cultivated in Europe, particularly in Belgium, France, and England, as well as North Africa and the Azores

HARVEST SEASON Chamomile flowers, which are reminiscent of daisies (a yellow central disk with white petals), were traditionally grown as lawn substitutes because they spread so willingly and make such a nice sunny ground cover. They are a perennial flower that leafs out in January, blooms from late spring to early June, and goes to seed by October before going into winter hibernation. Commercially, they are harvested by hand a few times during their blooming season. Then they are dried in the open air or in a dryer within a few days' time.

PARTS USED Flowers

ABOUT Chamomile, or Roman chamomile, is a member of the daisy (Asteraceae) family and is named for the Greek word meaning "earth apple" due to its fruity scent. Of course, there are a number of other daisy-like plants that go by the same name, like *Matricaria chamomilla* (also known as German chamomile). They are frequently used interchangeably in teas and medicinally. The Roman variety I use is more common in England and has a calming effect.

Chamomile's essential oils are also used in a number of ways, including in herb beers, bitters, candies, desserts, and liqueurs. Try infusing some into cookies or ice cream for a sweet treat. Aside from their culinary uses, its oils are also utilized in hair dyes (specifically for blondes), mouthwash, shampoos, and sunscreens.

FAMILIAR USES

Chamomile sabayon
Chamomile tea
Sorbet and ice cream
Shortbread cookies
Crème brûlée

NOTE

Toasting not recommended

RECOMMENDED PAIRINGS

- Infused vodka
- Manhattan
- Soba noodle soup
- Roasted carrots
- Poached pears

SPICE PAIRINGS

cardamom, clove, orange peel, sage, vanilla

RECIPE IDEAS

1. Infuse a handful of chamomile flowers in hot heavy cream, strain, and refrigerate until cold. Whip the infused cream with sugar for a floral whipped cream.

2. Sprinkle chamomile flowers into boiling chicken stock and use to cook couscous.

3. Mix light brown sugar with ground chamomile and use for baking or in hot beverages.

QUICK BLEND
Daisy

Use this blend to season dried apricots poached in port wine and serve as a garnish for cheese. It also adds a floral element to lobster cream sauce.

Makes about ⅓ cup/21 grams

¾ cup/15 grams chamomile flowers, ground
1 pod/2 grams vanilla bean, chopped and ground
2 teaspoons/2 grams pink pepperberries, ground
Scant ¾ teaspoon/2 grams ground sumac

CHIPOTLE

CAPSICUM ANNUUM

A dried, smoked jalapeño that adds complexity to savory and sweet dishes

FLAVOR & AROMA I love that chipotles have smoky notes with medium heat. They are one of the spices I use often for cooking vegetables to give them a meaty or "grilled" taste. They also add a lot of depth and color to the finished dish. More than just for Mexican or Latin American dishes, they are great ground and sprinkled on cooked or raw dishes. Because of the powder's complex notes, it's also a perfect addition to desserts.

ORIGIN ☞ Native to Central America and Mexico ☞ Cultivated mainly in the Chihuahua state of Mexico, but also in Veracruz, Oaxaca, and Sinaloa, and in the United States in South Texas and southern New Mexico

HARVEST SEASON Chipotles are a great example of how an ingredient can be good, but also completely different, when fresh or dried. Most people do not realize (I was included in this group for many years) that a chipotle is just a dried and smoked jalapeño chile (in the nightshade, or Solanaceae, family). Traditionally when making chipotles, jalapeños are left on the plant as long as

possible, until they are deep red and beginning to dry out. They are then harvested at the end of the growing season, in the early fall (though many modern farmers grow their chiles in greenhouses for multiple harvests throughout the season). As has been done since pre-Aztec Mexico, they are always placed inside a smoking chamber heated by a firebox and smoked for several days. Once dry, chipotles become wrinkled and obtain a dull, deep brown color.

PARTS USED Dried whole chiles

ABOUT The technique of smoke-drying jalapeños is an early example of food preservation used back in Mesoamerica, even before the Aztecs, though the name *chipotle* does come from their word *chilpoctli*, meaning "smoked chile." Christopher Columbus most likely encountered these chiles on his trip to the New World and brought them back to Spain, where they would later spread to Europe, India, and beyond. The fact that they

are preserved would have made it possible for them to survive the long journey.

Today, chipotles are still predominantly from Mexico, where they produce two varieties: *morita*, which is mostly what you'll find in the United States, and the larger *meco*, which is used domestically. I get my chipotles from Mexico and New Mexico, and I personally prefer the *morita* variety, which is darker in color.

Whichever you use, chipotles add a wonderful medium heat to many dishes including smoky salsas, cooked sauces, scrambled eggs, pickled vegetables, and even brownies. You've probably seen them, or used them, canned in adobo sauce, a rich marinade of tomato, dried chiles, brown sugar, onions, vinegar, garlic, and other spices. Traditionally, you may also find them reconstituted and stuffed with delicious, savory fillings.

TRADITIONAL USES

Authentic to Mexico
Adobo marinade
Mole sauce
Chipotle grilled chicken
Black beans with chipotles
Tinga de pollo (chicken in chipotle-tomato sauce)

NOTE
Toasting not recommended

RECOMMENDED PAIRINGS
Bean soup
Pimento cheese
Tomatillo salsa
Fish tacos
Grilled flank steak

SPICE PAIRINGS
annatto, cumin, ginger, oregano, tomato powder

HEAT INDEX
Medium heat

RECIPE IDEAS
1. Sprinkle ground chipotle into equal parts lemonade and beer for a spicy shandy.
2. Stir ground chipotle into red wine vinegar and serve with deep-fried chicken wings.
3. For a smoky, hot shakshuka, season simmering tomato sauce with ground chipotle and crack a couple of eggs into it.

QUICK BLEND
Chihuahua

Season ground pork with this smoky blend while cooking it with fresh corn and tomato paste and use as a side dish or in tacos. It also perks up a savory ratatouille.

Makes about 2 tablespoons/18 grams

1 tablespoon/5 grams coriander seeds, toasted and ground
¾ tablespoon/8 grams ground chipotle
½ tablespoon/3 grams smoked sweet ground pimentón
1 teaspoon/2 grams ground cinnamon, preferably Vietnamese

CHIVES

ALLIUM SCHOENOPRASUM

The long, mild green tops of a
particular member of the onion family

FLAVOR & AROMA Chives are great when used fresh in raw dishes or in low-temperature cooking (think omelets). But, because fresh chives can become bitter when cooked, dried chives are a good solution. You can add dried chives to stuffing and sauces while still preserving their fresh, mild onion notes. I buy mine already sliced, and I like to leave them like that to give crunch to a blend or a dish. If you want to use fresh chives, you can safely assume that 1 teaspoon dried chives equals about 2 teaspoons snipped fresh chives.

ORIGIN ☞ Native to Northern Europe ☞ Cultivated in Austria, Canada, France, Italy, the Netherlands, Switzerland, the United Kingdom, Germany, and the United States

HARVEST SEASON A perennial member of the amarylis (Amaryllidaceae) family, cylindrical hollow chives can grow 1 to 2 feet high and have a tendency to spread out over time. They are ready to harvest about a month after transplant or 2 months from seeding by either cutting the leaves down to the ground (for multiple harvests), or pulling the whole plant, bulb and all. Globular purple flowers, which are also edible, will open in the late spring.

Commercially, clumps are hand harvested and rows are machine harvested during the summer months. They are then cleaned, sorted, trimmed, and typically cut into uniform pieces when sold fresh. For dried herbs, which I use specifically, the cut pieces are freeze-dried to preserve the flavor and bright green color, which would be lost if the chives were air-dried.

PARTS USED Stems (leaves) and flowers

ABOUT Chives, or garden chives, are one of several varieties that can be found across Europe, Asia, and North America because they seed and spread easily, sprouting up along riverbanks and wet areas. Not to be confused with *Allium tuberosum,* which are garlic, or Oriental, chives, the chives I am referring to here have been around for thousands of years and have likely adorned your baked potatoes at some point.

Thought to have originated in the northern temperate zones, where they grew wild in areas of Northern Europe and ancient Greece, garden chives later spread throughout European gardens as an easy-to-grow ingredient and were eventually brought to North America. They weren't really cultivated commercially until after the Middle Ages.

Chives are essential to the classic French herb blend fines herbes, which also includes tarragon, parsley, and chervil. The mild, tender stems of chives can be chopped, snipped with scissors, or used dried and added as a garnish or at the end of cooking to salads, potatoes, deviled or scrambled eggs, soups, herb sauce for fish, dips, and cream cheese.

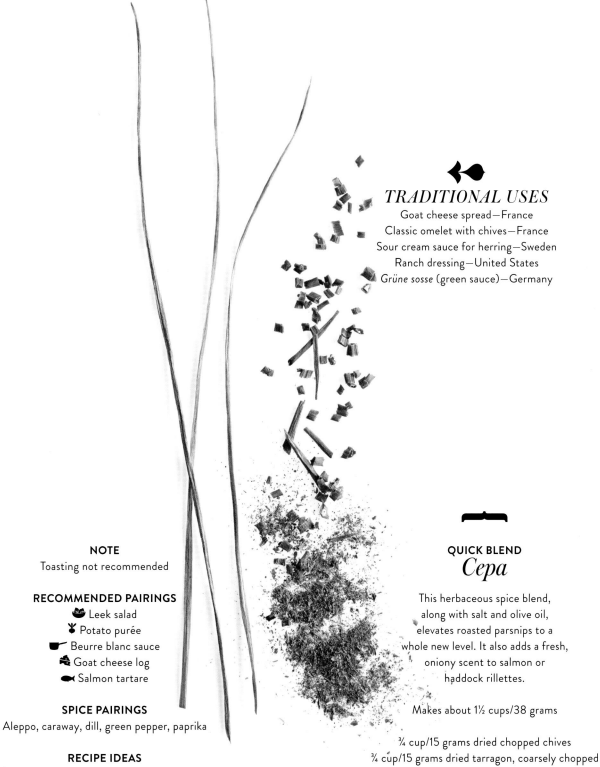

TRADITIONAL USES

Goat cheese spread—France
Classic omelet with chives—France
Sour cream sauce for herring—Sweden
Ranch dressing—United States
Grüne sosse (green sauce)—Germany

QUICK BLEND
Cepa

This herbaceous spice blend,
along with salt and olive oil,
elevates roasted parsnips to a
whole new level. It also adds a fresh,
oniony scent to salmon or
haddock rillettes.

Makes about 1½ cups/38 grams

¾ cup/15 grams dried chopped chives
¾ cup/15 grams dried tarragon, coarsely chopped
2 teaspoons/2 grams dried dill
2 teaspoons/2 grams crushed dried mint
1⅓ teaspoons/4 grams nigella seeds

NOTE
Toasting not recommended

RECOMMENDED PAIRINGS
Leek salad
Potato purée
Beurre blanc sauce
Goat cheese log
Salmon tartare

SPICE PAIRINGS
Aleppo, caraway, dill, green pepper, paprika

RECIPE IDEAS
1. Mix dried chopped chives with feta cheese and
olive oil and use in baked penne pasta.
2. Combine dried chopped chives with bread crumbs, garlic powder,
and olive oil and sprinkle on sautéed mixed mushrooms.
3. Stir ground chives into simmering heavy cream and
use as a base for a pasta primavera sauce.

CILANTRO

CORIANDRUM SATIVUM

The dried leaves of the equally loved and loathed pungent green herb

---

FLAVOR & AROMA Cilantro has a few things stacked against it. The name actually comes from the Greek word *koris,* meaning "bedbug," due to the plant's notoriously pungent smell. And while many people from across the globe love its citrusy, peppery flavor, others describe the taste as bitter and soapy. To be fair, recent studies suggest the plant's natural aldehydes are to blame. But for the rest of us who couldn't live without its fresh, floral, and herbaceous notes, it is wonderful when added freshly chopped to salsas and chutneys or the whole leaves—either fresh or dried and ground—stirred into soups and stews.

One of my blends, Shabazi N.38, is made with 70% dried cilantro. I wanted to capture the essence of the Yemenite *zhoug* (a green chile and cilantro condiment), and the dried cilantro allows me to preserve the quality of the traditional wet paste in a powder form.

ORIGIN ☞ Native to the Mediterranean, North Africa, and Western Asia ☞ Cultivated in the Mediterranean, Morocco, Latin America, and United States

HARVEST SEASON For climates with hot summers, cilantro grows best when sown in the fall. The herb generally peaks around February and March, but can be harvested gradually throughout the year. Or, if sown April through May, it will flower from June to August. Cilantro is ready to harvest 40 to 60 days before it flowers and goes to seed (the seeds are also known as coriander).

PARTS USED Leaves and root (cilantro); seeds (coriander)

ABOUT The leaves of the cilantro or coriander plant are one of the most widely used herbs in the world and are essential to Middle Eastern, Latin American, Indian, Thai, and Chinese cuisines. It resembles parsley in appearance (being a member of the parsley, or Apiaceae, family) and is also commonly referred to as Chinese parsley or coriander, which is actually the seed (page 102).

Native to the Mediterranean and Middle East regions, cilantro has been referenced in historical texts for thousands of years. Ancient Sanskrit, Egyptian papyrus records, and even the Bible have mentions of it. It is even sometimes said that cilantro root, not horseradish, was used as the bitter herb for Sephardic Jews during Passover. There was a time when cilantro was commonly used all over Europe, but with the exception of some Spanish and Portuguese dishes, it was replaced by parsley. The thin root, which has an earthy, deep flavor, is used in traditional Thai dishes.

At La Boîte, I prefer using cilantro from Israel—and not just because I am from there; the quality is just great. Vibrant green, with a wonderful scent, it comes to me already dried and crushed but not ground. This allows me to keep it either coarse or grind it fine if needed. I also like the fact that it is processed under kosher regulations that ensure no insects or bugs have come along for the ride.

TRADITIONAL USES

Curry paste (cilantro root)—Thailand
Zhoug (chile paste)—Yemen
Shawarma spice blend—Middle East
Chermoula marinade—North Africa
Tomatillo salsa verde—Mexico

NOTE
Toasting not recommended

RECOMMENDED PAIRINGS
Fruit salad
Creamed spinach
Béchamel sauce
Split pea soup
Pasta primavera

SPICE PAIRINGS
caraway, clove, garlic, green chiles, onion

RECIPE IDEAS
1. Season melted unsalted butter with crushed dried cilantro leaves and lemon juice and drizzle over steamed broccoli.
2. In a blender, purée cooked chickpeas, crushed cilantro leaves, lemon juice, olive oil, and cracked blacked pepper for a quick green hummus.
3. Combine crushed dried cilantro leaves with fresh ground pork, season with salt and pepper, and use to make meatballs.

QUICK BLEND
Cilantro Verde

This brightly flavored spice blend makes a quick salad dressing when mixed into extra-virgin olive oil. It is also great for roasted baby eggplants.

Makes about ¾ cup/19 grams

½ cup/10 grams crushed dried cilantro
2½ tablespoons/5 grams crushed dried basil
Scant ¾ teaspoon/2 grams ground amchoor
Scant ½ teaspoon/1 gram fine sea salt
Scant ½ teaspoon/1 gram black peppercorns, coarsely ground

SOFT STICK, CASSIA,
OR VIETNAMESE CINNAMON

CINNAMOMUM ZEYLANICUM OR CINNAMOMUM VERUM/
CINNAMOMUM CASSIA/CINNAMOMUM LOUREIROI

*Warm spices made from the barks
of young tree stems*

FLAVOR & AROMA Of all the spices I use—and I don't say this lightly—cinnamon would probably be on my top ten list. I always say that it brings sweetness to savory foods and a savory element to desserts. Because of its clove-like scent and warm flavor, it can trick our brains into thinking that dishes made with cinnamon have sugar even if there is none.

Countries like Morocco embrace cinnamon in their savory dishes to mellow the gamy notes of lamb. Aside from the bark, which is the part we are most familiar with eating, the hard-to-find buds have a cinnamon flavor whether eaten as is or used in cooked dishes. Cassia, which is very similar, has an even stronger aroma, and an astringent flavor that's sharper than that of cinnamon. They are often used interchangeably.

ORIGIN ☞ Native to Burma (cassia), Sri Lanka (soft stick cinnamon), and Southeast Asia (Vietnamese cinnamon) ☞ Cultivated in Vietnam and southern China (cassia), Sri Lanka, Seychelles, Indonesia, and Madagascar (soft stick cinnamon), and Vietnam (Vietnamese cinnamon)

HARVEST SEASON Both cinnamon and cassia are the stripped inner bark of a number of species in the laurel (Lauraceae) family. The trees are grown for a couple of years and then chopped down to stumps that push up a number of bushy new shoots from the base. After rainy season, these shoots are cut. The outer bark is then scraped off and discarded and the inner bark carefully pulled off into rolls. These rolls naturally curl, or become quills, as they are laid out in the warm sun to dry.

PARTS USED Cinnamon: whole or ground quills of dried bark, and buds

Cassia: dried whole or ground quills of dried bark, unripe fruits (cassia buds), and tejpat leaves

ABOUT Cinnamon deserves a book of its own. I love it. One of my main goals here is to explain that cinnamon is not just for dessert; you can use it for so much more than just Thanksgiving and the holiday season. Sadly, most people only know of cinnamon as the extreme notes and flavors it lends to sticky cinnamon buns, sweet baked goods, and flavored coffees and drinks. These, for the most part, are made with artificial extracts that do not do justice to this elegant and fragrant spice.

I mainly use three types of cinnamon at La Boîte: cassia, soft stick, and Vietnamese. The soft stick variety (true cinnamon), also known as Sri Lanka cinnamon, is very delicate, yet most people do not know about it. In Mexico, where it is called *canela,* it is used in chocolate dishes and sauces. This is the variety I mainly use at La Boîte.

Cassia, or Chinese cinnamon, is most familiar and is an essential ingredient in Chinese five-spice powder (page 296). It is easier and cheaper to harvest and process, and it is also very rich in essential oil, which makes it so pungent and fragrant. It works really well whole in long-cooked dishes or those cooked on high heat. Its buds, which resemble cloves, impart a warm, mellow flavor to sweet Asian pickles and teas, but are hard to come by.

Vietnamese, or Saigon, cinnamon is actually more closely related to cassia. This variety comes mainly ground since the bark is very thick and hard to grind. You can, however, buy Saigon bark in some specialty stores and use it whole in soups and stews. I love how pungent yet complex it is.

Cinnamomum tamala leaves, often referred to as Indian bay or tejpat leaves, are used predominantly in North Indian and Mughlai cuisines. They impart a wonderful musky aroma to slow-cooked *korma*s and garam masala.

TRADITIONAL USES
Squab pastilla (pigeon pie)—Morocco
Phở (noodle soup)—Vietnam
Moussaka (meat and potato casserole)—Greece
Garam masala (spice mixture)—India
Apple pie—United States

NOTE
Toasting not recommended

RECOMMENDED PAIRINGS
 Lamb kebabs
Tomato sauce
Chicken tagine
Pork dumplings
Rhubarb crumble

SPICE PAIRINGS
caraway, cardamom, clove, cumin, ginger

RECIPE IDEAS
1. Mix ground Vietnamese cinnamon with unsweetened cocoa powder and use to season lamb meatballs.
2. Season thick wedges of kabocha squash with ground soft stick cinnamon and sherry vinegar before roasting in the oven.
3. Warm ground cassia with olive oil, add shaved Brussels sprouts, garlic, and lemon juice, and serve over fresh penne pasta.

QUICK BLEND
Canela

Season diced apples and tomatoes with this blend while cooking slowly over low heat for a warm, spiced condiment to serve with grilled meat or fish.

Makes about 3 tablespoons/21 grams

3 sticks/10 grams soft stick cinnamon, ground
1 tablespoon/5 grams ground Vietnamese cinnamon
1 teaspoon/2 grams cumin seeds, toasted and ground
Scant ¾ teaspoon/2 grams sweet pimentón
Scant ¾ teaspoon/2 grams Aleppo chile flakes

CLOVES

SYZYGIUM AROMATICUM

A powerfully scented dried flower bud that is destined for more than just your holiday ham

—

FLAVOR & AROMA If you are lucky enough to have a clove tree, or have access to the leaves, they are great for roasting meat, fish, and vegetables. Clove can be very powerful, so if you are using ground clove, add a little at a time. Whole cloves will release their sweet, bitter, and somewhat peppery flavor and warm, sweet scent as you cook, and you can remove them before serving to keep a milder flavor. They are also visually appealing, which is why you usually see them decorating whole, bone-in ham or oranges during the holiday season.

They are part of the sweet spices—like cinnamon, nutmeg, and mace—and I like to use them equally in sweet dishes and with savory meats and vegetables. Try adding one clove to your tea and you might give up sugar over time.

ORIGIN ☞ Native to the Maluku Islands in Indonesia ☞ Cultivated primarily in Indonesia, but also in India, Madagascar, Zanzibar, Pakistan, Sri Lanka, and Tanzania

HARVEST SEASON The clove tree, which yields after the seventh year from planting, flowers September through November in the plains and December through February in higher altitudes. Clusters of unopened, bright

red flower buds are pulled off by hand in bunches or shaken off by skilled local farmers who often climb trees up to 50 feet high to harvest the buds. After the crop is sorted and separated from the leaves, they are both left out in the sun to dry for about 3 days, until they turn a golden-brown color, wafting an incredible heady scent into the air.

PARTS USED Flower buds and leaves

ABOUT Cloves, which belong to the myrtle (Myrtaceae) family, originated on the Maluku Islands of Indonesia (also known as the Spice Islands). These coveted dried flower buds have been cultivated for some two thousand years, but only became popular during the Colonial Period. The Portuguese brought them to Europe in the fifteenth century and had control over them until the Dutch took them over in the seventeenth century, dominating the trade with a fearsome monopoly. They actually ordered all trees, with the exception of those on a few islands, to be

destroyed. Afo, the name of what is believed to be the oldest clove tree in the world, somehow survived all this and still reigns from Ternate some four hundred years later.

In the late 1700s, a Frenchman—appropriately named Pierre Poivre (see page 18)—brought stolen clove seedlings back to France, and then Zanzibar, where the industry would thrive for years. It wasn't until the cigarette industry began using cloves that Indonesia would become the main exporter once again.

Growing up, I only knew about ground clove. My knowledge was limited to its use as a remedy for toothaches, and that it was generally good for baking and desserts. It was only later that I discovered how well it works with savory dishes and that whole cloves are far superior to most ground ones. When ground, it is an essential ingredient to a number of classic spice blends, including French quatre épices (page 298), Indian garam masala (page 297), and Chinese five-spice powder (page 296).

I get my cloves whole from Sri Lanka. A good way to evaluate the quality is making sure the tip of the clove is still attached and slightly soft to touch. The stem should be dark and not faded in color.

TRADITIONAL USES
Quatre épices—France
Candied walnuts—Turin, Italy
Five-spice powder—China
Honey-baked ham with cloves—United States
Mulled wine—Europe and United States

NOTE
Toasting not recommended

RECOMMENDED PAIRINGS
Punch
Sunchoke purée
Roast pork tenderloin
Apricot chutney
Poached figs

SPICE PAIRINGS
cardamom, cinnamon, cumin, fennel, rose

RECIPE IDEAS
1. Mix equal amounts of ground cloves and confectioners' sugar and use to dust fresh scones.
2. Season grated apples with ground cloves and balsamic vinegar and serve with pork chops.
3. Marinate lamb collar or shoulder with ground cloves and pomegranate juice before braising.

QUICK BLEND
Maluku

Season thinly sliced savoy cabbage with this fragrant blend and apple cider before sautéing and serve as a warm side dish for roasted meat. This mix also adds a spiced element to an old-fashioned.

Makes about 3 tablespoons/19 grams

1½ tablespoons/10 grams cloves, ground
1 tablespoon/5 grams juniper berries, ground
½ tablespoon/3 grams ground galangal
½ teaspoon/1 gram ground licorice root

CORIANDER

CORIANDRUM SATIVUM

The seeds of the cilantro herb, with an entirely different, woodsier flavor profile

———

FLAVOR & AROMA Moroccan coriander seeds have a sweet, woodsy, spicy fragrance with a warm flavor. Indian dhania has a slightly sweeter and stronger aroma, with more obvious nuttiness and citrus notes. Because each variety is so different, I often mix half of each in my spice blends. But where the seeds really shine is when they are coarsely ground. Large pieces, when chewed, are a great addition to the texture of a dish. Because India only sells a small quantity each year, I always stock up in advance.

ORIGIN ☞ Native to the Mediterranean, North Africa, and Western Asia ☞ Cultivated in India, South Asia, Morocco, Canada, the United States, and Eastern Europe

HARVEST SEASON There are two types of coriander: the smaller-seeded Moroccan variety and larger-seeded Indian dhania variety. The light brown, rounder Moroccan seeds are much more common and, oddly enough, are mostly harvested in Canada. They are grown as a spring crop and harvested in 115 to 120 days. Dhania, which is yellow with a longer, more oval shape, is grown as a winter crop, with a shorter time to maturity, 100 to 110 days.

PARTS USED Seeds (coriander); leaves and root (cilantro)

ABOUT Coriander is a heat-loving annual of the parsley (Apiaceae) family, along with carrots, fennel, and caraway. It's one of the few spices that is completely edible, from its lanky root to its citrusy leaves (see cilantro, page 96), and seeds. Its instantly recognizable aroma has been coveted for centuries across India, Asia, Eastern Europe, and the Middle East, where it is essential to many authentic cuisines, including Indian curries, flavored Russian and Scandinavian liqueurs, pickles, tagines, and baked goods. Its essential oils are used in soaps, perfumes, and cosmetics and are said to be applied medicinally for digestion. Coriander is also used as a healthy source of dietary fiber, iron, and magnesium.

India, which is a significant producer of coriander, actually consumes most of what it harvests domestically, so what you buy at the store typically ends up being the Moroccan, or European, small-seeded variety. Canada is also a major producer of the small-seeded variety, which is where the United States gets its lion's share. Of course, we grow quite a bit here as well.

TRADITIONAL USES

Pickle and meat brine—United States and Europe
Beer brewing—Belgium
Cured fish such as gravlax and herring—Scandinavia
Harissa (chile paste)—Tunisia and Morocco
Dukkah (herb, nut, and spice condiment)—Egypt

NOTE

Toasting recommended

RECOMMENDED PAIRINGS

Mojito
Cream of mushroom soup
Ratatouille
Grilled pork chops
Seared tuna

SPICE PAIRINGS

cumin, fennel, mint, rose, tarragon

RECIPE IDEAS

1. Combine coriander seeds with egg whites and granulated sugar
and bake until crispy for a salad topping.
2. Sprinkle ground coriander on halved strawberries with a drizzle
of lime and a pinch of cayenne. Macerate for 10 minutes
before serving with ice cream.
3. Coat a log of fresh goat cheese with a handful of
coarsely ground coriander and poppy seeds.

QUICK BLEND
Cousbara

Marinate thin slices of duck breast with this blend, honey,
and lime juice before cooking. It also adds great texture
and woodsy, citrus elements to spinach salad.

Makes about ¼ cup/24 grams

3 tablespoons/15 grams coriander seeds, toasted and coarsely ground
½ tablespoon/5 grams fennel seeds, toasted and coarsely ground
1 teaspoon/3 grams white sesame seeds, toasted
Scant ½ teaspoon/1 gram granulated dried lemon peel

CUBEB

PIPER CUBEBA

A slightly bitter, tongue-numbing pepper with a signature tail

FLAVOR & AROMA The cubeb is a complex pepper. First, it barely has any heat (a 3 on a scale of 1 to 10). But what strikes me most are the fresh, nearly resin-like elements I get every time I open a jar. Once you taste it, you'll initially discover some bitter notes, then later, a refreshing, slightly numbing sensation. Some say the cubeb is a warm, camphoraceous cross between a pepper and allspice. One of the best ways to explore this spice is with citrus.

I get my cubeb from Java, but there is also a wild variety growing in Madagascar called voatsiperifery (*Piper borbonense*) that is much more floral and citrusy; the Madagascar variety is very hard to get. The false cubeb pepper from Central Africa, known as ashanti pepper (*Piper guineense*), has a similar appearance to cubeb, but a more reddish color and a less bitter flavor. The best way to tell the difference is that the cubeb has a curved tail and the ashanti's is straight.

ORIGIN ☞ Native to Java, Indonesia ☞ Cultivated mainly in Java and other Indonesian islands, but also Africa and India

HARVEST SEASON Cubeb is the immature fruit of a tropical, climbing perennial vine in the pepper (Piperaceae) family that often grows in coffee plantations. The vine produces a number of small white flowers along central spikes that turn into a collection of berries. They are gathered in the early summer before they ripen and laid out in the sun to dry, turning from a spring green to a wrinkled brown-black.

PARTS USED Dried immature fruits

ABOUT The first time I encountered cubeb, also known as tail pepper or Java pepper, was after culinary school during my time in France. Although it was commonly used in Europe in the sixteenth and seventeenth centuries as a substitute for black pepper, there is really no sign of it now, particularly in the West. For some odd reason—maybe the bitterness—it lost its charm and appeal.

Even though centuries ago cubeb was traded by Arab merchants, making its way to India and then Europe, Javanese growers are said to have sterilized the berries through scalding, to retain their monopoly. It must have worked; they are still the main exporters. Though originally grown for medicinal purposes, the cubeb became popular as an ingredient for its peppery notes. I like the many North African usages that help balance gamy meats and sweet-dried fruits and spices.

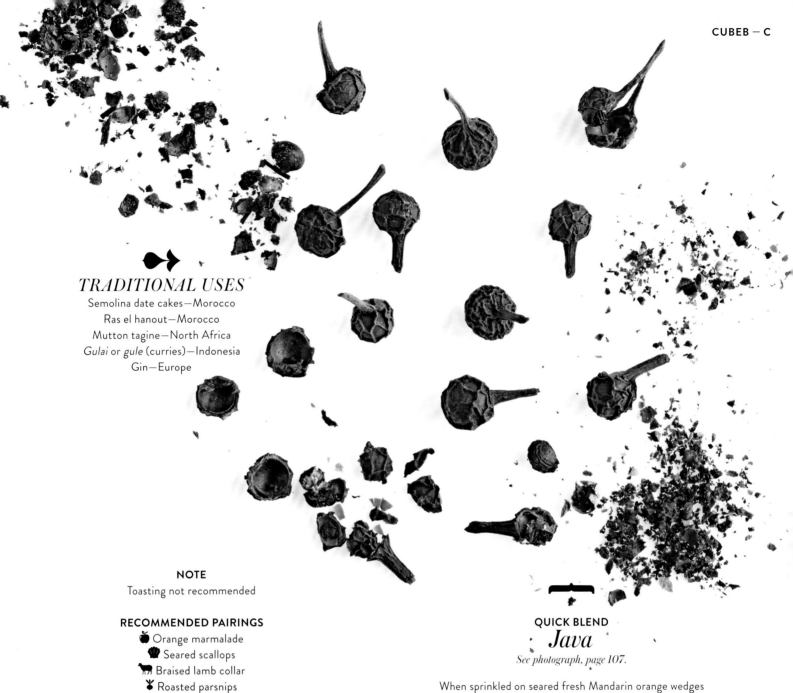

TRADITIONAL USES
Semolina date cakes—Morocco
Ras el hanout—Morocco
Mutton tagine—North Africa
Gulai or *gule* (curries)—Indonesia
Gin—Europe

NOTE
Toasting not recommended

RECOMMENDED PAIRINGS
 Orange marmalade
 Seared scallops
 Braised lamb collar
 Roasted parsnips
 Lemon pie

SPICE PAIRINGS
clove, lemongrass, nutmeg, orange peel, pink pepperberries

RECIPE IDEAS
1. Infuse simmering milk with cubeb berries and
use for a béchamel sauce.
2. Season thin slices of duck breast with ground cubeb,
ground ginger, and soy sauce before cooking.
3. Combine ground cubeb with rice wine vinegar, sesame seeds,
and orange zest and use to season a cold soba noodle salad.

QUICK BLEND
Java
See photograph, page 107.

When sprinkled on seared fresh Mandarin orange wedges
and deglazed with white wine, this refreshing, peppery blend
is the perfect accompaniment for meat, fish, or
a scoop of ice cream. It's also great on seared scallops.

Makes about ⅓ cup/24 grams

Scant ½ cup/2 grams kaffir lime leaves, ground
3 tablespoons/15 grams cubeb berries, ground
1 tablespoon/5 grams star anise, ground
1 teaspoon/2 grams ground mace

CUMIN

CUMINUM CYMINUM

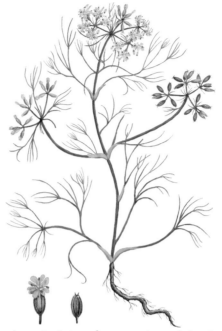

A meaty, intensely aromatic seed that is either craved or disliked

---

FLAVOR & AROMA Cumin has a heavy scent and a nutty, peppery taste (not to mention appearance) that's redolent of caraway. Even though it has been used by so many for so long, its notorious animal sweat scent—or, as I call it, "subway spice"—doesn't exactly make it popular with everyone. But it is this very characteristic that makes it so important to many dishes. Its leathery, savory note gives a meat-like scent to vegetable dishes and creates the sensation of grilling, while its salty notes pleasantly balance sweet or sour dishes. I even like to sprinkle cumin seeds into a salad or on cooked dishes for a flavorful crunch. Because of its intensity, use it sparingly.

ORIGIN ☞ Native to Egypt and the Levant ☞ Cultivated mainly in India, but also in China, Syria, Iran, Pakistan, Morocco, Afghanistan, Turkey, and Latin America

HARVEST SEASON In India, where cumin is grown as a winter crop, seeds are sown from October through early December and harvested from February onward. In Syria, Iran, Turkey, and Afghanistan, cumin is sown January through March, and is ready for harvesting from June through July. Cumin is the seed of an annual herb belonging to the parsley (Apiaceae) family and blooms small white or pink flowers. These delicate flowers wither, giving way to seeds that turn from dark green to brownish-yellow, signaling they are ready to harvest. Typically still harvested by hand, the plants are threshed to remove the seeds, which are laid out in the sun or in a dryer, and finally winnowed before being packaged.

PARTS USED Dried seeds and flowers

ABOUT Cumin has made its mark on world cuisines and medicines dating back to ancient Egypt around 5000 BC, where it is said to have been one of the ingredients used to mummify pharaohs. Its name can be found throughout history, from ancient Mesopotamian cuneiform to first- and second-century medical writings referencing its health benefits. Cumin is even mentioned in the Old and New Testaments, where it was both a seasoning and a currency for paying tithes. Medicinally, cumin has been used for a variety of ailments and needs, including improved immunity, as a diuretic, for respiratory disorders and anemia, and, oddly enough, as an aphrodisiac.

As for its part in enhancing food, it is essential to a number of traditional cuisines and is typically found in Indian, Middle Eastern, Mexican, Portuguese, and Spanish dishes. India is the largest producer and consumer of cumin (*jeera*) in the world, keeping and using 70% to 80% of what it grows. India's government-regulated quotas only allow it to be exported after domestic needs are met. While you can also find great-quality Syrian and Moroccan cumin, the instability of these regions makes these varieties harder to come by. Turkey produces fine cumin as well, but I prefer the Indian variety since it is more pungent with even more savory notes.

TRADITIONAL USES

Chutney—India
Jeera pani (cumin-water drink)—India
Vegetable tagine—Morocco
Leyden cheese—The Netherlands
Kümmel liqueur—Germany

NOTE
Toasting recommended

RECOMMENDED PAIRINGS
Yogurt dressing
Lentil stew
Roasted cauliflower
Chicken tagine
Grilled lamb chops

SPICE PAIRINGS
caraway, cardamom, cinnamon, coriander, fennel

RECIPE IDEAS
1. Combine cumin seeds with Dijon mustard and rub onto a beef roast before cooking.

2. Season Greek yogurt with ground cumin, lemon juice, and a splash of olive oil for a simple, delicious vegetable dip.

3. Mix together cumin seeds, honey, and sherry vinegar and use to coat whole carrots before roasting.

QUICK BLEND
Komino
See photograph, pages 112–113.

This blend is great for dry marinating a whole rack of lamb before roasting it; serve it with yogurt sauce made with a pinch of the blend. It also adds a warm, savory element to Israeli couscous.

Makes about 3 tablespoons/22 grams

1½ tablespoons/10 grams cumin seeds, toasted and coarsely ground
1 tablespoon/5 grams coriander seeds, toasted and coarsely ground
1½ heaping teaspoons/5 grams caraway seeds, toasted and coarsely ground
1 teaspoon/1 gram crushed dried oregano leaves
Scant ½ teaspoon/1 gram black peppercorns, coarsely ground

BLACK CUMIN (KALA JEERA)

BUNIUM PERSICUM/BUNIUM BULBOCASTANUM

A pungent, nutty, and floral spice often confused with many others

---

FLAVOR & AROMA For years all I knew was regular cumin (page 108). It wasn't until more recently that I discovered the mellower, slightly floral, and fresh notes of black cumin (kala jeera). The fruit's distinctive aroma is heavy and strong, and when crushed, almost piney and a bit less earthy. The taste is nutty, peppery, warm, pungent, and reminiscent of caraway. Its slightly smoky notes enable you to use it in vegetarian dishes to impart the flavor of meat. Because the seeds are so thin, I think they are even better when eaten whole in salads or sprinkled on cooked dishes for an added crunch with a hint of saltiness. Some say the root, which is eaten like a vegetable in Kashmir, tastes like sweet chestnuts.

ORIGIN ☞ Native to Central Asia and North India ☞ Grows mainly in Kashmir

HARVEST SEASON Black cumin is cultivated on a small scale but grows wild predominantly in Kashmir, India. The seeds, which are sown October through November, germinate after the snow melts around March and April. The crop matures in late July or August when its delicate white flowers finally open. When

the seeds turn brown, the stalks are carefully collected in the morning, and often sun-dried for a few days to ensure better maturity and storage. Dried plants are threshed by hand or machine, and then cleaned by winnowing.

PARTS USED Dried seeds, essential oils, and roots

ABOUT There is often confusion between *kala jeera* (*Bunium persicum*), which is also known as black caraway or zira, and other spices, including the cheaper and less pungent *shahi jeera*. *Nigella sativa* (page 188), from the Ranunculaceae family, goes by the same name, but has a bitterer, pungent flavor profile and a seed that is smaller, pointed, and black. It's also commonly mistaken for caraway seed, due to its similar crescent-shaped appearance and dark brown color. But despite its identity crisis, the black cumin I am referring to here belongs to the Apiaceae family, alongside its parsley, dill, and fennel brethren, and is a more expensive variety than the more well-known

white cumin (*Cuminum cyminum*). Confused yet? Join the crowd.

During the sixteenth and seventeenth centuries, black cumin was a popular ingredient in Mughlai cooking, donning the name *shahi jeera,* meaning "imperial cumin." During the Mughal rule of northern India, their cooking blended Iranian and Middle Eastern ingredients with local methods, influencing much of the cuisine. Today, roasted black cumin seeds are used as a delicious addition in breads, while their essential oils are often used for seasoning pickles, sauces, and even sweets.

The oils are also widely used in Iranian folkloric medicine as an anti-inflammatory and for pain relief, while its seeds are commonly applied as a diuretic and to remedy digestive problems. Even with all this culinary and medicinal history in parts of the world, the spice remains relatively unknown elsewhere. My hope is that more people will explore it.

TRADITIONAL USES

Biryani (mixed rice dish with meat or
vegetables)—North India
Korma (mild curry dish)—North India
Maharashtrian masala bhat (spiced rice dish)—India
Bahārāt (spice blend)—Saudi Arabia
Kibbeh (meat-stuffed fried
croquette)—Middle East

NOTE
Toasting recommended

RECOMMENDED PAIRINGS
Rum punch
Potato salad
Grilled cheese sandwich
Rice salad
Grilled salmon

SPICE PAIRINGS
curry leaves, fennel, ginger, onion, turmeric

RECIPE IDEAS

1. Sprinkle kala jeera on sliced apples and add grated carrots,
yogurt, and lemon juice for a quick salad.

2. Add a handful of kala jeera to a quart of boiling water with a few slices
of lemon and cut strawberries. Served chilled as an aromatic iced tea.

3. For an Indian-inspired egg dish, sprinkle a few pinches of kala jeera
and feta cheese on an omelet while it is cooking.

QUICK BLEND
Black & Yellow

Marinate shrimp with this blend before grilling or sautéing in a pan. It
also adds a pungent, fresh flavor to yellow bean and radish salad.

Makes about 3 tablespoons/19 grams

2 tablespoons/10 grams kala jeera, toasted and coarsely ground
½ tablespoon/5 grams ground turmeric
1 teaspoon/3 grams fennel seeds, toasted and coarsely ground
Scant ½ teaspoon/1 gram cayenne powder

CURRY LEAVES

MURRAYA KOENIGII

The fresh or dried leaves often confused with, but infinitely better than, the powder they inspired

FLAVOR & AROMA Curry leaves have bitter notes combined with an herbaceous, pine-like scent that adds richness to stews, soups, and roasted vegetable dishes. I buy green fresh leaves from California and dry them immediately in-house to preserve their best qualities; predried leaves are often tasteless and old. I use them as an herb component in some of my curry-style blends, but I also like to pair them with sweet elements such as cinnamon and honey. You can add whole leaves while cooking or grind them to powder.

Keep the stems, dry them, and then add them to hot coals while grilling to get a wonderfully scented smoke. If you can get them fresh, you can even muddle them like mint in cocktails.

ORIGIN ☞ Native to India ☞ Cultivated in India, South and Southeast Asia, and in the United States in Hawaii

HARVEST SEASON Bright green curry leaves come from the strongly aromatic deciduous *Murraya koenigii* tree in the rue (Rutaceae) family. Leaves should be harvested before the plant flowers, from July through August, at which point their quality decreases. Though mostly grown in tropical regions, in places where there is a winter harvest, leaves should be gathered before the frost.

PARTS USED Leaves

ABOUT Curry leaves are not necessarily part of curry powders or pastes. Those are mostly British inventions inspired by the flavors of Indian cuisine that actually contain a variety of spices, sometimes including cumin, coriander, black pepper, chiles, and fenugreek. True curry leaves are prized in Indian and South Asian cuisines for their intensely aromatic, warm flavor. In fact, they are rarely found far from these locales.

In Sri Lanka, they are typically fried with chopped onion when making curry and are used in South India's predominantly vegetarian fare in lentil and vegetable curries, or in the spicy-sour rice dish *bisi bele bhaat*. They are found in North Indian stuffed samosas, and are roasted to give texture to soups in Cambodia. From long-simmered meat stews in Kerala to pickles, curry leaves add an irreplaceable element no powder will ever come close to.

TRADITIONAL USES

Fish curry—Kerala, India
Mango curry—Sri Lanka
Coconut chutney—India
Maju krueng (sour soup)—Cambodia
Roti canai (flatbread) with butter prawns—Malaysia

NOTE

Toasting not recommended

RECOMMENDED PAIRINGS

Braised eggplant
Clam chowder
Poached lobster
Braised pork shoulder
Steamed cod

SPICE PAIRINGS

ajowan, cardamom, coriander, cumin, garlic

RECIPE IDEAS

1. Season a snapper fillet with salt, pepper, and olive oil
and place on a piece of foil lined with a handful of
dried curry leaves before wrapping and baking.
2. Add dried curry leaves to diced butter, melt over low heat,
and use the infused butter to baste a roast chicken.
3. Purée dried curry leaves, lemon juice, mustard seeds,
and grapeseed oil in a blender for a vinaigrette.

QUICK BLEND
Muraya

See photograph, page 117.

This Asian-inspired blend, along with coconut milk, makes a
sweet-savory addition to braised eggplant, especially when served
with a drizzle of lime juice and sprinkled with chopped cilantro.
It also adds a savory element to toffee pudding for dessert.

Makes about ⅓ cup/16 grams

2 cups/8 grams dried curry leaves, ground
1½ tablespoons/3 grams dried cilantro leaves, crushed
1 tablespoon/3 grams dried basil leaves
1 teaspoon/2 grams Sichuan pepper, ground

DILL

ANETHUM GRAVEOLENS

A slightly pungent, herbaceous spice made from dried leaves or seeds

FLAVOR & AROMA Dill offers fresh, herbaceous notes, while its seeds have a sweeter scent and a slightly bitter taste. I like to use dried dill for seared fish and seafood because it remains tasty even when charred, while fresh dill will burn and make food bitter. I also enjoy it in meat or vegetable stuffing since it doesn't oxidize and there is no risk of fermentation. You can even grind it into powder to flavor sauces, soups, and dressings. Its seeds, which would easily be confused with anise seeds were it not for their aroma, are great whole or ground in baked goods or on roasted vegetables or legumes.

ORIGIN ☞ Native to Russia, the Eastern Mediterranean, and Western Asia ☞ Cultivated mainly in India and Pakistan, but also in Denmark, Romania, the Netherlands, the United Kingdom, Hungary, Germany, Holland, Egypt, Fiji, Mexico, Canada, and the United States

HARVEST SEASON Dill's slender, dark green, threadlike leaves look similar to fennel fronds (without the often unpopular licorice flavor), and the plant can grow up to 2 feet tall. This member of the parsley (Apiaceae) family is harvested for its leaves before the plant develops tiny white or yellow flowers 8 to 12 weeks after seeds are sown. In Europe, fresh dill is usually grown in the spring, but it can also be grown as an overwintering crop in some areas. Seeds are harvested when the majority of a plant's seeds are mature, since they tend to ripen at different times.

When the fresh herbs and seeds are processed commercially, they are usually air- or freeze-dried to maintain their aroma and some of their essential oils. Traditionally, they are dried in the shade, turned regularly, and then threshed.

PARTS USED Leaves and seeds

ABOUT Poor dill. Neither the dried herb nor the seed gets enough love or attention. Most dill is used fresh, and even though its seeds are great, they are used in very few recipes anywhere. You probably recognize fresh dill in potato or chicken salads, but dill seeds are used in Indian curries and masala spice blends. They have been used as an ingredient even as far back as dynastic Egypt, Ancient Greece and Rome, and Mesopotamian civilizations. At La Boîte, I get my dried dill herb and seeds from India or Egypt and always look for new ways to use them.

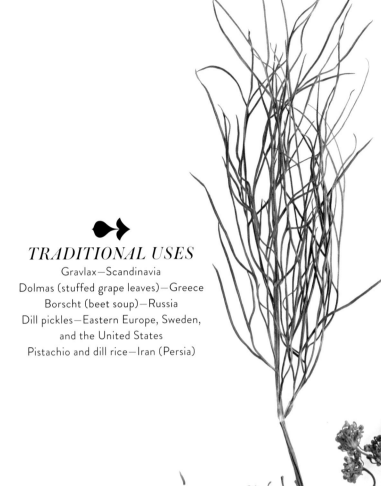

TRADITIONAL USES

Gravlax—Scandinavia
Dolmas (stuffed grape leaves)—Greece
Borscht (beet soup)—Russia
Dill pickles—Eastern Europe, Sweden,
and the United States
Pistachio and dill rice—Iran (Persia)

NOTE

Toasting not recommended

RECOMMENDED PAIRINGS

- Tuna salad
- Sautéed zucchini
- Cooked barley
- Leek velouté
- Baked trout

SPICE PAIRINGS

fennel, onion, oregano, pomegranate, tarragon

RECIPE IDEAS

1. Mix dried dill and dill seeds into a hot celery root purée and
add crumbled feta cheese to serve as a side dish.
2. Brush thin strips of puff pastry with egg wash and sprinkle
with a few pinches of dill seeds, dried dill, and shredded cheddar
before baking to make cheese straws.
3. Combine chopped raw beets, dill seeds, red wine vinegar,
salt, and shallots for a beet tartare.

QUICK BLEND
Shamir

Season cooked shredded chicken with
this blend, along with mayonnaise,
lemon juice, and chopped scallions (green parts only)
to make a sandwich spread, or use the blend to add
an herbaceous element to steamed fish or shrimp.

Makes about ½ cup/23 grams

½ cup/10 grams dried dill
1 tablespoon/5 grams dill seeds
½ tablespoon/5 grams poppy seeds
Scant ¾ teaspoon/3 grams nigella seeds

EPAZOTE

DYSPHANIA AMBROSIOIDES OR CHENOPODIUM AMBROSIOIDES

The fresh or dried oregano- and lemon-scented leaves essential to Mexican fare

FLAVOR & AROMA For most of us, it is hard to find fresh epazote since it is rarely imported from its main growing regions in Mexico and Central America. You can, however, buy it in its dried form and still enjoy its notes of oregano, pine, lemon, and sometimes mint. Dried epazote should be cooked; its flavor really develops when the leaves are added to long braises and stews. It also works great in marinades, and I especially like to pair it with savory spices such as cumin and caraway. It's safe to assume that 1 teaspoon of dried epazote equals 6 or 7 fresh leaves.

ORIGIN ☞ Native to Central America, South America, and southern Mexico ☞ Cultivated in Central America, South America, and southern Mexico, as well as areas of Europe and the United States

HARVEST SEASON The epazote plant is a member of the amaranth (Amaranthaceae) family and can grow up to 4 feet tall with oblong leaves that are about 5 inches in length. Leaves can be harvested at any point after the plant is established, up until the flowers open, July through October (about 55 days after plants emerge). Cutting back the center stem (which promotes a bushier regrowth) and harvesting leaves often can extend harvests. Leaves are dried for longer preservation.

PARTS USED Leaves

ABOUT Epazote also goes by the names wormseed, Jesuit's tea, Mexican tea, and paico. In Spanish, *epazote* means "skunk sweat," which is probably why it makes such a good pest repellent in the garden.

As an ingredient, it is mostly found in Mexican cuisine, including bean dishes—partly because it's delicious but also because it is a friendly carminative. Its pungent flavor is essential to dishes of the Yucatán region and traditional Mayan dishes like mole verde sauce and authentic refried beans (not to be confused with the modern interpretation found north of the border). It is also a common element in soups and salsas.

TRADITIONAL USES

Authentic to Mexico
Classic black beans or pinto bean stew
Mole verde
Cheese tamales
Quesadillas
Wild mushroom enchiladas

NOTE

Toasting not recommended

RECOMMENDED PAIRINGS

Sautéed fava beans
Broccoli soup
Barley risotto
Fish tacos
Braised oxtail

SPICE PAIRINGS

chipotle, clove, cumin, lemon peel, sesame

RECIPE IDEAS

1. In a blender, purée cooked spinach leaves with dried epazote, some sour cream, salt, and ground chipotle to make a dip.
2. Marinate cubed lamb shoulder in epazote leaves, chopped garlic, and lime juice before braising.
3. Season thick sweet potato wedges with olive oil, salt, and ground epazote and roast.

QUICK BLEND
Paico

This herbaceous, tangy blend is perfect for a fish taco marinade, or you can sprinkle it on roasted cauliflower. It also adds a touch of heat to corn chowder.

Makes about ½ cup/23 grams

½ cup/15 grams crushed dried epazote
3 tablespoons/15 grams coriander seeds, toasted and ground
½ tablespoon/5 grams ground sweet pimentón
1 teaspoon/3 grams ground ancho chile

ESPELETTE

CAPSICUM ANNUUM

A sweet-hot chile grown by rigorous standards exclusively in and around the French town for which it is named

PARTS USED Dried chiles

FLAVOR & AROMA What I love about the Espelette chile is that the heat component is met with citrus notes, a sweet, acidic taste, and a vibrant orange color. You can use Espelette in almost anything savory or sweet, cold or hot, raw or cooked, and it works. Its slightly coarse texture also adds a nice surprise.

ORIGIN ☞ Native to South and Central America and later the French commune of Espelette, Pyrénées-Atlantiques ☞ Cultivated exclusively in the French commune of Espelette, Pyrénées-Atlantiques

HARVEST SEASON Espelette chiles, a nightshade in the Solanaceae family, are planted in the spring and harvested by hand—only when the color and flavor are considered perfect—beginning August 14 and ending, by law, at the end of November. Traditionally, they are strung onto *cordes,* or *ristras,* and hung outside over balconies and along the walls of homes to dry. Some are still sold this way to home cooks or as a kitchen decor. Today, they are mainly dried in large dehydrators and then ground to a precise degree.

ABOUT This is a prime example of how, every once in a while, farmers can come together and create something really good. Named for its native region, the Espelette chile (also called piment d'Espelette) has been grown in the Basque country for many years by a small number of farmers. But because crops would vary from one farmer to the next, the chiles had inconsistent characteristics.

About twenty years ago, farmers from fewer than a dozen communes collectively decided to create rules and regulations on how these chiles should be grown, harvested, and processed. The result was a French AOC (Appellation d'Origine Contrôlée) geographical origin recognition in 2000, followed by a European PDO (protected designation of origin) label in 2002. This ensures that only chiles grown in the region and processed accordingly can be sold as Espelette.

Farmers wishing to begin growing Espelette peppers get their seeds from one of the approved farmers, who also serves as a mentor or teacher. The regulations are very strict in terms of when farmers can sprout the seeds and plant them in the ground. For instance, once plants are in the ground, they can only be irrigated once. Farmers then send a sample of each batch anonymously to a jury to be tested. If the color, taste, scent, and grinding degree are approved, they will be allowed to add a special seal to signify that these are certified Espelette chiles. Today, piment d'Espelette is the first and only spice in France with these labels.

This chile is a mainstay of Basque cuisine, largely replacing black pepper in recipes. Traditionally it is used to conserve meat and is found in *marmitako* (fish stew) and *axoa* (a veal and tomato dish) and is often sold pickled. An annual festival held in Espelette in October to celebrate this remarkable chile greets thousands of guests.

TRADITIONAL USES

Authentic to the French Basque region
Pipérade (tomatoes, peppers, and onions)
Pickled Espelette chiles
Basquaise (braised dish)
Jams and jellies
Bayonne hams (cured ham)

NOTE

Toasting not recommended

RECOMMENDED PAIRINGS

● Olive frittata
🥗 Endive and goat cheese salad
🦆 Duck cassoulet
🍜 Mushroom gnocchi
🥟 Orange sorbet

SPICE PAIRINGS

anise, cinnamon, cumin, orange peel, rosemary

HEAT INDEX

Light to medium heat

RECIPE IDEAS

1. Make a jam with fresh strawberries, whole pistachios,
lemon juice, sugar, and ground Espelette to add a touch of heat.
2. Toss cooked whole chickpeas with ground Espelette, olive oil,
lemon juice, and salt and serve with roasted peppers and grilled bread.
3. Stir ground Espelette into a little lemon juice and top with
a splash of tequila and ice cubes for a quick cocktail.

QUICK BLEND
Basque

Braise white beans with cured chorizo and this
blend and serve it with poached eggs and grilled bread.
It also adds a sweet, hot element to carrot purée.

Makes about ⅓ cup/28 grams

¼ cup/5 grams crushed dried marjoram
3 tablespoons/15 grams Espelette pepper flakes
½ tablespoon/3 grams anise seeds, ground
1 teaspoon/3 grams granulated dried orange peel
Scant ¾ teaspoon/2 grams caraway seeds, ground

FENNEL AND LUCKNOW

FOENICULUM VULGARE AZORICUM

A heady, anise-scented spice made from the seeds, pollen, and leaves of the entirely edible plant

FLAVOR & AROMA Fennel is one of my most beloved spices. Part of its beauty lies in the fact that the whole plant is used, from the bulb as a vegetable to the stem and, of course, the seeds, and even the pollen. There is no waste. The pollen is the most prized and delicate (not to mention expensive) part, and the crunchy aromatic seeds are great whole or ground, toasted or not. I buy the bold, licorice-flavored Florence fennel, or *finochio*, from India and Turkey. In India, there is also a special variety that is a bit harder to get and lesser known, called Lucknow, named after the town of the same name. It is sweeter and more delicate. I love combining both kinds.

Dried fennel seeds are also used a lot in sausages and cured meats. They add a slight pine note, bitterness, and herbaceous taste that help cut fatty ingredients, hot dishes, or acidity. If I could, I would probably include fennel in every blend I make, so I often have to force myself not to use it.

ORIGIN ☞ Native to the Mediterranean ☞ Cultivated mainly in India, but also in Europe, Turkey, and the United States

HARVEST SEASON Fennel, a member of the parsley (Apiaceae) family, can grow 2 to 5 feet tall and has fragrant thin fronds that look similar to dill. Seeds sown in the spring for summer harvest often bolt too early, so plantings in July or August are often preferred for a fall crop instead. When grown for their bulbs, they take 12 to 14 weeks to reach harvest time. When sown for their oval-shaped, anise-scented seeds, umbels are cut when seeds are fully ripened (usually fall of the second season), then laid out in partial shade to dry. Seeds are separated from the stems, cleaned, and stored in bags for market.

PARTS USED Leaves, flowers, pollen, stems, and seeds

ABOUT As a native of Italy, Florence fennel seed was carried by Roman armies throughout Europe, where it would later be used to flavor English sack mead (a fermented honey drink). Emperor Charlemagne liked it so much that he mandated it be grown on imperial farms. Its increasing popularity helped it to naturalize throughout Europe, Asia, and North America, where it is mostly grown in California.

Fennel, specifically Florence fennel, is an herb that gives us a few different ingredients. The bulbous stem, which has a celery-like texture but anise-like flavor, is sliced or diced and used as a vegetable, either raw, as in chicken salads, or added at the end of cooking and perhaps served alongside delicate fish. The wispy fronds liven up salads, sauces, and shellfish. In Provence, the stems create a bed to nestle and perfume whole baked fish.

Often confused with anise seeds, fennel seeds add stronger aromatic notes of licorice to Indian five-spice mixture, absinthe, pickles, and Italian sausages. In places like India, fennel seeds are even consumed whole as a digestive. They are one of my secret weapons to cleanse my palate after tasting many spices—especially the hot ones. It's not surprising that it is also used to flavor natural toothpaste. The pollen, which has an even more intense anise aroma, is harder to find but gives a fresh flavor to seafood, grilled vegetables, and even breads. I urge you to have some form of fennel in your kitchen at all times.

TRADITIONAL USES

Fennel seeds only
Finocchio sausage—Italy
Porchetta (stuffed, rolled, and roasted pork)—Italy
Black bread—Russia
Garam masala (spice blend)—India
Five-spice powder—China

NOTE
Toasting recommended

RECOMMENDED PAIRINGS
🌾 Farro risotto
🥬 Roasted Brussels sprouts
🍄 Mushroom cream sauce
🐟 Baked sea bream
🐔 White wine–braised chicken

SPICE PAIRINGS
caraway, cumin, mustard, nigella, oregano

RECIPE IDEAS
1. Sprinkle thinly sliced zucchini with fennel pollen, sea salt,
olive oil, and lemon juice for a zucchini carpaccio.
2. Mix an equal amount of fennel seeds, sesame seeds, and mustard
seeds and use to coat a tuna loin before quickly searing it.
3. Combine one part fennel seeds with two parts panko (Japanese bread
crumbs) and use to bread chicken cutlets before cooking.

QUICK BLEND
Ferula
See photograph, page 126.

This anise-scented blend is great for seasoning sautéed
mixed wild mushrooms with white wine. It also brightens
up a pork roast with wilted arugula.

Makes about ¼ cup/29 grams

2 tablespoons/15 grams fennel seeds, toasted
and coarsely ground
1½ tablespoons/10 grams Lucknow seeds (or caraway), toasted and
coarsely ground
1 teaspoon/3 grams black mustard seeds
Scant ½ teaspoon/1 gram fennel pollen

FENUGREEK

TRIGONELLA FOENUM-GRAECUM

A savory, maple-scented spice made from dried or fresh leaves and seeds

FLAVOR & AROMA You've probably had fenugreek a number of times in your life but just didn't know it. It is often found in curry powders and other Indian spice blends. This, for the most part, is due to its sweet yet oniony scent, but also because it has a starchy quality that is good for thickening soups, stews, and marinades. Its flavor is often compared to that of pungent maple syrup or burnt sugar. Fenugreek seeds are much more subtle and even nutty when toasted, while the leaves have a bitter scent.

ORIGIN 👉 Native to southeastern Europe and western Asia 👉 Cultivated mainly in India, North Africa, and the Mediterranean

HARVEST SEASON When harvested for its clover-like leaves, fenugreek is a cut-and-come-again crop. Though you can eat the bitter microgreens, the plant is typically harvested in India for its milder full-grown leaves about 3 weeks after sprouting, and then dried or eaten fresh. There, they clip the young shoots and leaves, allowing the plant to regrow for another harvest or two. In places like Europe and Canada, where fenugreek is grown for its amber-colored triangular seeds, 30-inch plants with white flowers and sickle-shaped pods give way to seeds during the fall.

PARTS USED Leaves and seeds

ABOUT A member of the pea (Fabaceae) family, fenugreek also goes by the monikers Greek hay, Greek clover, and bird's foot. In India and the Middle East you can find the fresh leaves sold in markets and destined for soups and stews. I get my seeds from India and dried leaves from Turkey, where they use them for spice blends and cured meats.

In Indian vegetarian fare, the fresh leaves are often chopped and added to naan dough, and in parts of East Africa and the Middle East, they are used like spinach. Dried leaves are an essential element in *ghormeh sabzi* (Iranian lamb stew), while dried seeds bring a bittersweet note to Indian curries, *sambar* (South Indian gravy), and spice blends.

It is believed that fenugreek seeds are a very healthy spice, good for circulation and blood pressure. I personally brew some seeds with hot water—only for a few minutes to avoid bitterness—and drink the golden-colored water hot or cold. It is very calming and good for digestion. You can use the same seeds for a few rounds and later use the softened seeds in a salad.

TRADITIONAL USES

Hilbeh (fenugreek and garlic condiment)—Yemen
Basturma (dried cured beef)—Turkey and Armenia
Çemen (meat rub)—Turkey
Chapatti (flatbreads)—India
Panch phoron (Indian five-spice blend)—Bengal

NOTE
Toasting recommended

RECOMMENDED PAIRINGS
Garlic purée
Chickpea soup
Bulgur salad
Lamb skewers
Apple chutney

SPICE PAIRINGS
cumin, mace, orange peel, pimentón, star anise

RECIPE IDEAS
1. Purée dried fenugreek leaves with arugula, hazelnuts, and olive oil in a blender for a pesto sauce.
2. Brew fenugreek seeds with honey and orange peel in boiling water in a French press and serve hot or cold.
3. Season sliced duck breast with ground fenugreek and cook with pitted fresh cherries.

QUICK BLEND
Methi

This bittersweet blend will elevate hot or cold roast beef
or can be stirred into a sweet potato purée.

Makes about ¼ cup/30 grams

½ cup/5 grams dried fenugreek leaves, ground
1 tablespoon/15 grams fenugreek seeds, toasted and ground
½ tablespoon/5 grams ground sweet paprika
½ tablespoon/3 grams dried garlic slices, ground
Scant ¾ teaspoon/2 grams chile flakes, preferably Urfa

GALANGAL

ALPINIA GALANGAL

*A gingery, peppery spice made from a
dried rhizome*

FLAVOR & AROMA Apart from Southeast Asian cuisine, most people, including professional chefs, don't know much about galangal. Ginger is often used in its place because the two share a lot of the same elements, but mostly because ginger is just more readily available. But make no mistake: they are not the same. Galangal has a sweeter, less powerful scent and a sharp, spicy-sweet taste that I actually prefer.

Fresh galangal root is hard, which makes it tricky to use. And because grinding it requires heavy-duty equipment, I buy all of mine already dried and ground. Greater galangal, which comes from Java, is milder than the lesser galangal from China. I love using it with seafood, fruits, and cocktails because it brings a sweet scent and tasting note to dishes without using sugar.

ORIGIN ☞ Native to Indonesia ☞ Cultivated in Malaysia, Laos, Thailand, and China

HARVEST SEASON Galangal is a tropical plant from the Zingiberaceae, or ginger, family that thrives when sown at the beginning of monsoon season (typically May through June). Orange-brown rhizomes grow clumps of stalks reaching 6 feet high that bloom greenish-white flowers with red berries. The rhizomes can be harvested as early as 18 months or up to 42 months from planting. The plant shoots and roots are removed, and the rhizomes are dug up and laid out to dry in the sun for 3 to 5 days.

PARTS USED Rhizomes

ABOUT Galangal is essential to Southeast Asian cuisine and can be found in a number of familiar dishes—though you may not even realize it. In Thailand and Laos, it is typically used in its fresh form, sliced, chopped, or ground with a mortar and pestle in *tom kha gai* (chicken-coconut soup), *tom yum* (spicy-sour soup), curries, and sauces.

When dried and ground, the way I use it in my blends and in cooking, galangal is found in the Malaysian soup *laksa*. In its native Indonesia, it accompanies chiles, ginger, garlic, and turmeric in the spicy beef stew *rendang*. Even the Moroccan staple ras el hanout gets its peppery-sweet essence from ground galangal. And while some would have you believe ginger is a worthy substitute, there really is no replacing it.

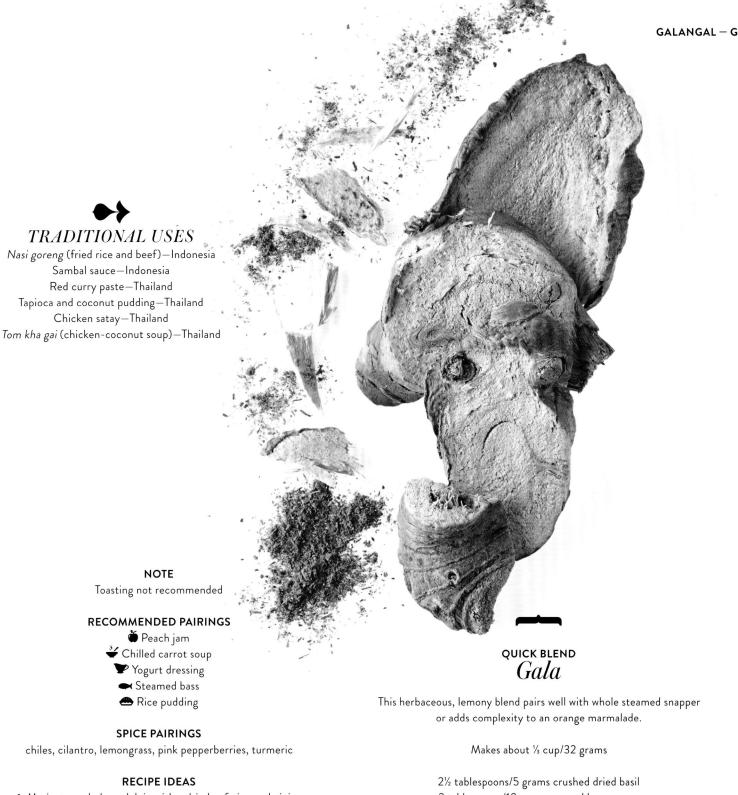

TRADITIONAL USES

Nasi goreng (fried rice and beef)—Indonesia
Sambal sauce—Indonesia
Red curry paste—Thailand
Tapioca and coconut pudding—Thailand
Chicken satay—Thailand
Tom kha gai (chicken-coconut soup)—Thailand

NOTE

Toasting not recommended

RECOMMENDED PAIRINGS

🍎 Peach jam
Chilled carrot soup
Yogurt dressing
Steamed bass
Rice pudding

SPICE PAIRINGS

chiles, cilantro, lemongrass, pink pepperberries, turmeric

RECIPE IDEAS

1. Marinate a whole pork loin with a drizzle of pineapple juice and 2 pinches of ground galangal powder before grilling.
2. Sprinkle pear wedges with ground galangal and drizzle with lemon juice to serve with cheese.
3. Stir a pinch of ground galangal into your favorite martini for an exotic twist.

QUICK BLEND
Gala

This herbaceous, lemony blend pairs well with whole steamed snapper or adds complexity to an orange marmalade.

Makes about ⅓ cup/32 grams

2½ tablespoons/5 grams crushed dried basil
2 tablespoons/10 grams ground lemongrass
1½ tablespoons/15 grams ground galangal
Scant ¾ teaspoon/2 grams cayenne powder

GARLIC

ALLIUM SATIVUM

The distinctively pungent and permeating spice made from dried garlic bulbs

---

FLAVOR & AROMA Fresh and dried garlic are equally great options for adding a lingering, warm, spicy-sweet flavor and scent to almost any dish. When used fresh, its notes are completely dependent upon the way it is prepared: minced garlic is not the same as mashed (the latter is more potent), just as roasted garlic is nothing like raw.

Oxidation causes these variances, which is why I love using dried garlic. It adds a different dimension of texture—particularly when granulated or sliced—and doesn't ferment, oxidize, or send up green shoots on your kitchen counter. Dried garlic, including garlic powder, elevates and adds richness to stews, gravies, marinades, pickles, and cooking liquids. Dry some yourself for something altogether different from what you buy in a jar.

ORIGIN ☞ Native to Central Asia ☞ Cultivated mainly in China and California, but also in Argentina, Mexico, India, and South Korea

HARVEST SEASON In places with cold winters, garlic is ideally grown as an overwintering crop planted in the fall before the first frost and harvested around the middle of July. In warmer climates, it can be planted in the spring for fall harvest, but it can be more challenging to get the same output. Garlic bulbs are pulled when more than half the leaves have yellowed and bent over, around 9 months from planting.

Small farms usually harvest by hand, while commercial growers have mechanized systems for large-scale bulb collection. Once out of the ground, garlic bulbs are hung to dry (sometimes braided) or stacked in fields in drier areas to allow the papery skins to form a protective, storage-ready barrier that better avoids rotting. Bulbs are then dehydrated in slices and granules and later made into powder.

PARTS USED Bulbs

ABOUT Garlic is a member of the amarylis (Amaryllidaceae) family and has been favored for thousands of years for its pungent flavor and many medicinal uses. There are records of it being cultivated in ancient China as a stimulant. There are illustrations of it in ancient Egyptian crypts from as early as 3700 BC. And there have been garlic bulbs found during archaeological excavations of Crete's Knossos Palace dating from 1850 BC to 1400 BC.

There are two main varieties of garlic: the hardneck variety, which gives us those delicious springtime scapes (a mild garlic flower shoot) and larger but fewer cloves, and the softneck type, which produces more but smaller cloves. What you mostly find in the grocery store are the fresh and dried versions of the latter.

Garlic is not what you would expect to find in a spice book, because most of us buy fresh garlic for cooking. As with many other spices in this book, dried garlic can work better in certain dishes. In ancient times, garlic was not available year-round, so some of it was dried to be used off-season. The problem with dried garlic is that some manufacturers—whose names I won't mention—sell whole heads of garlic ground with the skin and roots intact to add weight and save time. This is just not tasty and is often why most people have a bad experience with dried garlic. It delivers a nasty aftertaste that lasts for hours.

I am here to try to correct that. Some granulated garlic is actually of good quality. You want to make sure it has a light cream color—a white hue indicates that papery skins were included. The best course is to buy dried garlic flakes, because they are pure, and then grind them as needed. I love garlic, and buying it dried makes it even more accessible for use in spice blends, and because it is shelf stable, it will not oxidize with time or ferment after a few days. I buy domestic garlic as well as Chinese during times when the United States cannot produce enough of it.

TRADITIONAL USES

Garlic salt—Worldwide
Barbecue rub—United States
Adobo spice blend—Mexico
Fried rice—China
Merguez sausage—North Africa

NOTE

Toasting not recommended

RECOMMENDED PAIRINGS

Minestrone
Macaroni and cheese
Roasted sunchokes
Fish kebabs
Braised lamb shank

SPICE PAIRINGS

Aleppo, basil, fennel, ginger, thyme

RECIPE IDEAS

1. Mix all-purpose flour with a little garlic powder
and use to bread pork or chicken cutlets.
2. Combine equal amounts of granulated garlic, oregano,
and finely grated Parmesan to use on pizzas and in pastas.
3. Incorporate garlic powder into your favorite waffle recipe
and serve with fried chicken and honey mustard.

QUICK BLEND
Shoum

Stir this blend into yogurt and use for marinating lamb chops
or chicken thighs to keep them moist on the grill. I also like the
pungent, savory notes it gives to sautéed mushrooms.

Makes about ⅓ cup/28 grams

3 tablespoons/15 grams dried garlic slices, coarsely ground
1½ tablespoons/5 grams dried savory leaves
1 tablespoon/5 grams dried thyme leaves
½ tablespoon/3 grams dried green peppercorns, coarsely ground

GINGER

ZINGIBER OFFICINALE

A fragrant, peppery spice made from the knobby rhizome

FLAVOR & AROMA I love the peppery notes ginger brings. It also delivers fresh, floral, and even warm flavors that tone down very savory dishes, which is why you'll often find it used with heavy meats and game. Because of these elements, and its sort of cooling effect, it translates well in both sweet and savory foods.

I like to bring bright accents into my blends, but fresh ginger can be harsh and aggressive. Ground ginger is like pepper without the heat and is sometimes much easier to use, particularly because you don't need to use a lot of it. I also love it in beverages such as tea, lemonade, and even a simple glass of water. Since it is very hard to grind—it requires heavy-duty equipment—most people buy it ground. It also dissolves better and faster in dishes. At La Boîte, I only use high-quality ground ginger from India.

ORIGIN ☞ Native to China ☞ Cultivated mainly in India, but also in China, Japan, Indonesia, Nigeria, Jamaica, and other islands of the West Indies, and more recently Australia (Queensland)

HARVEST SEASON Ginger is a knobby, tan-colored rhizome in the ginger (Zingiberaceae) family that is typically planted May through June. The plant produces white-and-pink flower bud clusters that bloom yellow. Rhizomes are harvested between December and February, when the stems begin to dry. They are lifted out from the ground using a fork, cleaned from their roots, and either kept fresh or dried and ground.

PARTS USED Rhizome

ABOUT The name *ginger* dates back some three thousand years to the Sanskrit word meaning "horn root" due to its appearance. It is native to China, where it began its journey through parts of Asia to West Africa, the Caribbean, India, and eventually Europe in the first century.

Ginger is often associated with Asian cooking but is found in many other cuisines. For many years ginger used outside of Asia was mostly dried because it was easier to transport. Now you can easily find knobs of fresh ginger in stores. Whether it is chopped, sliced, grated, shredded, minced, or ground into a paste, you'll find it adding its signature bite to Korean kimchi, Indian spiced teas and coffees as well as curries, Jamaican ginger beer, Japanese pickles, and Thai garlic-ginger paste.

Dried ginger is found more in European and Middle Eastern cuisines thanks to the caravan routes that delivered it there. Traditional spice mixtures such as ras el hanout, berbere (page 296), and *chaat masala* would be completely amiss without it. You'll also find it in some of your favorite sweet indulgences, including candied ginger, ginger ale, ginger wine, gingersnaps, and *speculoos* cookies.

TRADITIONAL USES

Five-spice powder—China
Pickled ginger—Japan
Gingerbread—United States
Quatre épices—France
Chai tea—India

NOTE

Toasting not recommended

RECOMMENDED PAIRINGS

Hot chocolate
Vietnamese phở
Tomato chutney
Applesauce
Coconut cake

SPICE PAIRINGS

cardamom, cinnamon, clove, lemongrass, turmeric

RECIPE IDEAS

1. Mix ground ginger into an egg-and-milk batter for French toast.
2. Combine 2 parts ground ginger with 1 part sweet paprika
and use to season roast potatoes.
3. Purée cooked parsnip with ground ginger.

QUICK BLEND
Zangvil

Marinate a duck breast with this blend before roasting it,
or add it to your favorite coleslaw salad for a pungent, peppery kick.

Makes about ⅓ cup/30 grams

3 tablespoons/15 grams ground ginger
1 tablespoon/5 grams coriander seeds, toasted and coarsely ground
½ tablespoon/3 grams anise seeds, toasted and coarsely ground
1½ heaping teaspoons/5 grams caraway seeds, toasted and ground
½ teaspoon/1 gram ground cinnamon
Scant ½ teaspoon/1 gram cayenne powder

GRAINS OF PARADISE

AFRAMOMUM MELEGUETA

A peppery, herbaceous spice made from pyramid-shaped seeds

FLAVOR & AROMA Grains of paradise were once highly praised, but subsequently forgotten about. Back in the Middle Ages, when it was hard to get pepper from India and Indonesia and everything outside of Europe was considered exotic, these little African grains were in high demand. Their woodsy aroma and light peppery heat offered a great substitute. This might be due to the fact that they are in the same family as ginger.

Even today there is not much of it growing, so it is not always easy to find. We have access to every pepper we can think of, so grains of paradise are more of a novelty item than a necessity. But I love their scent and flavor. The mild heat with herbaceous and even cardamom notes is great with meat and fruit, but you can add the grains whole or ground to many dishes.

Avid cooks use them to replicate traditional North African dishes. They also get lots of love from the beer and distilling industries. You can enjoy them whole, toasted, or coarsely ground, which reveals the white flesh inside. Unlike with pepper, you will need quite a few grains in order to get the full effect.

ORIGIN ☞ Native to West Africa ☞ Cultivated in Ghana and Nigeria

HARVEST SEASON The leaves of this tropical plant resemble bamboo. When its ginger-scented, trumpet-shaped flowers emerge, they produce reddish-brown pods (similar to cardamom) that contain seeds inside a pulpy gel. Seedpods are ready to harvest 9 to 11 months after planting (between February and June), when they turn from green to red. Seeds from immature green pods do not have the same coveted pungency. Pods are then dried in the sun for about a week.

PARTS USED Seeds

ABOUT This perennial plant in the ginger (Zingiberaceae) family thrives in the swampy Grain Coast of West Africa. It goes by a number of monikers, including guinea grains, alligator pepper, and melegueta pepper, but shouldn't be confused with the Brazilian malagueta pepper of the Solanaceae family.

Grains of paradise trekked the spice route, caravanning across the Sahara to Europe in the thirteenth century, where it would become a prized spice used in place of pepper until Vasco da Gama replenished European supplies. Even Queen Elizabeth I used it for spicing wines until King George III made that practice illegal.

Though it lost its charm in Europe and is relatively unknown in the West, it continues to be used in Middle Eastern and North and West African cuisines. In North Africa, it is found flavoring rum and brandy, and it adds a slightly bitter, warm bite to Tunisian stews and Moroccan spice blends. In Ghana, you'll find it in sauces, soups, and meats. Try it in a dipping sauce; on grilled meats, braised lamb, eggplant, sausages; and in grain dishes.

TRADITIONAL USES

Qâlat daqqa (spice blend)—Tunisia
Ras el hanout (spice blend)—Morocco
Meat stews—Ghana
Cordials—England
Aquavit—Scandinavia

QUICK BLEND
Malguetta

Season thick-cut sweet potato wedges with this blend before roasting them. It also adds a delicious woodsy flavor to grilled whole branzino.

Makes about 3 tablespoons/24 grams

1½ tablespoons/15 grams grains of paradise, toasted
1 tablespoon/5 grams cubeb berries, coarsely ground
1 teaspoon/2 grams cloves, ground
Scant ¾ teaspoon/2 grams granulated dried orange peel

NOTE
Toasting recommended

RECOMMENDED PAIRINGS
🥣 Okra stew
🐟 Snapper tartare
🌱 Sautéed English peas
🐑 Lamb curry
🥧 Apple crumble

SPICE PAIRINGS
basil, cardamom, cinnamon, galangal, paprika

RECIPE IDEAS
1. Combine equal parts coarsely ground toasted grains of paradise, millet seeds, raisins, and dried cranberries for a sweet-and-savory trail mix.
2. Fold a handful of toasted grains of paradise into banana bread batter before baking.
3. Sprinkle toasted grains of paradise on orange segments and thinly sliced turnip for an interesting salad.

GUAJILLO

CAPSICUM ANNUUM

A medium-heat dried chile with complex notes of berry and a hint of smoke

---

FLAVOR & AROMA Guajillo peppers are one of the most used peppers in Mexico. What I love about them is the approachable heat and sweet berry taste with a tannic or pine-like element. They can sometimes even have light smoky notes from drying in the sun. This makes them a great addition to many dishes and spice blends. You can use the peppers whole or ground for more flavor, or soak the dried chiles in warm water, strain, and then grind them into paste to use for cooking or sauces.

ORIGIN ☞ Native to Mexico, particularly Durango, Aguascalientes, and San Luis Potosí ☞ Cultivated in Mexico, Peru, China, and the United States (specifically California and New Mexico)

HARVEST SEASON In their fresh form, guajillos are called mirasol chiles, from the Spanish word meaning "looking at the sun." The name derives from the fact that guajillos grow upright, unlike the many varieties of peppers that grow hanging down. Guajillos can reach up to 6 inches long and about 1 inch wide, turning a deep red-burgundy color when ready to harvest in October. They are picked when fully ripe and are traditionally sun-dried.

PARTS USED Whole chiles

ABOUT Guajillo, meaning "little gourd," gets its name from the rattle sound the seeds of the dried chile make when shaken. Just don't confuse it with its fellow nightshade (Solanceae), the cascabel chile (page 80), known for its similar attribute. Guajillos are a mainstay of authentic Mexican cuisine, often complemented by the plum notes of the ancho chile (page 50) in certain dishes.

Though still mostly used in traditional Mexican recipes, guajillos have certainly made their mark on southwestern fare in New Mexico, Texas, and Arizona.

These dried chiles are usually found whole and are typically soaked and blended to make burnt-red enchilada sauce or combined with anchos for a spicy dark red mole sauce. When left dry, they can be crumbled and used in meat—especially chicken—rubs, or stirred into rich stews and soups. The spicy bite that they deliver earned these chiles their other occasional moniker, *travieso,* meaning "mischievous." Try adding some to a fruity dessert to see for yourself.

TRADITIONAL USES

Authentic to Mexico
Guajillo chile sauce
Mole sauce
Stuffed chicken rolls
Beef stew
Chilaquiles al guajillo
(fried eggs served over tortillas with red sauce)

NOTE
Toasting not recommended

RECOMMENDED PAIRINGS
Tomatillo salsa
Cod soup
Caramelized red onions
Broiled flank steak
Cherry cobbler

SPICE PAIRINGS
caraway, cilantro, cumin, epazote, garlic

HEAT INDEX
Medium heat

RECIPE IDEAS
1. In a blender, purée soaked guajillo chiles with fresh garlic, olive oil, lemon juice, and salt for a fast chile paste.
2. Slice dried stemmed guajillo chiles and toss with Brussels sprouts and orange zest while pan-frying.
3. Use ground guajillo chile to thicken your favorite salad dressing.

QUICK BLEND
Little Gourd

This blend delivers heat and complexity to delicate mushroom or artichoke raviolis. It also enlivens braised collard greens with a fiery bite.

Makes about ½ cup/58 grams

⅓ cup/40 grams ground guajillo chiles
1½ tablespoons/10 grams caraway seeds, toasted and ground
1½ heaping teaspoons/5 grams green cardamom pods, toasted and ground
1 teaspoon/3 grams freshly grated nutmeg

HIBISCUS BLOSSOM

HIBISCUS SABDARIFFA

A tart, floral, and colorful spice from the dried roselle flower

FLAVOR & AROMA I used to think that hibiscus flowers were something reserved for gardening. It was only later that I discovered the great scent, flavor, and color they impart to hot or cold teas. I remember drinking sweet, chilled *karkadé* tea as a child in Egypt and loving it.

When using hibiscus, you will first notice the beautiful rose-burgundy color and floral aroma. As you taste it, you get sour, tart, and even sweet flavors. I like to use it with fish, vegetables, and fruits. Although you can enjoy it as is without cooking, I think you really get the full effect by applying heat or at least letting it infuse into a hot liquid.

ORIGIN ☞ Native to West Africa ☞ Cultivated mainly in Sudan, China, Thailand, and Mexico

HARVEST SEASON The hibiscus fruit, which consists of the bright red calyx and seedpod at the base of the flower, is picked toward the end of the year when it is mature and plump (after about 6 months). Calyxes are traditionally laid out in the sun to dry, and leaves are harvested 6 to 8 weeks after planting, 2 or 3 times during the growth cycle.

PARTS USED Leaves and flowers

ABOUT There are a number of hibiscus varieties, but *Hibiscus sabdariffa,* more commonly called roselle, has been cultivated for centuries as a vitamin C–rich spice and for its strong fibers, used for jute or cordage. A member of the mallow (Malvaceae) family, it also goes by Jamaican sorrel, java jute, and Florida cranberry due to its similar flavor and color.

The roselle's calyx is cooked down to make sauces like Senegalese *bëkëj,* beverages, jams, chutneys, preserves, pies, and ice cream. In the West Indies, it's used in wine making, flavored rum syrup, and cakes. In Central America, particularly during Christmastime, you'll find people sipping ruby red hibiscus drinks.

The green leaves also have their appeal. In Mali, leaves are boiled to make sauce, and they are essential to Burmese *chin baung kyaw* curry. Leaves are also used as a spicier version of spinach in Senegalese *thiéboudiène* (a fish rice dish).

TRADITIONAL USES

Salad dressing—Mexico
Jus de bissap (hibiscus tea)—Senegal
Karkadé tea—Egypt
Candied flowers in syrup—Australia
Chicken soup—Philippines

NOTE

Toasting not recommended

RECOMMENDED PAIRINGS

Rum punch
Tomato salad
Mustard vinaigrette
Grilled swordfish
Cherry clafoutis

SPICE PAIRINGS

anise, ginger, juniper, mint, pink pepperberries

RECIPE IDEAS

1. Drop a few whole dried hibiscus flowers into simmering salted water and use to boil sweet potatoes.
2. Infuse ground hibiscus into your favorite vodka for a few weeks and use to create fun floral cocktails.
3. Poach whole pears in simmering white wine with honey and a few whole dried hibiscus flowers for a sweet-tart dessert.

QUICK BLEND
Rose Mallow

Sprinkle this floral blend over thick-cut slices of daikon radish and braise them with vermouth and chicken stock. It also makes a sweet-tart addition to chilled strawberry soup for dessert.

Makes about 3 tablespoons/24 grams

½ cup/15 grams hibiscus flowers, coarsely ground
1 tablespoon/5 grams ground galangal
2½ pods/3 grams star anise, ground
Scant ½ teaspoon/1 gram cayenne powder

HORSERADISH

ARMORACIA RUSTICANA

A sinus-opening spice made from an intensely aromatic, pungent root

———

FLAVOR & AROMA Horseradish is part of the same family as wasabi and mustard, which explains its heat and pungent aroma. The dried roots allow me to introduce mild heat, but also fresh notes and flavors, to blends. A lot of the effect comes from the fact that the scent hits you long before you taste it.

Both fresh and dried horseradish have their advantages: The sharpness of fresh horseradish does not last very long unless combined with vinegar, but that sometimes takes away from the pure penetrating taste. When ground—it's rarely sold dried whole—it stores longer, dissolves more easily, and allows you to harness its unmistakable flavor without using a wet ingredient. It can also handle higher cooking temperatures than fresh roots, which would typically lose their flavor under the same heat. Note, you might need a bit more dried horseradish than fresh to get the full effect. If you brave making fresh horseradish sauce at home, be sure to open a window.

ORIGIN ☞ Native to southeastern Europe and western Asia ☞ Cultivated in Central and Eastern Europe, and the United States (mainly Illinois)

HARVEST SEASON Horseradish is a perennial of the Brassicaceae, or cabbage, family that is usually grown as an annual and cultivated for its long, white taproot. Its fleshy root is planted in the spring and grows large, shiny, dark green leaves and whitish flowers that bloom in the summer months. Though traditionally planted and harvested by hand, about half of commercial crops are harvested with converted potato diggers or similar equipment in the fall, with the rest left in the ground to overwinter for a spring harvest.

PARTS USED Young leaves and roots

ABOUT This lingering, aromatic root has been an essential element of European fare since before the Renaissance, after which it spread to Scandinavia and England. By the late 1600s, horseradish was found on nearly every table in England, used as an accompaniment for beef and oysters. By the early 1800s, it was found across the North America's northeast, having been cultivated there by early settlers, and from there made its way west. The horseradish industry thrived east of the Mississippi River, where it is still chiefly grown, in Illinois.

Even today, horseradish is prized as a readily available condiment—particularly because you can substitute the fresh and dried forms—and a fiery addition to the cuisines of its origin. Austrians mix it with grated apples and lemon juice for a condiment called *Apfelkren,* and it is commonly served with tongue or roast beef in Germany. Also, the next time you dip a cooked shrimp in sweet, spicy cocktail sauce, you may recognize horseradish from the aroma that hits you head-on. You've probably most often eaten horseradish in place of actual wasabi (page 286). This traditional Japanese condiment is made from a root of the same family, but its scarcity makes horseradish (usually mixed with mustard and food coloring) a somewhat comparable replacement.

Growing up in Israel, I mainly saw horseradish once or twice a year alongside the words *gefilte fish* (or filtered fish, as a friend calls it jokingly). It is, for the most part, always combined with cooked beets, vinegar (which keeps the fresh root from oxidizing), and sugar as a European Jewish classic. The spicy-yet-sweet condiment works perfectly with the poached carp patties and smoked fish of my childhood and is especially welcome when eating a lot of matzoh bread. After all, we still add it to the Passover seder plate as a bitter herb.

TRADITIONAL USES

Tartar sauce—Worldwide
Potato purée—Worldwide
Cocktail sauce—Worldwide
Easter Day soup—Poland
Bloody Mary—United States

NOTE

Toasting not recommended

RECOMMENDED PAIRINGS

Tartar sauce
Steamed asparagus
Pot roast
Poached cod
Crab boil

SPICE PAIRINGS

celery seeds, juniper, mustard, orange peel, paprika

RECIPE IDEAS

1. Sprinkle ground horseradish onto ground
beef patties before grilling for spicy burgers.
2. Purée cooked beets in a blender with ground horseradish
and salt and serve with heavy cream mixed with a bit of
ground horseradish for a simple borscht.
3. For a spicy salad, combine cooked shredded chicken,
mayonnaise, capers, and ground horseradish.

QUICK BLEND
Raifort

This blend is great in goulash-style beef or veal stew,
or for adding an aromatic kick to macaroni and cheese.

Makes about ¼ cup/33 grams

1½ tablespoons/15 grams ground horseradish
1½ tablespoons/10 grams ground sweet paprika
½ tablespoon/5 grams celery seeds, ground
½ tablespoon/3 grams dried garlic slices, coarsely ground

HYSSOP

HYSSOPUS OFFICINALIS

*The dried leaves and flowers of the
fennel- and anise-scented "holy herb"*

FLAVOR & AROMA I remember picking hyssop leaves and flowers in the fields near our house in the Galilee. We would bring them home to dry out on a piece of news-paper so we could use them on flatbreads, grilled meats, and in tea. This variety of hyssop has fennel, mint, and anise notes and can even be used to replace anise in some recipes. It has a slight but pleasant bitterness, with some peppery hints as well.

Whether you are using fresh or dried hyssop leaves (the flowers are more rare), they work great when roasting and grilling. Since the leaves are relatively small, you can keep them whole. If you're going to cook with them, a little goes a long way.

ORIGIN ☞ Native to southern Europe, North Africa, and Western Asia ☞ Cultivated in the Balkans, Turkey, the Mediterranean, and North America

HARVEST SEASON Of the many hyssop varieties (all members of the mint, or Lamiaceae, family), this one is a vibrantly hued shrub with dark green leaves and woody stems that reach up to 2 feet high. In early summer and again in early fall, fragrant flowers bloom in blues, pinks, and sometimes white, signaling harvest times. Stalks with flower tips and leaves are cut and dried out on pallets or in stacks in a cool, dry place, which takes just under a week. They are usually kept out of the sun to prevent oxidation and loss of color. Once dried, the leaves and flowers are removed, finely chopped, and packaged.

PARTS USED Dried leaves, young shoots, and flowers

ABOUT What was once lauded as a holy herb—the literal Greek and Hebrew translation—used to ward off illness, cleanse churches, and symbolize humility in religious paintings has become a roadside weed. Brought to North America by early European colonists, its anise-scented flowers once framed monastery gardens as ornamental hedges. Now it has naturalized and spread to unlikely places.

While it may not have a storied history in the culinary world, its present and future are bright. Just as its sweet nectar attracts bees and butterflies, its flavors make it a must-have for chefs and home cooks alike. Hyssop's ability to balance the richness of fatty dishes makes it great with roasts, veal and chicken stews, and cheeses. Where it really shines is in infusions: try using it to make tea, jams, custard, and fruit syrups. It's also found in the French liqueur Bénédictine.

TRADITIONAL USES

Fruit compote—France
Herbes de Provence (spice blend)—France
Chartreuse liqueur—France
Za'atar (spice blend)—Middle East
Yogurt soup—Syria

NOTE

Toasting not recommended

RECOMMENDED PAIRINGS

Baked goat cheese
Farro salad
English pea soup
Roasted bell peppers
Duck skewers

SPICE PAIRINGS

Aleppo, garlic, lemon peel, paprika, sumac

RECIPE IDEAS

1. Season grated potatoes with coarsely ground dried hyssop and use to make latkes.
2. Marinate thick-cut slices of beefsteak tomato with olive oil and ground dried hyssop before grilling.
3. Combine equal parts whole dried hyssop, sage, and mint leaves and steep in boiling water for an herbal tea.

QUICK BLEND
Poivre d'Ane

Make croutons with this floral blend: just sprinkle it on diced bread along with grated pecorino cheese and a drizzle of olive oil before baking. It's also great on grilled vegetable skewers and with roasted beets.

Makes about 3 tablespoons/28 grams

Scant ½ cup/15 grams dried hyssop leaves, coarsely ground
½ tablespoon/5 grams nigella seeds
½ tablespoon/5 grams ground sumac
½ tablespoon/3 grams pepperoncino flakes, or other mild chile flakes

JALAPEÑO

CAPSICUM ANNUUM

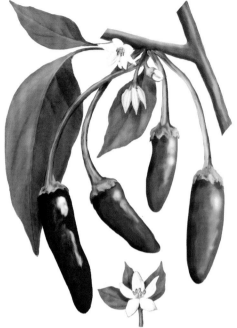

A highly versatile, ubiquitous fresh or dried medium-heat chile

FLAVOR & AROMA Although jalapeño chiles are mainly used fresh, they are also dried into flakes or ground, or smoked and dried to make chipotles (page 90). When they're fresh, most of the fire is in the seeds, so you can adjust the heat by removing them or keeping just a few.

I love it in all its forms, but for spice blending I rely on the ground green powder. It retains a very fresh scent with a lot of heat and some acidic notes. Although we are living in a time when the highest heat is often the most coveted, the jalapeño still brings a complex taste and scent that contributes to great blends and dishes.

ORIGIN ☞ Native to Mexico ☞ Cultivated mainly in Mexico in Veracruz (near Papantla), Oaxaca, and Chihuahua, but also in Costa Rica and the United States in Texas and the Southwest

HARVEST SEASON Jalapeño plants are in the nightshade (Solanaceae) family and can grow up to 3 feet tall, producing around 30 pods per plant. During the growing period, which takes 70 to 80 days, pods are harvested when still green and sometimes with small cracks. When they turn red at full maturity, they are more often used for smoking or as a less desirable fresh chile. Traditionally, they are grown as a hot-weather summer crop, but modern greenhouses make them available to us year-round.

PARTS USED Whole chiles

ABOUT The jalapeño is named for Xalapa, the capital city of Veracruz, where it was originally cultivated. In Mexico, jalapeño generally refers to pickled peppers; when fresh, they are often called *cuaresmeño*, even though this is a distinct but very closely related chile. Only in the United States is it always a jalapeño—except when smoked and dried, of course. It may be one of the most ubiquitous and versatile chiles, but it is still predominantly found in Mexican and southwestern fare.

Crisp, fresh chiles are halved and stuffed; roasted whole; diced and added to salsas, cornbread, and long-cooked beans; or used as a condiment to deliver heat to any dish. They are also found canned and pickled and used in the southwestern style on cheese-smothered tortilla chips, made into spicy jellies, or infused (try tequila) and muddled into cocktails.

Using dried flakes or ground jalapeño opens up a whole new world of cooking, where you can easily dissolve the spice into sauces and dressings, or even it sprinkle over popcorn without the issues you get when adding a wet ingredient—everything that is meant to be crisp stays crisp. Plus you get the added benefit of extended shelf life, so you always have a little extra heat on hand. There are endless ways to use this approachable, but not to be underestimated, chile.

TRADITIONAL USES

Authentic to Mexico and the American Southwest
Jalapeño poppers
Green escabeche
Guacamole
Tomatillo salsa
Quesadillas

NOTE
Toasting not recommended

RECOMMENDED PAIRINGS
Mango salad
Chimichurri
Snapper ceviche
Fried eggplant
Pork sliders

SPICE PAIRINGS
cilantro, cumin, garlic, oregano, pimentón

HEAT INDEX
Medium heat

RECIPE IDEAS
1. Mix ground jalapeño with lime juice, olive oil, and honey
and drizzle over cubed fresh watermelon and crumbled feta cheese.
2. In a food processor, purée blanched peeled fava beans,
garlic, avocado, and lemon juice, season with salt and
ground jalapeño, and serve with raw vegetables.
3. Season halved cherry tomatoes with ground jalapeño, olive oil,
and salt before quickly broiling and serving over just-cooked pasta.

QUICK BLEND
Veracruz
See photograph, page 148.

Sprinkle this hot and tangy blend onto a crab and green
papaya salad. You can also rim your cocktail glasses with
it to add bite to mojitos and margaritas.

Makes about 3 tablespoons/23 grams

1 tablespoon/10 grams ground jalapeño
1 tablespoon/5 grams crushed dried basil leaves
½ tablespoon/5 grams granulated dried orange peel
1 teaspoon/3 grams ground amchoor

JASMINE FLOWER

JASMINUM OFFICINALE

The sweet-smelling spice made of flowers and unopened buds

FLAVOR & AROMA When you think of jasmine, it's easy to conjure thoughts of tangled green vines speckled with white flowers, or steaming cups of fragrant tea. While this flower is traditionally used for teas, I love using it in delicate spice blends to highlight the floral notes in dishes. In order to fully appreciate it, you will need to let it infuse into liquid or apply low to medium heat when cooking. In its dried form, it retains only a hint of the fresh flower's heady aroma, but it is certainly still present. Since it is a delicate item and the flowers will eventually dry and turn to powder, I recommend buying small amounts at a time.

ORIGIN ☞ Native to the Himalayas and China ☞ Cultivated mainly in China, but also in France, Spain, Italy, North Africa, and the Middle East

HARVEST SEASON Beloved as a long-blooming garden plant, jasmine typically flowers June to September. The white or yellowish flower buds are harvested when fully developed, but unopened, in the early morning or evening, and then dried and packaged. Fresh flowers are plucked for distilling and their essential oils used in perfume.

PARTS USED Flowers and buds

ABOUT *Jasminum officinale,* also known as common jasmine or poet's jasmine, is one of more than seven hundred flowering plants in the olive (Oleaceae) family. This perennial climbing vine is lauded for its permeating sweet aroma, which is prized in the perfume and aromatherapy industries. In the kitchen, fresh and dried edible buds make their presence known and remembered most notably in hot teas and desserts.

In Chinese flowering teas, jasmine buds are the centerpieces of handwoven bundles of green or black tea leaves that bloom when steeped in hot water. For a modern twist, buds add their distinct aroma when infused into simple syrups for cocktails. Jasmine tea is also used to flavor sorbets, financiers, cupcakes, and even ice pops.

FAMILIAR USES

Infused oil
Ice cream
Vinaigrette
Cookies
Lemonade

NOTE

Toasting not recommended

RECOMMENDED PAIRINGS

Carrot juice
Nectarine jam
Steamed brown rice
Maple glaze
Panna cotta

SPICE PAIRINGS

anise seeds, basil, ginger, pink pepperberries, white pepper

RECIPE IDEAS

1. Sprinkle dried jasmine flowers into simmering apple cider
and reduce to make a syrup for dressings or pancakes.
2. Combine heavy cream, sugar, and ground jasmine,
whip, and serve with brownies.
3. Infuse warm grapeseed oil with dried jasmine flowers
to make fragrant jasmine oil for salads and fish.

QUICK BLEND
White Flower

This aromatic, peppery blend works wonders when added to
simmering cream for poaching lobster tail or shrimp.
It also gives a fragrant floral element to lemon curd.

Makes about ⅓ cup/22 grams

Scant ¾ cup/10 grams dried jasmine flowers, ground
3 tablespoons/3 grams crushed dried basil leaves
1 tablespoon/5 grams pink pepperberries, ground
1 teaspoon/3 grams ground dried pomegranate seeds
½ teaspoon/1 gram Sichuan pepper, ground

JUNIPER

JUNIPERUS COMMUNIS

A resinous, pine-scented spice from the seed cone of a juniper shrub

FLAVOR & AROMA Juniper is mainly known as an essential ingredient in gin and aquavit, as well as for its annual appearance during the winter holiday season in the West. Because it works so well with game, most people unfortunately don't use it much during the rest of the year.

I get my juniper from Europe, particularly Yugoslavia and Albania, and love that the berries are still a bit soft and I can even chop them with a knife. Because they are still oily—a sign of good quality—they can also serve as a binding agent in a blend. I also love the piney resin notes that they bring with a touch of sweetness, and the bright, sharp scent they give spice blends or dishes.

If you have access to fresh berries, you might be lucky and get ahold of some of the branches too. Add them to the fire when smoking meat or fish, or simply nestle some in with roasted chicken while basting it. Whole or ground dried juniper berries are also perfect for roasting root vegetables or poaching fruits.

ORIGIN ☞ Native to the British Isles ☞ Cultivated in Europe, North America, and Asia, and naturalized across the Northern Hemisphere

HARVEST SEASON *Juniperus communis,* or the common juniper, is a low-growing, wide-spreading shrub in the cypress (Cupressaceae) family. Its spherical, berry-like seed cones, what we know as juniper berries, turn from green to a blue-black when ready to harvest in the fall. This process can take 2 to 3 years. They are often harvested from the wild in Europe, where they are laid out to dry and turn a purple-black color before being taken to market.

PARTS USED Seed cones (berries) and sometimes branches

ABOUT Juniper berries have been used medicinally as far back as ancient Egypt and more recently by the Navajo people as a treatment for diabetes. As a culinary ingredient, particularly as a gin flavoring, juniper berries made their debut somewhere before the seventeenth century. The gin we are familiar with today is based on the traditional liquor of the Netherlands, genever, or Dutch gin. It was actually intended to calm soldiers during the Eighty Years' War (in which the Netherlands fought for independence from Spain), but understandably became a favorite among the British for imbibing.

Over the centuries, juniper berries became a mainstay in European cuisines and spirits. They are an essential element of the traditional Finnish ale *sahti,* the farmhouse ales of Scandinavian countries, and in the Slovak juniper brandy known as borovička. In Northern Europe, juniper accents pâté, game (specifically venison, hare, and game birds), sauces, stuffing, pork, and poultry. Try adding a few crushed berries to your pickling liquid or mulling spice for something altogether different.

TRADITIONAL USES

Gravlax—Scandinavia
Rotkohl (sweet and sour red cabbage)—Germany
Hasenpfeffer (hare or rabbit stew)—Germany
Sauerkraut and choucroute garnie (fermented
cabbage condiment with salted
meats)—Alsace, France
Venison stew—Europe

NOTE
Toasting not recommended

RECOMMENDED PAIRINGS
Potato salad
Apple slaw
Whole roasted veal rack
Red wine and beef sauce
Beer-braised chicken

SPICE PAIRINGS
bay leaf, cinnamon, nutmeg, sage, star anise

RECIPE IDEAS

1. Infuse a bottle of white wine vinegar with a handful of juniper berries and 4 bay leaves to make bright, earthy dressings or sauces.

2. Stir ground juniper berries into sour cream seasoned with chopped dill, salt, and pepper to serve with cold smoked fish.

3. Combine equal amounts of toasted ground caraway seeds and ground juniper and use to season whole roasted carrots with prunes.

QUICK BLEND
Ar-Ar

Season a whole turkey with this fragrant blend before roasting,
or use it to sharpen cider-braised red cabbage.

Makes about ⅓ cup/32 grams

½ cup/10 grams dried rosemary leaves, coarsely ground
3 tablespoons/15 grams juniper berries, coarsely ground
1 tablespoon/5 grams star anise, ground
1 teaspoon/2 grams ground mace

KAFFIR LIME

CITRUS HYSTRIX

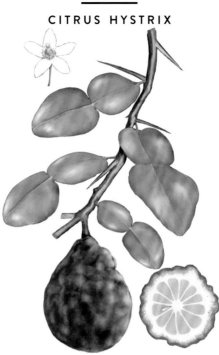

*The intensely fragrant fruit and
hourglass-shaped leaves of a citrus plant*

FLAVOR & AROMA I was introduced to kaffir limes, or makrut, while working with Olivier Roellinger in France, of all places. We used to buy what is known as *combava* in French every weekend from the one and only Asian supermarket in the area. I remember being blown away by how potent and fragrant the fresh leaves were and the amazing citrus scent given off by the fruit's rind and juice. We would infuse the leaves in grapeseed oil over low heat and then use that oil to finish delicate broths or lightly cooked fish. The rind was grated into crab salads before serving.

I love the fresh scent and floral notes of both dried and fresh kaffir limes. Although they are from the citrus family, they bring very little acidity to a dish or blend once dried. They are also amazing at balancing flavorful seafood or ingredients like garlic and onion. There is not a lot of juice in the kaffir lime and it can be slightly bitter, so you only need to use a little bit of it. If using the fresh leaves as a garnish, you should remove the inedible central vein first. When using whole leaves to impart a refreshing aroma to soups or stews, you can leave them intact and discard before eating.

Both the fruit and leaves are also great dried and offer a solution for the off-season or in places that cannot get them fresh. Since I cannot find a good source for dried leaves and fruit, I dry both at La Boîte. I buy the fruits during peak season and air-dry them, which can take five months, and then grind them into powder as needed, or use them whole for broths. The leaves are available year-round in the United States. They take a few days to dry and then can be ground as needed.

ORIGIN ☞ Native to Southeast Asia ☞ Cultivated in Southeast Asia, Australia, and the United States (California and Florida)

HARVEST SEASON The leaves of this bushy citrus plant (a member of the rue, or Rutaceae, family) have two lobes connected by a tough central vein. They can vary in size from a fraction of an inch to several inches long and can be picked throughout the year as needed. The wrinkly, knobby, pear-shaped fruit is dark green when at its peak—it will fade to a yellowish green when past its prime—and is ready for harvest beginning in the fall.

PARTS USED Leaves, fruit, and rind

ABOUT You may have only discovered this small, wrinkled citrus fruit more recently in some trendy mixologist concoction, but it's been a mainstay of Southeast Asian cuisine for many years. Its fragrant leaves, zest, and small squeeze of juice add an essential citrus element that's not quite lemon and not quite lime to Indonesian sambals, Thai soups, and Malaysian laksas.

When crushed, its leaves impart aromatic natural oils to Thai green curry paste, in which the leaves are ground with a mortar and pestle along with cilantro roots, galangal, lemongrass, garlic, shrimp paste, Thai chiles, and spices to add a tangy citrus element to meats and eggplant. When thinly sliced, leaves are added to savory fish paste and green beans to be fried into cakes or are used to give a pop of color and a brightness to beef penang. Kaffir lime is indispensable as the sour element of the fundamental Thai flavors.

TRADITIONAL USES

Flavored rum—Martinique
Rougail (spice paste condiment)—Mauritius
Tom kha gai (coconut soup)—Thailand
Soto ayam (chicken soup)—Indonesia
Kroeung (spice and herb paste)—Cambodia

NOTE
Toasting not recommended

RECOMMENDED PAIRINGS
Crab spring rolls
Shrimp coconut soup
Pad thai
Steamed bok choy
Pork and peanut meatballs

SPICE PAIRINGS
basil, galangal, garlic, lemongrass, turmeric

RECIPE IDEAS
1. Infuse dried kaffir lime leaves in simmering orange juice, strain, chill, and use the juice for mimosas.
2. Grate some dried kaffir limes with a Microplane over seared scallops.
3. Marinate green beans with olive oil, garlic, and ground kaffir lime leaves before grilling.

QUICK BLEND
Combava

Try stirring this citrus-scented blend along with lime juice into coconut milk and eggplant soup. It is also great for giving duck a bright, fresh seasoning before roasting.

Makes about ⅓ cup/21 grams

2 cups/10 grams dried kaffir lime leaves, ground
1 tablespoon/5 grams ground lemongrass
1 tablespoon/3 grams crushed dried basil leaves
½ tablespoon/3 grams ground galangal

LAVENDER

LAVANDULA ANGUSTIFOLIA/LAVANDULA × INTERMEDIA/LAVANDULA STOECHAS

*A perfumy spice made from purple
flower buds and gray-green leaves*

———

FLAVOR & AROMA For the most part we think of lavender in soap and sachets, not as a spice or cooking ingredient. Because it is very strong and pungent, using it with food can be tricky. If done right, however, it is wonderful.

The Provence region of southeast France remains the main source of lavender in the world. At some point its fragrant flowers and sometimes bitter leaves or stems found their way into food; the root is the part used for extracts.

Today, you can find many chefs adding lavender to various dishes. I am often challenged to incorporate floral and sweet-scented notes into blends, and lavender flowers allow me to do it. Its flower buds, which have hints of mint and citrus, can also be candied and added to salads and desserts.

ORIGIN ☞ Native to countries bordering the Mediterranean Sea ☞ Cultivated mainly in Provence, France, but also in parts of Europe, China, New Zealand Australia, Tasmania, and the United States

HARVEST SEASON Lavender flowers typically bloom from mid- to late June through early July. When harvested for drying, the flowers are gathered by hand when the first few florets begin to open. For essential oil crops, they are harvested with special machinery when they are half in bloom. Leaves can be harvested at any point during the growing season. With 70% to 80% water content, lavender takes a week or two to dry.

PARTS USED Flowers and leaves

ABOUT The name *lavender* actually comes from the Latin word *lavare,* meaning "to bathe" or "to wash," and it has stuck by its name throughout history. It was one of the herbs used to prepare the holy essence in the biblical Temple; the Greek naturalist Dioscorides lauded its medicinal attributes in the first century AD; and the Greeks and Romans often used it in their herbal baths. It was also essential to ancient Egyptian incense.

Of the nearly forty species of lavender worldwide (all part of the mint, or Lamiaceae, family), the three you'll most likely find used for dried flowers and for its heady essential oils are *L. × intermedia* (a hybrid mostly grown for oil), *L. stoechas* (Spanish lavender), and *L. angustifolia* (English lavender), the most widely cultivated. All of these are readily available as dried spices and are easily grown in home gardens for fresh cuttings.

Herbes de Provence, a blend of rosemary, fennel, herbs, and lavender, is the best-known culinary usage and is used for vegetable dishes, lamb, and desserts. Lavender adds an aromatic element to sweet pastries and whipping cream, and you can even mix it with sugar for making scones or jam. For savory dishes, try adding it to lamb stew or roasted pheasant and chicken, or even rice.

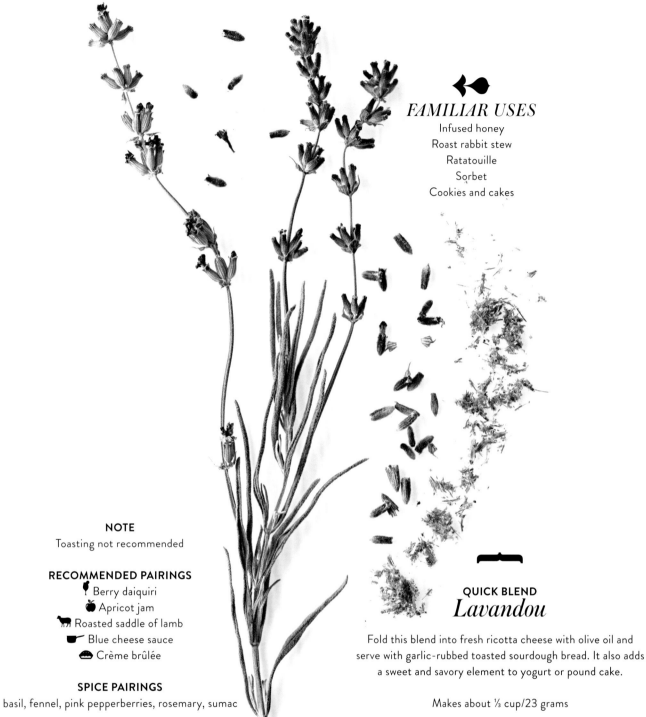

FAMILIAR USES

Infused honey
Roast rabbit stew
Ratatouille
Sorbet
Cookies and cakes

NOTE
Toasting not recommended

RECOMMENDED PAIRINGS
Berry daiquiri
Apricot jam
Roasted saddle of lamb
Blue cheese sauce
Crème brûlée

SPICE PAIRINGS
basil, fennel, pink pepperberries, rosemary, sumac

RECIPE IDEAS
1. Season cubed veal, diced tomato, and a bit of white wine with ground lavender for a fragrant stew.
2. Combine equal amounts of ground lavender and sugar and use in any baked good recipe like scones, muffins, and biscotti.
3. Add a handful of dried lavender flowers to simmering port and use to poach fresh figs.

QUICK BLEND
Lavandou

Fold this blend into fresh ricotta cheese with olive oil and serve with garlic-rubbed toasted sourdough bread. It also adds a sweet and savory element to yogurt or pound cake.

Makes about ⅓ cup/23 grams

½ cup/10 grams dried lavender flowers, ground
1½ tablespoons/5 grams dried savory leaves
1 tablespoon/5 grams coriander seeds, toasted and coarsely ground
½ tablespoon/3 grams ground ginger

LEMON BALM

MELISSA OFFICINALIS

*A bright green,
fresh-scented herb*

FLAVOR & AROMA Lemon balm is part of the mint family, but as the name suggests, it has a lemon scent and slightly acidic taste. Unlike mint, it is not always available fresh because of low demand and lack of awareness—most of it is used for the pharmaceutical industry or in cosmetics. This delicate, fragrant herb is much easier to buy dried online, and I highly recommend using it.

It is great when steeped in hot or cold teas, stirred into soups or stews, or as a marinade for lamb or fish. It does lose some of its flavor in cooking, so incorporate it at the end, or just add some fresh leaves to fruit juice. I buy dried lemon balm domestically.

ORIGIN ☞ Native to southern Europe, the Mediterranean, Western Asia, and North Africa ☞ Cultivated worldwide

HARVEST SEASON These perennial plants in the mint (Lamiaceae) family can grow 2 to 3 feet high and have spring-green leaves that look like larger mint. Leaves are harvested early in the season, around May and June, before clusters of small white-yellow flowers boom and go to seed.

PARTS USED Leaves

ABOUT Lemon balm, which also goes by melissa balm and bee balm, has been a curative herb for some two thousand years, used in the Middle Ages as a calming ingredient for reducing stress and easing discomfort. Early colonists brought this lemon-scented plant from southern Europe to North America to make herbal teas, to use as a substitute for lemon in jams, and to attract honeybees—the Greek word *melissa* actually means "honeybee."

Just as it was used all those years ago, lemon balm is often combined with other calming herbs like chamomile for a soothing effect. But it also complements a variety of fresh fruits like melon or pineapple and adds a citrus element to vinaigrettes, scones, pies, cheesecakes, sauces for fish, poultry stuffing, herb butters, and sandwiches. It adds brightness and a touch of summertime to any dish, any time of the day.

FAMILIAR USES

Spiked punch
Simple syrup
Roast chicken
Apple desserts
Ice cream

NOTE
Toasting not recommended

RECOMMENDED PAIRINGS
🍎 Quince jam
🥗 English pea salad
🌾 Quinoa
🐟 Steamed cod
🥄 Beurre blanc sauce

SPICE PAIRINGS
cubeb, ginger, licorice, vanilla, white pepper

RECIPE IDEAS
1. Season portobello mushrooms with olive oil and ground lemon balm leaves, sauté in a pan, and serve with fresh ricotta cheese.
2. Marinate an arctic char fillet with olive oil and a few pinches of ground lemon balm leaves, broil, and serve with horseradish cream.
3. Infuse dried lemon balm leaves in white wine with chopped shallots and pepper and use as a base for lemony béarnaise sauce.

QUICK BLEND
Melissa

This coarsely ground blend gives texture to a nectarine and pistachio salad or can even be stirred into an olive oil dressing for a lemon-pepper flavor. It also adds a bright, citrus note to seared scallops.

Makes about ⅓ cup/22 grams

2 cups/10 grams dried lemon balm leaves, coarsely ground
1 tablespoon/5 grams pink pepperberries, coarsely ground
½ tablespoon/5 grams yellow mustard seeds, coarsely ground
Scant ¾ teaspoon/2 grams ground amchoor

LEMONGRASS

CYMBOPOGON CITRATUS

A bright, fresh, lemony spice made from the lower stalks of a tropical grass

FLAVOR & AROMA Growing up in Israel, I often found myself picking lemongrass from my family's garden. Now that I live in New York City, I have to buy it at the store like everyone else. In the past, I would use fresh lemongrass in tea and for cooking various recipes, but there always seemed to be a bit left over that would slowly dry in the fridge. I was surprised to find that even dried lemongrass leaves were still fantastic. Now I just buy it every once in a while and intentionally dry some so that I do not have to go shopping for it all the time.

Dried lemongrass obviously has fresh lemon notes, but it also has some sweet scents and rose-like aromas with a clean citrus taste. It is not as sharp as a lemon, but rather more rounded. For it to really shine, you need to mix it with a hot or cold liquid or apply some heat.

Most dried lemongrass comes from Asia, and I like to buy it whole or at least in large pieces so I can make sure nothing was added to it when it was ground. Even though it's a fairly well-known ingredient, most people still think of it as something you only find in tea or Asian dishes. I hope that it will find its place among the more common herbs and spices. It adds something entirely unique to savory dishes, desserts, and drinks.

ORIGIN ☞ Native to South India, Ceylon, or Indonesia ☞ Cultivated in Eastern and Western Asia, India, Mexico, the United States (particularly Florida and California), Central America, Brazil, Australia, Western Africa, and the West Indies

HARVEST SEASON Lemongrass is a perennial tropical grass that is harvested every 3 to 4 months. During harvest time, the entire tuft or clump of grass (Poaceae family) is cut at the base; the stems are separated from the leaves and then cleaned and bundled or dried. For most home gardens, a lemongrass plant is easily grown, is attractive, and provides plenty of stalks throughout most of the year.

PARTS USED Fresh or dried lower part of the stalk and leaves

ABOUT Lemongrass was most likely used in Asian cuisine as a flavoring agent right from its beginning. In the late 1800s, India began cultivating and distilling lemongrass, or *choomana poolu,* for its favored aromatic citronella oil. The oils were also coveted in the Philippines in the seventeenth century, but it wasn't until the early to mid-1900s that it became commercially cultivated in Haiti and the United States (mainly in Florida).

To this day, it remains a staple of Southeast Asian cuisines. You'll find it in the Nonya cooking of Singapore, Vietnamese salads, Thai curries and soups, and the Indian coffee called *chukku kaapi,* and adding lemony notes to fish and poultry, stews, flavored syrups, and drinks.

The bottom few inches of fresh lemongrass stalks are either crushed and left whole to infuse braising liquids, broths, and teas, or the woody outer layers are peeled off and the tender inner parts are finely chopped and cooked in stir-fries or added to curry paste and marinades. The tough, inedible leaves can also be tied and added to rice or the cavity of poultry for a fresh aromatic. Dried lemongrass has a less intense flavor but is wonderfully fragrant when used in cooking liquids or mixed into dressing, spice rubs, and desserts.

TRADITIONAL USES

Spicy lemongrass chicken—Malaysia
Bumbu (spice blend)—Indonesia
Tom yum (spicy-sour soup)—Thailand
Lemongrass green tea—Africa
Bò nhúng dấm (fondue)—Vietnam

NOTE
Toasting not recommended

RECOMMENDED PAIRINGS
Fried rice
Shrimp kebabs
Fish curry
Shredded pork salad
Coconut pudding

SPICE PAIRINGS
basil, coriander, garlic, ginger, turmeric

RECIPE IDEAS
1. Dust fresh diver scallops with ground lemongrass, salt, and pepper and sear in coconut oil.
2. Combine ground lemongrass with ground chicken meat and chopped salted peanuts and use for sliders.
3. Stuff a whole red snapper with a handful of coarsely chopped dried lemongrass leaves, fresh cilantro, and sliced fresh garlic before roasting.

QUICK BLEND
Limonit
See photograph, page 163.

Season cubes of pork loin with this blend and sauté with fresh pineapple and cashew nuts. It is also a great way to add brightness to a mango and shrimp salad.

Makes about ⅓ cup/30 grams

3 tablespoons/15 grams ground lemongrass
2½ tablespoons/5 grams crushed dried basil leaves
1 tablespoon/5 grams coriander seeds, toasted and ground
1½ heaping teaspoons/5 grams crushed Aleppo chile flakes, or mild chile flakes

LEMON MYRTLE

BACKHOUSIA CITRIODORA

The "more lemony than lemon"
leaves of an evergreen tree

FLAVOR & AROMA Outside of its native homeland, lemon myrtle doesn't have much notoriety. But that is starting to change. Some describe it as having an even more lemony scent than actual lemons. It also has some sweet and floral notes, which make it very complex. It works great wherever you can think of using lemon and adds brightness to savory dishes, desserts, and drinks. It is very potent, so you have to be careful not to let it overpower a blend or dish.

I buy Australian lemon myrtle, and it comes coarsely ground or crushed. My personal theory is that since the leaves are so lightweight, commercial producers prefer crushing them so that they can pack more in the bags or boxes.

ORIGIN ☞ Native to Queensland, Australia ☞ Cultivated mainly in Queensland and the north coast of New South Wales

HARVEST SEASON Lemon myrtle is an evergreen shrub or tree with dark green leaves that can be picked year-round. Mechanical harvesting is used in commercial plantations where they dry leaves to be sold as a spice or distilled for essential oils. Fragrant, feathery flowers bloom in the fall.

PARTS USED Fresh and dried leaves

ABOUT Also known as the sweet verbena tree, lemon myrtle, a member of the myrtle (Myrtaceae) family, is native to the coastal rain forests of Australia. It is a major producer of citrol, the oil responsible for the leaves' signature lemon flavor and scent. By comparison, lemon myrtle has more than 90% citrol, whereas lemons only have about 5%, which means it actually tastes more like the fruit than the fruit itself. It has the most intense lemon aroma of any spice in the world.

This citrusy, tangy flavor makes it a go-to ingredient for a variety of foods and drinks in which you would use lemongrass or lemon rind. It is delicious in meat rubs, fish or chicken marinades, pasta dough, and pancake batter. It's also a great replacement for acidic lemon juice in milk-based foods where curdling is a concern. Try adding it to sorbet, ice cream, or cheesecake for problem-free lemon desserts.

TRADITIONAL USES
Authentic to Australia
Prawns with lemon myrtle
Shortbread
Whole baked fish
Roast chicken
Chile marinade

NOTE
Toasting not recommended

RECOMMENDED PAIRINGS
Chai tea
Duck consommé
Sautéed green beans
Steamed grouper
Raspberry pie

SPICE PAIRINGS
cinnamon, clove, coriander, fennel, long pepper

RECIPE IDEAS
1. Combine equal parts ground dried lemon myrtle leaves and shredded unsweetened coconut and use to season stir-fried noodles.
2. Fold ground dried lemon myrtle leaves into softened butter and use for cooking a flounder fillet.
3. Infuse ground dried lemon myrtle leaves in warm milk, then chill and use for breakfast cereal.

QUICK BLEND
Sweet Verbena

Use this warm, fresh blend to season cubed sweet potatoes before roasting and puréeing with salted butter. It also makes a fragrant addition to fresh-cut cantaloupe melon.

Makes about ¼ cup/19 grams

2 tablespoons/10 grams ground lemon myrtle leaves
1 tablespoon/5 grams coriander seeds, toasted and ground
½ tablespoon/3 grams anise seeds, coarsely ground
½ teaspoon/1 gram ground cinnamon, preferably soft stick

LEMON PEEL

CITRUS × LIMON

*The unmistakably tart and acidic peel
of a lemon fruit*

FLAVOR & AROMA Lemon has a tart citrus flavor that is instantly recognizable and brightens any dish—whether baked goods, seafood, or roast chicken—unlike anything else. I like to use granulated dried lemon peel or whole dried lemon peel because it brings the same acidic and citrus notes to my blends or dishes without the wet aspect of fresh lemon juice. Dried lemon is not a replacement for fresh lemon, but it is conveniently shelf stable so it will last longer. Even dry, the peel still maintains a slight bitterness, though it is less intense than what you'll find in fresh lemon. Another benefit: it's also less likely to burn while cooking at high heat. The same is true for lime and any other citrus variety.

In the kitchen, more often than not we use lemon for its juice and throw the rest away. You'd be surprised by the delicious, highly versatile spice that is going to waste. We should all make an effort to peel or zest our lemons and dry the zest to use later in sauces, dressings, or stuffing.

ORIGIN ☞ Native to Asia and the Indian subcontinent ☞ Cultivated in countries around the Mediterranean Sea, South Africa, California, Chile, and Brazil

HARVEST SEASON Lemon trees bear fruit as early as the third year after planting. Since they usually bloom throughout the year, the fruit can be picked up to ten times in a year. Commercial growers often harvest lemons while still green, cure them, and then keep them in storage for months to be readily available. When grown for their essential oil-rich peels or for drying whole, they are heated to remove moisture and then processed.

PARTS USED Fresh or dried peel

ABOUT Believe it or not, lemon is actually an ancient natural hybrid of the original four citrus fruits—mandarin, pomelo, papeda, and citron—from some 20 million years ago. Citron, with its similar but larger appearance, is often confused with lemon but is a much more bitter citrus fruit. This member of the rue (Rutaceae) family has been recorded throughout history for its culinary and medicinal benefits, particularly in ancient Greece and Italy. It was even found in the ruins of Pompeii.

While its juice is prized for the refreshing yet sour taste it adds to dressings, beverages, pastries, and liqueurs, the outer yellow lemon peel has the highest oil content, which makes it best for baking. It's also our way to get that tangy lemony flavor into a spice jar. Freshly zested or dehydrated lemon peel—but not the pectin-rich bitter white pith beyond it—has an intensity that lends itself perfectly to a host of foods and drinks. Whether sprinkled on fish, stirred into pasta, or added to chutneys, pickles, tea, frosting, sorbet, or cocktails, lemon peel has no substitute.

TRADITIONAL USES

Preserved lemon—North Africa
Custard—United States
Limoncello—Italy
Vinaigrette—France
Lemonade—Worldwide

NOTE

Toasting not recommended

RECOMMENDED PAIRINGS

🍎 Marmalade
🐟 Snapper ceviche
🌾 Lemon risotto
🍝 Linguine with clam sauce
🥧 Sorbet

SPICE PAIRINGS

basil, black pepper, coriander, fennel, rosemary

RECIPE IDEAS

1. For a citrus-scented spaghetti, add granulated lemon peel to fresh pasta dough before rolling it.
2. Combine soft butter with granulated lemon peel and coarsely ground white pepper and use to sauté broccoli rabe.
3. Mix equal amounts of granulated lemon peel, ground mustard seeds, and turmeric and add white wine vinegar and salt to make a smooth homemade mustard.

QUICK BLEND
Citron

Season a whole bone-in leg of lamb with this blend before roasting. It also perks up steamed leeks and mustard dressings.

Makes about ¼ cup/30 grams

1½ tablespoons/15 grams granulated dried lemon peel
1½ tablespoons/5 grams dried rosemary leaves, coarsely ground
1 tablespoon/5 grams coriander seeds, toasted and coarsely ground
1 teaspoon/3 grams fennel seeds, toasted and coarsely ground
Scant ½ teaspoon/2 grams medium-grain sea salt, preferably fleur de sel

LEMON VERBENA

ALOYSIA CITRODORA OR ALOYSIA TRIPHYLLA

*The dried leaves of a lemon-scented
South American shrub*

———

FLAVOR & AROMA Lemon verbena
is found in many gardens where I grew up
in Israel. We would go outside and pick
a few leaves to use in hot or cold teas. It has
a strong, lemon scent but with more floral
notes, and lacks the acidic taste of the
citrus fruit.

Lemon verbena is an aromatic addition
to soups, stews, and roasted dishes, elevat-
ing them with camphor and licorice notes.
Because it does not grow during winter,
you will most likely find dry leaves much
more easily than fresh. I get my dried lemon
verbena from Israel and love using it whole or
ground. Its refreshingly crisp taste, especially
when served with mint, perks up any beverage,
salad dressing, or bread batter; it can be used
in place of lemon zest in some recipes. Dried
or fresh, lemon verbena leaves hold on to
their flavor throughout cooking and are great
at cutting the richness of fatty meats.

ORIGIN ☞ Native to South America,
particularly Chile and Argentina
☞ Cultivated in North Africa, parts
of Asia, Chile, the Mediterranean region
(including Israel), and France

HARVEST SEASON Lemon verbena
is a perennial bushy plant in the verbena
(Verbenaceae) family with long, pointed
leaves on branches that can reach 2 feet in
one season. Its leaves can be harvested spring
through fall, but before the winter frost, when
the plant dies back. Perfumy white flowers
bloom in late summer.

PARTS USED Leaves

ABOUT Lemon verbena is a native of
South America that was brought to Spain in
the seventeenth century by Spanish explorers, and to North America by a sea captain

a century later. In the early 1800s, it was
named for Maria Louisa, Princess of Parma—
you may find it being called herb Louisa for
this reason.

It flourishes in gardens and along roadsides, and its highly aromatic leaves have
long been used in perfumes and soaps. As a
spice, it pairs well with baked goods and jellies
and can even be used as a replacement for
oregano in fish and poultry dishes.

FAMILIAR USES

Lemon verbena sorbet
Tisane (herbal infusion)—France
Poached fish
Chicken soup
Lemonade

NOTE

Toasting not recommended

RECOMMENDED PAIRINGS

Mojito
Vermicelli-pork soup
Butter-lemon sauce
Orange-verbena roast chicken
Pear tart

SPICE PAIRINGS

fennel, ginger, pink pepperberries, sage, white cardamom

RECIPE IDEAS

1. Lightly coat a whole side of skin-on salmon with olive oil and then coat with dried lemon verbena leaves before covering and baking.

2. Sprinkle ground lemon verbena on pitted apricots and sauté with olive oil and honey for an aromatic cheese condiment.

3. Combine diced cucumber with yogurt, chopped fresh garlic, olive oil, salt, and ground lemon verbena and serve with roasted rack of lamb.

QUICK BLEND
Louisa

Use this blend to season thick-cut celery root before roasting it in the oven. It also adds fresh, crisp lemony notes to baked trout or branzino.

Makes about 3 tablespoons/19 grams

1½ cups/10 grams dried verbena leaves, ground
1½ heaping teaspoons/5 grams dried green cardamom pods, toasted and ground
1 teaspoon/3 grams pomegranate powder
Scant ½ teaspoon/1 gram white peppercorns, ground

LICORICE

GLYCYRRHIZA GLABRA

An instantly recognizable, anise-scented spice made from the root and rhizome of a licorice plant

FLAVOR & AROMA Licorice has long been used for medicinal purposes and, ironically, as a tobacco flavoring. In the food world it is mainly associated with the candy and liqueur industries. Luckily, more chefs and home cooks are learning to appreciate the floral notes and sweet anise flavors this ingredient offers.

I get my roots and ground licorice from Turkey. Since the taste can be a bit overwhelming, you will want to add just a little at a time to whatever dish you are preparing. If you are using the whole root—they look like short sticks—you will have to remove them before serving, since it is impossible to eat them. I also like to use the whole root as a skewer for meat or fish, particularly for grilling. In its dried and ground form, it will easily dissolve in hot or cold liquids.

ORIGIN ☞ Native to southeastern Europe and the Middle East ☞ Cultivated in the United States, Canada, and the Middle East and grows wild in parts of Asia and Europe

HARVEST SEASON Licorice plants are perennial shrubs in the pea (Fabaceae) family cultivated for their flavorful roots and rhizomes. They are harvested in the fall or winter after the tops die back, 2 to 3 years after planting. The roots are then shade-dried for about 6 months.

PARTS USED Dried rhizomes and roots

ABOUT When I was younger, all I knew about licorice was that it was a black candy in the form of a spiral ribbon. Of course, it does not grow like that in the fields. It is a woody, fibrous root that looks nothing like a confection. Actually, the candies rarely have much natural licorice in them at all. What you taste is most likely anise oil.

But, that also explains why I would occasionally see people chewing on a piece of what seemed to be a tree branch. It has been used as a breath freshener for a very long time.

Its use in the world of sweet treats dates back to sixteenth-century England, but it was also mentioned in the Greek Hippocratic texts as early as the fifth century BCE.

The Dutch add the root to water along with laurel licorice and shake it until frothy for a delicious beverage, and it is used in making the anise-scented liqueurs sambuca and pastis. Egyptians and Syrians also enjoy it in a cold drink called *erk sous*. In China, it is added to cooking liquids for soup and foods cooked in soy sauce, and it enhances five-spice powder in some dishes. As a ground powder, it is incredibly versatile and works great in poaching liquids, as a meat rub, or as a seasoning for vegetables and fruit.

TRADITIONAL USES

Root beer—United States
Tea—China
Pain d'épices (spice bread)—France
Drop candy—Netherlands
Braised snails—Morocco

NOTE

Toasting not recommended

RECOMMENDED PAIRINGS

🍩 Scones
🍎 Blueberry jam
🥣 Chilled cucumber soup
🥬 Celery gratin
🥧 Crème brûlée

SPICE PAIRINGS

ginger, orange peel, star anise, vanilla, white pepper

RECIPE IDEAS

1. Combine equal amounts of ground licorice, unsweetened cocoa powder, and ground ginger and use to dust roasted squash or cauliflower.

2. Sprinkle ground licorice into simmering salted water for poaching potato gnocchi.

3. Purée fresh peeled pears with lemon juice and ground licorice and serve as a sauce for fruit pie.

QUICK BLEND
Sweet Smoky Root

Braise short ribs with red wine, shallots, and a bit of this sweet-scented blend. It also adds a warm spice element to creamy carrot purée.

Makes about ¼ cup/26 grams

2 tablespoons/15 grams ground licorice rhizome
1 tablespoon/5 grams black cardamom pods, ground
½ tablespoon/3 grams cloves, ground
½ tablespoon/3 grams ground ginger

LONG PEPPER

PIPER LONGUM

An obscure, cone-shaped pepper with considerable complexity and heat

FLAVOR & AROMA Long pepper is a pepper! This pinecone lookalike is actually sort of an envelope holding many small peppercorns. It has complex musty notes of clove, nutmeg, pine, and sometimes vanilla, but it is still a pepper with heat. Because of its complex and unique aroma, most people prefer to use regular pepper (the close relative, *Piper nigrum*) in its stead. I find it fascinating when used in cooking, baking, drinks, and spice blends. It delivers so many layers plus the added heat, which I actually find to be secondary. It elevates simple raw fruits and vegetables, and opens up even more in longer-cooked dishes.

Because of its shape and the "envelope" that covers the mini peppercorns, you can easily use a Microplane to grate it over food before serving—a bit similar to the nutmeg process.

ORIGIN ☞ Native to South Asia ☞ Cultivated mainly in India, but also in Nepal, Sri Lanka, Timor, Indonesia, and the Philippines

HARVEST SEASON Long pepper comes from a flowering vine in the Piperaceae family. Its spikes look like tiny cattails, or long skinny pinecones dotted with dark brown fruits. These are harvested at their peak pungency, about 6 months after the spring planting, and are then thoroughly dried in the sun for 4 to 5 days.

PARTS USED Whole, dried spikes

ABOUT Long pepper, also known as pippali, Bengal pepper, and Indonesian long pepper, comes from the Deccan Plateau in the southern part of India. It is used interchangeably with the similar pepper (*Piper retrofractum*) that comes from Southeast Asia.

It has a rich history dating back to the ancient Indian Ayurveda texts, in which it was lauded for its medicinal purposes. Back during the Greek and Roman era, long pepper was expensive and prized. Even Theophrastus, the father of botany and a student of Aristotle,

distinguished it from black pepper, which was less popular at the time (around 400 BC). Then, with the discovery of the New World and the chile pepper—also confusingly referred to as long pepper—it lost its glory.

While it grows mainly on the islands of Indonesia, it has oddly enough been used for years in Ethiopian and North African cuisines. Due to the trade routes to Europe, and later to the rest of the world, Africa had easy access to it and adopted it as their own, using it in spice blends like ras el hanout and in Ethiopian stews. It was eventually transplanted to Kerala, where it now grows wild, and is predominantly prized for medicinal purposes, though you'll also find it adding its signature heat to vegetable pickles and lentil stews there. Long pepper is also found in Malaysian and Indonesian cuisines, in which it adds complexity and heat to dishes such as roasted meats and curries.

TRADITIONAL USES

Achar (pickles)—India
Pickling brine—India
Nihari (meat curry stew)—Pakistan
Berbere (spice blend)—Ethiopia
Fried rice—Indonesia

NOTE

Toasting not recommended

RECOMMENDED PAIRINGS

Fresh strawberries
Curried chicken salad
Fried oysters
Green curry
Chocolate ice cream

SPICE PAIRINGS

cubeb, ginger, hibiscus, kaffir lime, mace

RECIPE IDEAS

1. Stir ground long pepper into equal amounts of peanut butter and coconut milk and add lime juice and soy sauce for a quick satay sauce.

2. Season shaved raw Brussels sprouts with ground long pepper, olive oil, lime, and salt and serve as a salad.

3. For a spiced milk shake, add ground long pepper to vanilla ice cream, milk, and unsweetened shredded coconut before blending.

QUICK BLEND
Pippali

Season a striped or sea bass fillet with this blend before roasting in the oven with chopped fresh shallots and garlic. It also gives a peppery bite to crepe batter.

Makes about ¼ cup/24 grams

18 pieces/15 grams whole long peppers, ground
¼ cup/5 grams hibiscus blossoms, ground
½ tablespoon/3 grams ground ginger
½ teaspoon/1 gram ground lemongrass
5 dried kaffir lime leaves, ground

LOVAGE

LEVISTICUM OFFICINALE

*Root to seed, a fresh or dried spice with
a fresh celery flavor*

FLAVOR & AROMA When I arrived in France, I remember seeing in markets what looked like celery leaves, but with a much thinner stem and small root. I quickly learned to love the celery and parsley flavor, large leaves, and fresh, somewhat tangy taste of the lovage stem. The scent of lovage will also sometimes remind me of oregano. Because of these strong notes, it is great when dried and stirred into long-braised dishes, stews, and soups, but also when chopped fresh leaves are added to salads.

The seeds have a similar flavor, but with an added warmth. In the United States, you can find lovage in farmers' markets, and many people choose to grow it in their own gardens. What you'll find dried in jars, and what I use here, are the dried leaves.

ORIGIN ☞ Native to southern Europe ☞ Cultivated in central and southern Europe, and Asia

HARVEST SEASON Lovage is a perennial plant in the parsley (Apiaceae) family that can reach up to 8 feet tall. Its shiny, light green leaves should be harvested in spring and summer before the plant's yellowish flowers bloom, causing the leaves to become bitter. The flowers bloom in late summer, giving way to large edible seeds that mature in the fall.

PARTS USED Fresh and dried leaves, stems, roots, and seeds

ABOUT The French call lovage eternal celery, since it has leaves year-round. Some also call it Maggi's herb because of its similarities to the European bouillon cube brand—which contains similar celery flavor and aroma notes, but no lovage.

Popular since the Roman times, the raw leaves and stems of this plant have long been chopped and added to casseroles, seafood chowders, stuffing, and sauces. The stems are also often candied, as is done with angelica, and eaten as a dessert or used as cocktail straws for a sweet-salty treat. Lovage roots are mostly eaten as a vegetable, grated into salads along with the chopped fresh leaves. The small, crunchy seeds are typically used whole like fennel seeds, or ground into a fine powder.

TRADITIONAL USES

Seafood chowder—United States
Vichyssoise—France
Lovage cordial—United Kingdom
Tomato sauce—Northern Italy
Ciorbă soup—Romania

NOTE

Toasting not recommended

RECOMMENDED PAIRINGS

Bloody Mary
Parsnip velouté
Potato salad
Sautéed mushrooms
Lobster roll

SPICE PAIRINGS

caraway, fennel, savory, sumac, tomato powder

RECIPE IDEAS

1. Simmer beef broth with some dried lovage leaves and use for cooking a barley risotto.
2. Season cooked, diced shrimp with ground lovage and add lime, mayonnaise, and ketchup for a shrimp cocktail salad.
3. Stir ground lovage into Dijon mustard and mix with diced cold roast beef to make sandwiches.

QUICK BLEND
Liveche

See photograph, page 176.

This blend adds an herbaceous element to tomato, clam, and mussel stew and gives egg salad and tuna casserole a fresh, celery-like flavor.

Makes about 3 tablespoons/21 grams

½ cup/10 grams dried lovage leaves, ground
1 tablespoon/5 grams coriander seeds, toasted and ground
½ tablespoon/3 grams ajowan seeds, ground
1 teaspoon/3 grams ground sweet paprika

MAHLAB

PRUNUS MAHALEB

The nutty, somewhat bitter kernel of the
St. Lucie cherry

FLAVOR & AROMA Mahlab kernels are proof that sometimes the better ingredient is found inside the fruit, and the fruit itself is not that great. I am not sure where the idea came about to use the kernel of this distasteful sour cherry, but I am glad someone thought of it. These little cream-colored, drop-shaped kernels have a nutty, almond-like scent with bitter notes and a hint of fruit and vanilla.

The kernels are a bit delicate, so it is best to use them right away or refrigerate them. I would recommend buying them whole and grinding them yourself, but if you don't have the time, you can find the spice in powdered form at most Middle Eastern stores. Note, often the powder you buy has lost some of its flavor and aroma, but it still does the job.

ORIGIN ☞ Native to the Middle East and southern Europe ☞ Cultivated in Syria, Iran, and Turkey

HARVEST SEASON The cherries of this deciduous tree or shrub in the rose (Rosaceae) family turn from green to red and then to a dark purplish-black when fully ripe toward the end of the summer season. They are harvested specifically for the kernel, which is extracted from the pit and then dried.

PARTS USED Dried kernels

ABOUT Mahlab is made from the kernels of the fruit of the St. Lucie cherry tree. It has been used in the ground form for centuries in these regions and hasn't strayed far—it would be surprising to find it on a menu anywhere else.

It is mainly used in baking and confectionery, added to bread and pastry doughs particularly during religious holidays. During Greek Easter, it adds an intriguing flavor to the brioche-like braided sweet bread *tsoureki* and is served in the form of *kandil* rings during Turkish Islamic holy nights. It is also an irreplaceable ingredient in Armenian *chorek* (sweet rolls) as well as Arabic *ma'-amoul* (shortbread pastries). Apart from its role in baked goods, it can be found in Jordanian *nabulsi* cheese (brined sheep's- or goat's-milk cheese) and the Easter Day or Ramadan cheese pies served in Cyprus called *flaounes*.

TRADITIONAL USES

Vasilopita (cake)—Greece
Mahlepli simit (mini bagels)—Turkey
Pogača (bread)—Turkey
Ka'ak (savory cookies)—Middle East
Honey, mahlab, and sesame paste—Egypt

NOTE
Toasting not recommended

RECOMMENDED PAIRINGS
◉ Grits
❦ Broccoli quiche
🍝 Ravioli dough
🌾 Risotto fritters
🥟 Macaron

SPICE PAIRINGS
anise, caraway, cinnamon, clove, ginger

RECIPE IDEAS
1. Season oats, raisins, sunflower seeds, and cranberries with coarsely ground mahlab to make a topping for yogurt.
2. Mix equal amounts of fresh whipped cream and ricotta cheese, season with ground mahlab, sugar, and lemon zest, and serve with fresh cherries.
3. Dust chocolate truffles with ground mahlab and unsweetened cocoa powder for a complex, almond-like flavor.

QUICK BLEND
Wild Cherry

Use this blend to complement the nutty, fruit flavors of a Waldorf salad. It's also a nice addition to your warm morning oatmeal.

Makes about 3 tablespoons/16 grams

1 tablespoon/10 grams mahlab kernels, ground
½ tablespoon/3 grams anise seeds, ground
1 teaspoon/2 grams cloves, ground
½ teaspoon/1 gram ground cinnamon

MARJORAM

ORIGANUM MAJORANA

An oregano-scented, slightly bitter spice made from leaves and flower buds

FLAVOR & AROMA Marjoram is one of the herbs that grows wild in Israel, and as kids we would often go out for a walk to pick some to sprinkle over homemade flatbread seasoned with olive oil, destined for a wood stove. The leftover marjoram would dry in a few days and would be used to season grilled meats and fish, or in a quick tomato salad.

I love the combination of fresh sharp notes with a slight bitterness. Marjoram is often confused with its close relative oregano because of its similar flavor profile, but it is more delicate, with a spicy-sweet taste that goes well with vegetables and sauces. Although it loses some of its strength when dried, I still think it retains its best characteristics. I especially like grilling with it since it will char and add texture to the dish without the bitterness that can occur with fresh herbs.

ORIGIN ☞ Native to the Mediterranean and Western Asia ☞ Cultivated in the Mediterranean, Russia, Morocco, North Africa, India, China, and the United States

HARVEST SEASON Marjoram is a small, bushy perennial (or annual in cooler climates) in the mint (Lamiaceae) family with upright stems that bear oval, gray-green leaves. Fresh leaves can be harvested throughout the growing season up until winter. When harvested for drying, leaves are picked just after the flower buds form. The fragrant lavender or white flowers are a favorite of bees and butterflies.

PARTS USED Fresh or dried, leaves and flower buds

ABOUT Marjoram has certainly made its rounds throughout history. It is said to have been cultivated by the Egyptians as far back as 1000 BC; the ancient Greeks used it in teas and as a spice; and much later, it was an essential ingredient in beer brewing before hops came into the picture. Even today, it thrives in the hot climates of these regions— I buy mine from Egypt and Israel.

Its popularity as a slightly sharp, aromatic spice has made it a welcome crop in countries beyond its native soil, and it is easily grown in the home garden. Its long growing season makes it a good choice for anyone wanting to have fresh ingredients on hand.

Fresh or dried leaves add delicate, warm notes to braised vegetables, stews, stuffing, and Mediterranean meat and pasta dishes, but should be added toward the end of the cooking time. The plant's delicate flowers also add a fresh aromatic element to salads, poultry, and cheese. Try using it in place of oregano to taste the different elements it brings.

TRADITIONAL USES

Za'atar (spice blend)—Middle East
Grilled mutton—Jordan/Lebanon
Krautwurst (herb sausage)—Germany
Herbes de Provence (spice blend)—France
Braised cabbage—Central Europe

NOTE

Toasting not recommended

RECOMMENDED PAIRINGS

Calamari salad
English pea velouté
Leek gratin
Grilled sardines
Braised lamb shank

SPICE PAIRINGS

cumin, paprika, sumac, Urfa chile, yellow mustard

RECIPE IDEAS

1. For a grilled meat condiment, add ground marjoram to diced tomatoes, olive oil, garlic, and diced onion.
2. Whip fresh goat cheese with dried marjoram leaves and serve with fresh figs.
3. Combine ground marjoram with finely chopped green olives and season with lemon juice for a quick tapenade.

QUICK BLEND
Marjolaine

Season fresh-cut baby turnips with a bit of this blend and finish with olive oil and orange juice for an herbaceous salad or side dish. It also adds a welcoming sharpness to pizzas and pastas.

Makes about ⅓ cup/29 grams

½ cup/15 grams dried marjoram leaves, ground
1 tablespoon/3 grams dried mint leaves, ground
½ tablespoon/5 grams white sesame seeds, toasted
1⅔ teaspoons/5 grams fennel seeds, toasted and coarsely ground
Scant ½ teaspoon/1 gram crushed Aleppo chiles, or mild chile flakes

MASTIC

PISTACIA LENTISCUS

A pine-flavored resin that oozes from trees on the island of Chios

FLAVOR & AROMA Years ago, I would stare every day at this jar of mastic drops in my kitchen. A friend had given them to me, and I could not figure out what to do with them. Mastic has a pleasant pine note and a slightly bitter, fresh flavor, a bit like eucalyptus and mint. When chewed, it has a gum-like consistency, which is why it often replaces cornstarch or gelatin in recipes. After reading about the intense, very old process of harvesting it, I started exploring it in different dishes. It works very well in various bread doughs and cakes, as well as cheese and fish dishes.

Mastic, or mastiha, comes from the Greek island of Chios. At La Boîte, I have a blend named for the island honoring this underutilized spice and its place in Greek cuisine.

ORIGIN ☞ Native to the Mediterranean region ☞ Cultivated on the Greek island of Chios

HARVEST SEASON Mastic is a sticky resin that fills the rich veins just under the bark of the evergreen lentisk tree in the sumac (Anacardiaceae) family. When the trunk is cut or the bark is scored, the tree "weeps" or oozes resin in tears—hence the Greek name tears of Chios—or it collects in the trunk ready to be gathered. The resin is only produced once the tree is at least 5 years old. The tree can continue to produce for another 50 years or more. These tears of resin are collected, washed, and laid out to dry in the sun before being sold whole or ground into a powder.

PARTS USED Dried tears or ground resin

ABOUT Mastic is produced exclusively on Chios, which holds a monopoly on its production. Even though the tree grows throughout the Mediterranean, it is said to weep its resin tears only there. During Ottoman rule, the sultan and his harem loved chewing this gummy treat so much that, despite his iron fist during the Chios Massacre of 1822, he spared the people of Mastichochoria, where it was being cultivated. Even today, there are about twenty villages in this region on the southern part of Chios that still produce mastic.

It is mainly used in desserts and baking, but its gummy consistency makes it perfect for fruit and vegetable preserves, jams, and sauces as well. For sweet dishes, the Turks use it as a stabilizing ingredient in authentic *salep* pudding (made with flour from orchid tubers), Turkish delight, and *dondurma* (ice cream made with mastic and *salep*). It is also used as a stabilizer for meringue and is a key ingredient in cakes found in the western region of North Africa. Mastic adds fresh notes to beverages, breads, and desserts, and it plays an essential role in savory dishes, including some Egyptian soups—like the somewhat slimy *mulukhiyah* vegetable soup—and boiled meats.

When you are looking to buy some, you may find it called Arabic gum or Yemen gum, but neither should be confused with gum arabic, which comes from the acacia tree. If you are like me and spend too long staring at it without an idea of what to do with it, just try chewing some to freshen your mouth while you think it over.

TRADITIONAL USES

Nougat—North Africa
Sütlaç (rice pudding)—Turkey
Flaounes (Easter cheese pastry)—Cyprus
Mastic spread—Greece
Mastika liqueur—Greece

NOTE

Toasting not recommended

RECOMMENDED PAIRINGS

Radish salad
Mackerel escabeche
Fennel bulb purée
Goat cheese soufflé
Peach pie

SPICE PAIRINGS

cinnamon, fennel, orange peel, tarragon, thyme

RECIPE IDEAS

1. Stir ground mastic into simmering chicken stock with lemon juice and use to cook lamb meatballs.
2. Season mascarpone cheese with ground mastic, orange zest, and a bit of sugar and serve with waffles and berries.
3. For a fresh twist on your favorite gingersnap cookies, add a few pinches of ground mastic to the dough.

QUICK BLEND
Tears of Chios

Use this blend to season a tuna or hamachi crudo with capers and radishes. It is also great on feta cheese served with olive oil and toasted pine nuts.

Makes about ¼ cup/21 grams

1 tablespoon/10 grams ground mastic
1 tablespoon/3 grams dried dill
1 tablespoon/3 grams crushed dried basil leaves
1 teaspoon/3 grams yellow mustard seeds
Scant ¾ teaspoon/2 grams caraway seeds, coarsely ground

MINT

MENTHA SPECIES

A refreshing, peppery family of herbs destined for more than chewing gum and toothpaste

FLAVOR & AROMA There are many types of mint—about eighteen familiar ones and hundreds of hybrids. Mint has obvious fresh notes but also imparts a sharp, somewhat peppery taste to dishes. As with many other herbs, fresh mint loses some of its strength when used in long-cooked dishes and can even develop some bitterness. One of the benefits of using dried mint is that these challenges are not an issue. Dried mint actually holds up very well when cooked over a longer time. Think of it as hydrating the mint and bringing it back to life. It also will not oxidize, turn brown, or spoil quickly.

It is one of my favorite herbs. From a simple mint tea to whole leaves in a salad to ground meat and lamb dishes, it is always useful. Mint also cuts fatty notes, tones down harsh savory scents, and balances overly sweet aromas.

Fresh mint is sold everywhere and is in season year-round. At La Boîte, I get my spearmint from Israel and Egypt.

ORIGIN ☞ Native to southern Europe and the Mediterranean ☞ Cultivated worldwide

HARVEST SEASON Leaves can be fully harvested two to three times during the growing season or picked as needed. The flavor is best when harvested before it flowers.

PARTS USED Leaves and flowers

ABOUT Though it may seem that everyone loves mint, there is at least one person who never did. In Greek mythology, Persephone, Hades's beloved and the goddess of vegetation and flowers, became jealous when she caught him falling in love with a nymph. To punish them both, the goddess turned the nymph into the lowliest of plants, often trampled by passersby on roadsides. She named her Minthe.

But despite this one negative, mint is an indispensable herb that has spread uncontrollably across the globe and is coveted for the cooling and warming sensation it imparts in food and drinks. The two most prominent groups of the mint (Lamiaceae) family are peppermint and spearmint—I mainly use the latter in my spices. They both add fresh notes to mint jelly or lamb sauce, marinades, teas, and vegetable and poultry dishes.

In the Middle East, spearmint is chopped up and added to tabbouleh, and in England it is found in cold soups, lamb sauce, and tea. In Greece it is sprinkled over halloumi cheese, stuffed into dolmas (grape leaves), and stirred into the ubiquitous tzatziki (cucumber-yogurt sauce) to be served with grilled meat or used as a dip. Mint adds a cooling element to Asian curries, dipping sauces, and sambals, as well as Thai prawn salads. The Moroccan variety of mint is essential to Maghrebi tea from North Africa, which has a spearmint flavor and is made with green tea and sugar.

For sweeter dishes, mint brightens watermelon salad, fruit platters, chocolate confections, and, of course, Kentucky's favorite drink, the mint julep.

TRADITIONAL USES

Tabbouleh—Israel/Middle East
Ghormeh (stew)—Iran (Persia)
Mint tea—North Africa
Mint jelly—United Kingdom
Laab (meat salad)—Thailand

NOTE
Toasting not recommended

RECOMMENDED PAIRINGS
Tahini dressing
Lamb meat loaf
Mushroom burgers
Chicken potpie
Mint sorbet

SPICE PAIRINGS
basil, caraway, cardamom, green pepper, lavender

RECIPE IDEAS
1. Add dried mint leaves to olive oil and purée in a blender to make a refreshing mint oil for dressings and sauces.
2. Marinate guinea hen breast with yogurt and ground dried mint before grilling or roasting.
3. Combine equal amounts of ground dried mint, panko (Japanese bread crumbs), and grated Parmesan cheese and use to season spaghetti or roasted Brussels sprouts.

QUICK BLEND
Na'ana

Marinate duck legs with some of this blend before slathering them with pomegranate molasses and roasting them. It creates a cooling effect when cooking it with rice or wheat berries.

Makes about ½ cup/25 grams

Scant ½ cup/15 grams crushed dried mint leaves
2 tablespoons/5 grams dried dill
1 tablespoon/1 gram dried tarragon leaves, ground
½ tablespoon/3 grams dried onion slices, coarsely ground
½ teaspoon/1 gram ajowan seeds, ground

MUSTARD

BRASSICA JUNCEA/BRASSICA ALBA/BRASSICA HIRTA/BRASSICA NIGRA

Intensely pungent seeds that are great whole or ground

FLAVOR & AROMA Most people think of mustard as a yellow, turmeric-stained paste in a jar (I won't even mention squeeze bottles). We all eat it with hot dogs and sandwiches, but that's where it ends. The mustard seeds used to make the condiment we know and love are often neglected. In countries like India, the seeds are fried in oil and used to enhance vegetable dishes and curries. They are essential to various spice rubs and blends in Asia, and in the United States, mustard seeds almost always find their way into pickles and brines.

I love the fact that they can be used whole or ground and still deliver a great punch with a slight heat. At La Boîte, I mainly use yellow mustard seeds that come from Canada. This is not entirely surprising—mustard is a part of the cabbage family (Brassicaceae) and the climate in North America is favorable to growing it. Yellow mustard is the mildest of the mustard seed family, but it still offers an approachable heat and slight bitter element.

I also use black mustard and hot or Chinese mustard (a spicy variety of the yellow seed). Black mustard seeds are a bit stronger than yellow and are great when used whole. Though you'll typically find brown mustard seeds sold as "black mustard," they are not the same. Black mustard has largely been replaced by brown because of the challenges in harvesting it. The flavors are comparably pungent. Hot mustard is another variety that is a bit harder to get, but worth the effort. It packs an even more serious punch.

Whichever you choose, mustard is at its best when used whole and toasted and when added during longer-cooking dishes or to blends. It is also great ground since it keeps all of its flavors and aromas and can even help thicken sauces and stews.

ORIGIN ☞ Native to southern Europe and Western Asia (black and yellow mustard) and India (brown/hot mustard) ☞ Cultivated in the United States, India, Canada, China, and parts of Europe

HARVEST SEASON Mustard seeds are harvested about 4 months from sowing. In the United States, they are harvested in the summer, and in India, they are grown as a winter crop. When fully developed but not ripe, mustard seeds are harvested by cutting the stems. This timing is necessary to avoid seedpods from shattering and casting their seeds on the ground (black mustard is particularly notorious for this).

PARTS USED Seeds

ABOUT Mustard seeds seem unassuming to look at. They don't have an aroma until they are ground, and they don't show off their peak potency until you add water. Their natural enzyme, myrosinase, activates the glucosinolates (the component that produces the oil) when the seeds are broken and water is incorporated. Only then is that instantly recognizable, sinus-opening pungency released—the southern Indian method of dry-roasting seeds in oil doesn't do this.

Yellow mustard is less intense than other varieties and a favorite among Europeans and Westerners, found in pickling brines (page 298), sandwich spreads, barbecue sauce and rubs, marinades, and salad dressings. When ground, yellow mustard seed is actually white. It is only when it is combined with turmeric (along with wheat flour, water, and typically vinegar) in the ubiquitous condiment that it takes on the familiar golden hue.

Dijon mustard, on the other hand, is made without turmeric, with verjus instead of vinegar (making it less acerbic), and typically with the more pungent and smaller brown or black mustard seeds. They are traditionally found in Indian, Asian, and African cooking. Bengalis use mustard seed to make piquant cooking oil for fish and vegetables, and it is essential to *kasundi* (mustard sauce or relish) and curries.

Hot mustard seeds are smaller than yellow, brown, and black seeds but bring the most heat. You may recognize the seeds from the little condiment jar on the table of your favorite Chinese restaurant. When ground to a powder, Chinese mustard has a bite reminiscent of horseradish.

TRADITIONAL USES

Sambar powder (spice mixture)—India
Panch phoron (Indian five-spice blend)—Bengal
Mostarda (candied fruit)—Italy
Piccalilli (relish)—United Kingdom
Boston baked beans—United States

NOTE

Light toasting recommended

RECOMMENDED PAIRINGS

Artichoke dip
Pickled mackerel
Roast beef
Mustard–white wine sauce
Sautéed spätzle

SPICE PAIRINGS

allspice, bay leaves, caraway, cumin, ginger

RECIPE IDEAS

1. Season caramelized onions with yellow mustard seeds, honey, and vinegar and use as a condiment for charcuterie and cheese.

2. For a sweet-spicy arugula and spinach salad, top with toasted yellow mustard seeds, diced apples, golden raisins, and almonds.

3. Sprinkle ground toasted black mustard seeds into heavy cream that has been reduced on the stove until it thickens slightly and use as a sauce for poached fish.

QUICK BLEND
Sarso

Perk up a lentil salad by stirring in a bit of this blend, or use it to add heat and texture as a garnish for lentil soup. It is also a great addition to a grated carrot salad dressed with lime juice.

Makes about ¼ cup/34 grams

1½ tablespoons/15 grams yellow mustard seeds, toasted and coarsely ground
1 tablespoon/10 grams black mustard seeds, toasted
1½ heaping teaspoons/5 grams caraway seeds, toasted and ground
1 teaspoon/3 grams poppy seeds
Scant ½ teaspoon/1 gram Aleppo chile, or mild chile flakes

NIGELLA

NIGELLA SATIVA

A black, drop-shaped seed with herbaceous, oregano notes

FLAVOR & AROMA Nigella seeds are probably one of the most confused spices. Over the years I've heard nigella referred to as onion seeds, black cumin, black caraway, and fennel flower, among others. Let's just simply call them nigella or *kalonji* (from Hindi).

However you choose to name this spice, what it lacks in aroma—it has a just a hint of a savory scent—it makes up for in taste. Nigella seeds have an oregano-like quality with herbaceous notes, a slight bitterness, and a warm, toasted-onion flavor. I like to add them whole to salads, sauces, and even soups at the last minute just before serving. They are a great replacement for sesame seeds without the sweet element.

ORIGIN ☞ Native to the Mediterranean region ☞ Cultivated and found wild mainly in Egypt and India, but also in other parts of North Africa, western and southern Asia, Southern Europe, and the Middle East

HARVEST SEASON Nigella is an annual plant with delicate blue or white flowers that bloom in July. The fruit is a large seed capsule with up to seven follicles that contain small, pear-shaped white seeds—they only turn black when exposed to air. When the fruit matures in September, the capsules are gathered before they burst, and are then dried and gently crushed for the seeds to be collected.

PARTS USED Seeds

ABOUT Nigella is a member of the buttercup (Ranunculaceae) family with about 1,700 other species of flowering plants. With all the names these seeds are called, it's no wonder they are so easily confused. In particular, the crescent-shaped *kala jeera* (*Bunium persicum*), more commonly known as black cumin (page 110), also goes by the same name. Its near cousin, *Nigella damascena,* or love-in-the-mist, often tries to take credit for this spice, but its flowers and seeds are merely decorative.

Nigella sativa seeds were said to have been found in King Tut's tomb and have been used for thousands of years as a preservative, a spice, and, as the Prophet Muhammad claimed, a seed with healing powers. Whatever ability nigella may have to mend the ill, it certainly does wonders in savory pastries, pilafs, curries, vegetable dishes, and pickles. Nigella seeds also add great texture when sprinkled whole over baked goods or when added to dough. I like to call it the "Middle Eastern poppy seed" since it is used so much on the breads back home.

In Asia, nigella seeds are sometimes ground into a powder or left whole and mixed into spice blends. Most notably, nigella seeds add a welcome crunch and herbaceous character when substituted for *radhuni* in Bengali *panch phoron,* joining equal parts fenugreek, cumin, black mustard seeds, and fennel seeds.

TRADITIONAL USES

String cheese—Middle East
Potato stir-fry—Bengal
Naan bread—India
Korma (braised meat or vegetable
dish)—India
Preserved lemons—Morocco

NOTE
Toasting not recommended

RECOMMENDED PAIRINGS
Spinach omelet
Red onion salad
Barley risotto
Grilled calamari
Yogurt pound cake

SPICE PAIRINGS
caraway, lemon peel, mustard seeds, paprika, thyme

RECIPE IDEAS

1. Mix whole nigella seeds with whipped feta cheese, yogurt, chopped capers, and lemon juice and use as a condiment for crudités.

2. Sprinkle nigella seeds on cooked fava beans and season with olive oil and lemon juice for a bright, satisfying side dish.

3. Coat small cubes of raw tuna with olive oil, lemon, and nigella seeds and serve as an hors d'oeuvre.

QUICK BLEND
Ketazh

This savory, warm blend is great for seasoning lemon-roasted broccoli rabe. It also gives a wonderful texture to tuna salad when mixed with fresh mayonnaise.

Makes about 3 tablespoons/22 grams

1½ tablespoons/15 grams nigella seeds
1½ tablespoons/5 grams dried savory leaves, ground
1 teaspoon/1 gram crushed dried mint leaves
Scant ½ teaspoon/1 gram dried fennel pollen

ÑORA PEPPER

CAPSICUM ANNUUM

A sweet, earthy spice made from dried wine-red ñora peppers

———

FLAVOR & AROMA I first saw ñora peppers in Olivier Roellinger's kitchen in France. He was slowly infusing them in grapeseed oil to obtain a reddish, sweet, and fragrant finishing oil. I later learned about their various uses in Spanish cuisine, particularly in the rich, nutty-sweet-flavored romesco sauce and in making Spanish pimentón (page 218).

The small ñora pepper is very mild, sweet, and earthy and still maintains quite a bit of its natural oils, which lend a distinctly fatty taste. I like using it whole while roasting meats or vegetables, or soaking some in warm water, straining, and then puréeing with some garlic, cumin, and lemon juice. It is a good compromise for people who do not like extreme heat but are still looking for a pepper with a bit more character than your standard supermarket bell pepper. Unfortunately, it is mainly sold ground—it is so much better whole. I am lucky to be able to source them directly from Valencia, Spain.

ORIGIN ☞ Native to and cultivated in Guardamar in Valencia, Spain

HARVEST SEASON Ñora peppers are harvested by hand in the fall when they are fully ripe and red. They are then dried in the sun for several days until they turn a deep red wine color and are glossy and wrinkled. They are sold whole or ground.

PARTS USED Dried chiles

ABOUT Ñora peppers are one of the varieties of nightshade (Solanaceae family) that Columbus brought back to Spain from his expedition to the Americas. It is said he delivered them to a monastery in La Ñora of the Murcia province, and that the monks planted some of the first of these peppers (actually a bell pepper, not a chile) in Spain. They found that sun-drying the peppers allowed them to be stored longer, and that when dried, these little "ball" chiles added a rich flavor to their food.

Sometimes replaced by or confused with *pimiento choricero*, ñora peppers enhance Spanish rice dishes and rich *cocidos* (Spanish stews), and are absolutely essential to romesco sauce and *bacalao a la Vizcaína* (Basque-style baked cod). Ñora peppers impart a distinct red color that enlivens soups as well.

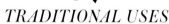

TRADITIONAL USES

Authentic to Spain

Chorizo

Arròs a banda (Valencian for "rice on the side")

Patates bravas (fried potatoes)

Paella

Galatian octopus

NOTE

Toasting not recommended

RECOMMENDED PAIRINGS

Bean salad

Arrabbiata sauce

Onion marmalade

Sausage and peppers

Grilled catfish

SPICE PAIRINGS

caraway, garlic, oregano, saffron, sesame seeds

HEAT INDEX

Light heat

RECIPE IDEAS

1. Combine ground ñora pepper with crumbled blue cheese, hazelnut oil, and red wine vinegar for a quick salad dressing.

2. Season a whole guinea hen with ground ñora pepper and olive oil before roasting.

3. To perk up a grilled cheese sandwich, make it with softened butter mixed with ground ñora pepper.

QUICK BLEND
Valencia

To add a sweet crunchy topping to salads, use this blend to season cubed bread and chopped almonds before toasting. It also gives a rich flavor and color to stir-fried rice.

Makes about ¼ cup/30 grams

2 tablespoons/15 grams ground dried ñora peppers

1 tablespoon/10 grams sesame seeds, toasted

½ tablespoon/3 grams ground ginger

½ teaspoon/1 gram ground garlic flakes

½ teaspoon/1 gram ground onion flakes

NUTMEG & MACE

MYRISTICA FRAGRANS

Two pungent, warm spices from the same plant

FLAVOR & AROMA I consider nutmeg a bargain because it offers two distinct spices in each seed: nutmeg is the kernel inside and mace is the reddish aril, or blade, that is wrapped around the seed's shell.

While most people just think of mace as a tear-inducing spray, it's actually a wonderfully pungent, warm spice that is similar in flavor to nutmeg. Mace is much more delicate, with some citrus notes, and is more oily in texture and scent, but both spices have a similar fragrance with light floral notes and can often be used interchangeably.

Although store-bought ground mace and nutmeg can be good (if the source is), it is preferable to buy whole nutmeg kernels and mace blades and grind or grate them as needed. Nutmeg can be grated using a classic grater—it looks like a round mini box grater—or a Microplane zester. I love using whole red mace blades, but they can easily be ground in a coffee grinder. At La Boîte, I buy from Grenada, Indonesia, and occasionally India. Make sure you look for evenly sized nutmeg with a uniform, smooth, unbroken surface, and without any black spots.

ORIGIN ☞ Native to the Banda Islands in the southeast Moluccas (the Spice Islands of Indonesia) ☞ Cultivated mainly in the Moluccas and the West Indies, but also South Africa, Grenada, and Sri Lanka

HARVEST SEASON Nutmeg and mace are found at the center of apricot-like fruits that grow on a tropical, dioecious tree in the nutmeg (Myristicaceae) family. These trees can reach about 75 feet high and typically yield fruit 8 years after sowing. From January to March and again from June to August, white-fleshed fruits ripen, splitting in two to expose a single red mace aril laced around a brown nutmeg seed. Mace is stripped from the seed, pressed flat, and dried. The seeds are dried in the sun for up to 8 weeks until the nutmeg kernel rattles in the shell. The shells are then broken, and the tan kernels are removed by hand.

PARTS USED Nutmeg kernels and mace arils

ABOUT Nutmeg and mace began their journey in the Spice Islands before being traded in Alexandria around the sixth century, and later joined the crusaders en route to Europe. Though they were mainly used medicinally in the early days, they would later become sought-after spices in Middle Eastern cookery.

Nutmeg's increased popularity by the fifteenth century gained the attention of Portuguese explorers, who traveled to the Spice Islands to gather seeds and take control of the islands. It wasn't until the seventeenth century that the Dutch took the islands over, with a strict monopoly on nutmeg and mace, raising the prices to extremes and unwittingly making themselves an easy mark for the English and French who sought those flavorful seeds. By the time the British took control, the seeds had already made their way to the Malay Peninsula, the West Indies, Mauritius, and, later, the Caribbean Islands.

To this day, the foods of these cultures are seasoned with both spices. In the Caribbean, nutmeg is added to pastries, jerk seasoning, eggnog, breads, and ice cream. In Indonesia, it is found in curries and sauces. In North Africa and the Middle East, you can find it in lamb dishes, and the Dutch add it to cabbage and cauliflower purées. It is also a key spice in blends, including ras el hanout and Tunisian five-spice powder.

Mace, which is more expensive than nutmeg, is used in savory dishes, including sauces, sausages, shellfish stocks, pickles, vegetable purées, meat pies, and chutney. It seasons North Indian *pulao*s (rice dish) and lamb, brings warmth to Indian garam masala (page 297), and adds a wonderful pungency to sweets from Asian cookies to American pies.

TRADITIONAL USES

Quatre épices—France
Béchamel sauce—France
Haggis—Scotland
Soto (soup)—Indonesia
Pumpkin pie—United States

NOTE
Toasting not recommended

RECOMMENDED PAIRINGS
Hot spiked cider
Cauliflower gratin
Shepherd's pie
Morel sauce
Quince tart

SPICE PAIRINGS
allspice, cardamom, clove, ginger, vanilla

RECIPE IDEAS
1. Season halved fresh figs with ground mace before quickly sautéing them in salted butter and brown sugar to serve with cheese.

2. Create a spiced citrus glaze for pork tenderloin by adding ground nutmeg to simmering grapefruit juice.

3. Sprinkle ground nutmeg and mace into a butternut squash purée and use as a sauce for al dente fettuccine pasta.

QUICK BLEND
Mashia

This blend adds warmth to red wine–braised veal stew, and I love it for roasting shallots or flat, sweet cipollini onions.

Makes about 3 tablespoons/30 grams

1½ tablespoons/15 grams freshly grated nutmeg
1 tablespoon/5 grams allspice berries, toasted and ground
½ tablespoon/5 grams ground mace
1 teaspoon/3 grams ground ancho chile
Scant ¾ teaspoon/2 grams ground sumac

OMANI LIME

CITRUS x AURANTIIFOLIA

A small, dried lime with earthy, citrus, and sour notes

FLAVOR & AROMA Black lime, Persian lime, noomi basra, limon amoni, or Omani—whatever you choose to call them, dried Omani limes are a must in every kitchen. They can be white or cream colored (sometimes brown) or dark black. In all cases, the result is a concentrated lime scent that is sweet and slightly fermented. The lighter variety is slightly more bitter than the black, which delivers a musky element. I love mixing them, half and half. They bring amazing sour notes to soups, stews, and long-cooked dishes without losing their acidic characteristic.

To use them whole, just pierce the pebbly skins or crush them, and drop them into cooking liquid. As the liquid passes through the lime, it softens and releases the tart, citrus notes within. Then just squeeze them at the end of cooking, before serving, to brighten even the richest stew.

They are not going to replace your fresh lemons or limes, but they certainly have their advantages. Omani limes keep for a very long time and you can use them in cooking without adding a lot of bitterness. I love simply grating them over raw or cooked dishes, adding them whole or crushed to roasting meats or vegetables, or just sprinkling a pinch of the ground spice into hot or cold tea.

ORIGIN ☞ Native to Oman ☞ Cultivated in Guatemala, Egypt, and in parts of Iran along the Persian Gulf

HARVEST SEASON Omani limes, a citrus in the rue (Rutaceae) family, are harvested when ripe year-round. They are boiled in salted brine and then dried in the sun until they look almost pebble-like. When dried, they become light tan to black in color with a dark, glossy center.

PARTS USED Dried fruit

ABOUT The Omani lime is about the size of a key lime and, when dried, becomes a walnut-size spice that is an essential ingredient in North India and the Persian Gulf countries. They are added whole to tagines, soups, and long-cooked stews. When ground into a powder, dried limes are one of the ingredients found in the Middle Eastern spice blend for *kabsa,* a rice-based dish popular in the Persian Gulf. Ground Omani lime is also used to season Indian basmati rice, fish, legumes, and stuffing. Their natural acidity cuts the fat in proteins, bringing life to meat and poultry dishes as well.

But even with their approachable flavor and versatility, Omani limes are almost exclusively used in Persian cuisine. The good news is, they have more recently begun receiving the popularity they deserve in the West and are becoming more and more relevant; the bad news is, that may come at the cost of quality. Because of new, higher demands and modernization, they are being placed in large ovens to dry faster—the sun is apparently not able to keep up. The result is great color, but a loss of flavor and essential oils. When shopping for Omani limes, you'll want to look for a lime that is still a little bit moist inside.

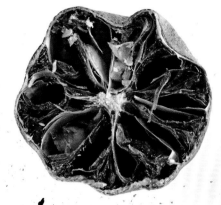

TRADITIONAL USES

Chicken *majboos* (rice dish)—Gulf/Middle East
Limon Omani tea—Middle East
Ghormeh sabzi (lamb and herb stew)—Iran (Persia)
Vegetable stew—Iran (Persia)
Khoresht ghaimeh (beef and split pea stew)—Iran
(Persia)

NOTE
Toasting not recommended

RECOMMENDED PAIRINGS
Matzoh ball soup
Whole roasted squab
Veal-lemon stew
Roasted black cod
Rice pilaf

SPICE PAIRINGS
basil, cardamom, dill, garlic, tarragon

RECIPE IDEAS
1. Using a Microplane, zest a bit of black Omani lime on a hot crab cake.
2. For a creamy, citrus-scented soup, add ground white or black Omani lime to cooked green lentils and purée.
3. Season pork chops with ground black or white Omani lime before grilling.

QUICK BLEND
Joon

Enliven rice or wheat berries by cooking them in chicken or vegetable stock seasoned with this blend, or sprinkle it over celery root before roasting.

Makes about ⅓ cup/31 grams

2 pieces/10 grams black Omani limes, ground
2 pieces/10 grams white Omani limes, ground
3 tablespoons/3 grams dried tarragon leaves, ground
2 tablespoons/5 grams dried dill, ground
1 teaspoon/3 grams fennel seeds, toasted and ground

ORANGE PEEL

CITRUS x SINENSIS

A fresh, sweet spice with a pronounced citrus aroma from the dried rind of an orange

FLAVOR & AROMA Most of us eat oranges or drink the juice, but the peel is often forgotten—a readily available spice we so quickly discard. As much as the fruit inside is coveted for its sweet juice, the peel is strongly aromatic with a pleasant, sweet scent and a bitter taste. The dried peel will not have any acidity at all, and depending on the quality of the orange, it can even add sweet notes to dishes.

You can very easily dry the oil-rich whole orange peel or zest (without the bitter white pith) on the counter for a few days, and then store it in a jar. Later, it can be used while roasting meat, fish, or vegetables, or it can be ground and added to dressings and sauces. I also like to thinly slice the orange (skin and fruit) and dry it out on the kitchen counter or between two pieces of parchment paper in a low oven. I use these dried slices to add great flavor and crunch to salads or as a cocktail garnish.

ORIGIN ☞ Possibly native to North India or China ☞ Cultivated worldwide, but mainly in the United States in California and Florida, and parts of the Mediterranean

HARVEST SEASON Oranges are harvested throughout the year. They are picked when ripe, and the peels are dried, making the spice more shelf stable than the fresh fruit itself.

PARTS USED Fruit peel

ABOUT No one seems to know for sure specifically where oranges are from, but many say these members of the rue (Rutaceae) family are from Southeast Asia (most likely China or India). Rich with vitamin C, enzymes, flavonoids, and phytonutrients, orange peel has been used medicinally since the second century BC, as noted in the *Divine Husbandman's Materia Medica,* a classic text in traditional Chinese medicine.

Columbus is said to have brought citrus seeds to the Caribbean during his second voyage in the late 1400s. But it wasn't until the 1769 that Father Junipero Serra and his Spanish friars planted the first orange seeds in California, which remains one of the largest producers of the fruit to this day. It became popular because California Gold Rushers with scurvy discovered that oranges battled their vitamin C deficiency. But it remains cherished because the fruit's bright, tart, and sweet flavor makes it an irreplaceable culinary ingredient.

Aside from the fruit, orange blossoms work wonders in the perfume industry, as well as in pastries and sweets. The fruit juice is on every breakfast table, but it is the peel that can be jarred as a spice to add freshness to both sweet and savory dishes. In Provence, the slow-simmered *daube de boeuf* (beef and red wine stew) gets a lift from orange peel, as do crème anglaise and crème caramel. Chinese master sauces, which are used again and again as ever-evolving cooking liquids, often include orange peel. It's also used to brighten teas, a variety of beverages, jams, jellies, fish, salad dressings, and sweets.

TRADITIONAL USES

Candied orange peel—United States
Gremolata (chopped herb condiment)—Italy
Negroni (gin aperitif)—Italy
Duck a l'orange—France
Shichimi tōgarashi (spice blend)—Japan

NOTE
Toasting not recommended

RECOMMENDED PAIRINGS
Mustard-orange vinaigrette
Roasted turnips
Veal osso buco
Butter-roasted scallops
Crepe soufflé

SPICE PAIRINGS
Aleppo, basil, caraway, fennel, pink pepperberries

RECIPE IDEAS
1. Add granulated dried orange peel to steel-cut oats and use as a citrus-scented breading for pork cutlets.
2. For a bright marinade, coat lamb shanks with olive oil and granulated dried orange peel before roasting.
3. Combine granulated dried orange peel with sautéed onions and crushed tomatoes for a sweet, citrusy sauce for pasta or meat.

QUICK BLEND
Tapuz

Sprinkle this blend on a chilled, cooked rice and chopped scallion salad. It also adds a citrusy, peppery element to carrot slaw.

Makes about ¼ cup/28 grams

1½ tablespoons/15 grams granulated dried orange peel
1 tablespoon/3 grams pink pepperberries, ground
1½ heaping teaspoons/5 grams caraway seeds, toasted and ground
1 teaspoon/3 grams nigella seeds
Scant ¾ teaspoon/2 grams white peppercorns, ground

OREGANO

GREEK (ORIGANUM VULGARE HIRTUM OR HERACLEOTICUM)/ TURKISH (ORIGANUM TYTTANTICUM)/MEXICAN (LIPPIA GRAVEOLENS)

A variety of warm, herbaceous herbs often best when dried

—

FLAVOR & AROMA I grew up seeing oregano in glass shakers at pizza places right next to jars of mediocre dried Parmesan, both for sprinkling on fresh pies. It was only many years later that I realized this herb, whether fresh or dried, has so much more to it. I love its warm, slightly bitter notes, and sometimes even little pine or peppery scents.

Oregano can often smell and taste better dried than fresh. As it loses its moisture content, its flavor and aroma become more concentrated. At La Boîte, I get my oregano leaves already crushed in large pieces, and I like to leave them as is to add texture to my blends.

ORIGIN ☞ Native to Mexico and Central and South America (Mexican oregano) and the Mediterranean and Western Asia (Greek and Turkish oregano) ☞ Cultivated in the Mediterranean and southern Europe (Greek and Turkish oregano)

HARVEST SEASON Oregano is a bushy perennial (or annual in colder climates) in the mint (Lamiaceae) family, which is planted in early spring. Leaves can be picked at any time. When harvesting for drying, oregano is best just after the flower buds form.

PARTS USED Leaves and flowers

ABOUT While it is challenging to pinpoint the storied beginnings of this herb, it has been used to add warmth to Mediterranean dishes for centuries. We can thank its cousin marjoram (page 180) for all the confusion. Southern Italy is often given credit for oregano's popularity, given its undeniably perfect pairing with tomato sauce, but it is also said to have been an essential ingredient of Greek and Mediterranean cuisine for just as long. It didn't even grace the dinner tables of North America until World War II, when GIs, having fallen in love with the savory, peppery flavor it gave to pizzas, brought it back from their travels.

There are a number of oregano varieties, most notably Turkish, Mexican, and Greek. I mainly use Mediterranean oregano from Turkey. It is a bit sweeter and less bitter than the Mexican kind and works well with meat dishes like lamb and barbecue. Mexican oregano is actually not oregano at all. It's a member of the verbena family, with more citrus notes that make it perfect for fiery chile-based dishes, moles, enchiladas, and beans.

Greek oregano brings whole grilled fish to life, especially when seasoned with lemon and olive oil. It is also what makes the ever-popular Greek salad more than just any salad, and what gives a recognizable earthiness to grilled meats like souvlaki (shish kebabs). It is also the variety most commonly associated with Italian fare; Greek oregano is a natural match for pasta sauces, garlic-laced dishes, seafood, roasted vegetables, and anywhere basil is used.

TRADITIONAL USES

Pizza topping—United States
Queso fundido (baked cheese)—Mexico
Chimichurri (green sauce)—Argentina
Classic marinara sauce—Italy
Flatbreads—Middle East

NOTE
Toasting not recommended

RECOMMENDED PAIRINGS
Roast pork belly
Lamb pie
Orecchiette and eggplant
Fried haddock
Tomato Provençal (stuffed baked tomatoes)

SPICE PAIRINGS
basil, garlic, orange peel, sumac, thyme

RECIPE IDEAS
1. Combine equal amounts of chopped walnuts and crushed dried oregano to give texture and depth to creamy polenta.
2. Add crushed dried oregano to warm, melted bacon fat and use as a base for a vinegary salad dressing.
3. Sprinkle crushed dried oregano into a mixture of crumbled feta cheese and olives and fold into penne pasta.

QUICK BLEND
Rigani
See photograph, page 201.

For a nutty, somewhat acidic flatbread topping, add a few pinches of this blend to diced halloumi cheese with minced garlic and diced tomatoes. It brings an herbaceous element to bulgur and feta cheese salad as well.

Makes about ½ cup/35 grams

Scant ½ cup/15 grams crushed dried oregano leaves
½ tablespoon/5 grams ground sumac
½ tablespoon/5 grams granulated dried onion
½ tablespoon/5 grams sesame seeds, toasted
1½ heaping teaspoons/5 grams fennel seeds, toasted and ground

PAPRIKA

CAPSICUM ANNUUM

A rust-red, mild to hot spice made from ground capsicums

FLAVOR & AROMA "Do you prefer color or flavor?" This question comes up often in conversations with my paprika suppliers. There are times when I am lucky to get both, but in some years, farms yield good flavor with muted tones. Some people prefer an intense, deep red color to impart a better visual element while cooking. Some, myself included, would rather have flavor in lieu of good looks. Since the quality of paprika peppers, as with all spices, is entirely dependent on nature and the growing environment, no two crops are exactly the same. I choose my Hungarian paprika based on a sweet scent and deep flavor, and I don't mind if it's darker or lighter as long as it delivers on taste. I also love that it comes in a range of heat levels, from mild to hot.

Paprika really shines when slightly heated or infused into a liquid. It is mostly sold already ground because of the labor-intensive process required to remove the stems and seeds and then grind it. You can buy whole mild chiles and grind them at home for a fresher result; it just means more work for you. Because of its powdery texture, paprika makes a great thickening agent for sauces and stews. Its vibrant color has been known to fix the appearance of any low-end tomato sauce as well.

I occasionally hear someone raving about Moroccan paprika, saying how great and unique it is. I'll let you in on a little secret: it's not some rare variety of paprika; they just add a touch of oil to it to give it a slightly humid aspect. That's what makes it so fragrant.

ORIGIN ☞ Native to the Americas and later Spain ☞ Cultivated in China, the Middle East, and Hungary

HARVEST SEASON These capsicums, in the nightshade (Solanaceae) family, are planted in early spring and harvested when they turn red and glossy in the summer and fall. Traditionally, as is still done in the Hungarian villages of Szeged and Kalosca, peppers are threaded on strings and hung along fences to dry, seeded and stemmed, and then ground by hand with a mortar and pestle. Today, mechanical stones and cylinders have replaced the laborious task of manual grinding.

PARTS USED Dried red capsicums

ABOUT The peppers used for making paprika are generally associated with two main sources: Spain, where it was first produced; and Hungary, where it has been produced since the seventeenth century. In Spain, paprika is known as pimentón (page 218).

What began as a spice used mainly by peasants became an essential ingredient and coloring agent in much of Hungarian cuisine. Szeged and Kalocsa produce some of the best paprika in the world and have competed against each other for the title of Paprika Capital for centuries. Here, capsicums are sun-dried instead of smoked, unlike some Spanish varieties. Red-hued Hungarian paprika is essential to its rich, meaty national dishes, including paprikás (chicken in paprika-infused roux) and *pörkölt* (meat stew) or *pacalpörkölt* (spicy *pörkölt* made with tripe).

In Hungary, paprika—particularly the hot variety—can be found on tables alongside salt shakers instead of pepper. It has become so popular that there is a bigger global demand than Hungary can fulfill alone, and let's not forget that pricing drives the market. Because of this, most paprika today comes from China, Peru, and some Middle Eastern countries.

TRADITIONAL USES

Goulash (meat and vegetable stew)—Hungary
Sofrito (sauce base)—Latin America
Chermoula (herb marinade)—Morocco
Fish stew—Portugal
Chorizo—Spain/Mexico

NOTE

Toasting not recommended

RECOMMENDED PAIRINGS

- Deviled eggs
- Crab bisque
- Sweet potato velouté
- Refried black beans
- Braised oxtail

SPICE PAIRINGS

caraway, cumin, garlic, ginger, thyme

RECIPE IDEAS

1. Add ground sweet paprika to reduced port wine and use to glaze a whole duck while roasting.
2. Combine ground sweet paprika with baked potato and use in your gnocchi recipe.
3. Season cooked chickpeas with ground hot paprika and fresh garlic for a pungent, perked-up hummus.

QUICK BLEND
Paprikash

Braise red cabbage with this earthy blend, along with red wine, smoky bacon, onions, and apples, or add it to savory pork stuffing for a touch of color and great texture.

Makes about ¼ cup/29 grams

2 tablespoons/15 grams ground sweet paprika
1½ heaping teaspoons/5 grams caraway seeds, toasted and ground
1 teaspoon/3 grams dill seeds, ground
1 teaspoon/3 grams white peppercorns, ground
1 teaspoon/3 grams juniper berries, ground

PARSLEY

PETROSELINUM CRISPUM

A fresh, mildly bitter herb commonly used as a garnish

FLAVOR & AROMA I like dried parsley for its herbaceous, mild peppery notes with a hint of sweetness and great green color. As with most dried herbs, it can be rehydrated in cooking liquid for a concentrated flavor without it burning or becoming bitter. Parsley is a versatile herb; it's always good to have a jar of dried leaves in your kitchen. It will lose its flavor and scent over time, but I never find it that difficult to use up before that happens.

I often think about the fact that I would need to fill my entire store from floor to ceiling with fresh parsley a few times a year in order to get to the final dried amount that I use in my blends. Thanks to my dried parsley supplier in Israel, I don't have to worry about that.

ORIGIN ☞ Native to the Mediterranean ☞ Cultivated worldwide

HARVEST SEASON Parsley is a biennial plant with bright green leaves on thin, edible stems. Beginning in the spring, stems and leaves are harvested from the outer part of the plant as needed until it sets seed or before it dies back in winter. When parsley bolts, or flowers, the leaves change shape and can become bitter.

PARTS USED Leaves, stems, and root

ABOUT There are two main varieties of parsley: curly leaf and flat leaf, which is also called French or Italian flat-leaf parsley, both members of the parsley (Apiaceae) family. You may recognize the former adorning the buffet or garnishing fresh fish at the grocery store. Curly parsley is more often used as a garnish for potatoes, rice dishes, fish, poultry, or sauces. The flat-leaf variety is arguably better for cooking and more commonly used to build flavor in stocks as part of a bouquet garni (herb bundle), or added to salads, sandwiches, soups, stuffing, eggs, and stews. The two are often used interchangeably and have been widely adopted across a number of world cuisines to add a pop of color to dishes.

In the Middle East, fresh flat-leaf parsley is chopped and mixed with tomatoes, lemon juice, onion, olive oil, bulgur, and mint for the Levantine vegetarian staple tabbouleh. The French sauté fresh parsley with garlic for a fragrant persillade to be served over oysters or escargot, or stirred into potatoes. With the addition of lemon zest, it enlivens osso buco alla milanese as a gremolata. In Brazil, it is chopped up and mixed with scallions and oil and used as a fragrant condiment called *cheiro verde* for meats, fish, soups, chicken, and rice dishes. Dried parsley is used in the Moroccan version of chermoula (marinade) served over grilled meat and fish.

There are other varieties: thick-stem parsley that resembles celery, and parsley root that looks more like a parsnip. Each has its place in the kitchen, but for seasoning I prefer fresh or dried flat or curly leaves. Parsley root is more common in Central and Eastern European cuisine than anywhere else. It's native to Germany, where they slow cook it in soups and stews or eat it raw like a carrot.

TRADITIONAL USES

Steak rub—United States
Jerk spice blend—Jamaica
Fresh sausage—Italy
Zhoug (hot chile condiment)—Yemen
Herbed goat cheese—France

NOTE

Toasting not recommended

RECOMMENDED PAIRINGS

Parsley pesto
Asparagus soup
Cauliflower fritters
Salmon kebabs
Salsa verde

SPICE PAIRINGS

cayenne, garlic, green pepper, mustard, tomato powder

RECIPE IDEAS

1. Mix ground parsley into an avocado purée for
a fresh green goddess dressing.
2. Sprinkle crushed parsley leaves between phyllo dough sheets,
spread with butter, and use to make potato samosas.
3. Combine dry cubed bread with a handful of crushed parsley leaves
and grind in a food processor for green, herbaceous bread crumbs.

QUICK BLEND
Petruzilia

See photograph, page 206.

Grill cucumber slices seasoned with this herbaceous blend
and add yogurt, lemon juice, olive oil, and goat cheese for a salad.
It also livens up whole boneless sardines before baking.

Makes about 1 cup/25 grams

¾ cup/15 grams crushed dried parsley
2 tablespoons/2 grams dried tarragon leaves, ground
½ tablespoon/5 grams celery seeds
2 teaspoons/2 grams crushed dried mint leaves
Scant ½ teaspoon/1 gram black peppercorns, coarsely ground

PEPPER

PIPER NIGRUM

Black, white, red, and green peppercorns are all fruits of the same evergreen climbing vine, just harvested at different times and handled in different ways.

Peppercorns are the most important spice in the history of the spice trade. What began as a simple vine growing off India's Malabar coast became the sole reason for lengthy sailing expeditions, drawn-out wars, and the carving out of trade routes. Pepper was traded for gold, was used to pay taxes, and single-handedly built and destroyed entire empires.

Similar to *terroir* in wine, the origin of each pepper variety imbues it with specific characteristics. The two main varieties, classified by where they are grown on India's Malabar coast, are Malabar and Tellicherry—which are actually grafted Malabar plants grown on Mount Tellicherry. More of a quality designation than anything else, Tellicherry is considered the best and largest of the two berries. That said, Malabar has arguably the better, fruitier flavor. Sichuan pepper (page 254) and pink pepperberries (page 220), on the other hand, are not true peppercorns nor in the same family (Piperaceae). The former is a berry from a mountain ash tree, and the latter is the fruit of the Brazilian pepper tree.

Along with salt, pepper is the most continuously used spice in the world. With endless sweet and savory uses, from seafood and wild game to cocktails and custards, it is no surprise that people went to such great lengths to get their hands on it.

ORIGIN ☞ Native to India's Malabar coast ☞ Cultivated in Malabar and other areas of India, Vietnam, Indonesia, Malaysia, Brazil, and Madagascar

PARTS USED Berries (peppercorns)

BLACK PEPPER

Most people take pepper for granted. There are many black pepper options today, and each offers something a little different. I invite you to find your favorite.

I always recommended buying black peppercorns and using a pepper mill or grinder to grind as needed. Unfortunately, there is a lot of adulteration when it comes to this spice, particularly if you buy it already ground. It can even have ground olive pits added to it to add weight for the sake of making more money. The practice is not dangerous for your health, but I like to season my food with pepper, not pits.

Indian Malabar is the most common black pepper variety and offers a robust flavor, scent, and degree of heat. Tellicherry is a higher-quality pepper with a larger berry that offers a bit of sweetness and notes of citrus. The Sarawak and Lampong varieties are smaller in size and are more piney with herbaceous notes. They are also similar to the Vietnamese (Phú Quốc) pepper, which has a lemony fragrance, and Cambodian (Kampot) pepper, which has a smoky finish.

HARVEST SEASON Black peppercorns are harvested January through March while they are still green and unripe and are then fermented or blanched, and sun-dried. This process turns them a dark brown/black color and wrinkles the skins.

GREEN PEPPER

You might stumble upon a can of green peppercorns in brine or at the supermarket, but chances are you have no idea what to do with them. Hint: They work best in sauces and stuffing.

Green pepper is not as hot as black or white pepper, and its herbaceous, fresh notes pair well with pork, sauces, fruits, and vegetables. Because it is harvested before it is ripe and air-dried or freeze-dried, green peppercorns easily break down into a powder; you can add whole ones to a salad without fear of breaking a tooth.

At La Boîte I mainly use Malabar green peppercorns, and I love adding them to blends to bring a fresh note with mild heat.

HARVEST SEASON Green peppercorns are harvested January through March when still unripe, and dried.

RED PEPPER

Don't confuse these with the more common pink pepperberries from Brazil (page 220); true red peppercorns are rare and expensive. One reason is that they are left on the vine longer to fully ripen, whereas black and green peppers are picked much earlier. The longer process, lower yield, and risk of loss—if they ripen too much, they fall to the ground—are the reasons for the heftier price tag.

I get them from three sources: Pondicherry in South India, Kampot in Cambodia, and Phú Quốc in Vietnam. The citrus scent with a touch of sweetness makes them great for seafood and fruit dishes, and when coarsely ground, they add a flavorful texture to cooked fish or roasted vegetables. When making a blend, I love combining them with herbs such as basil and tarragon for their fresh aromas and added complexity.

HARVEST SEASON Red peppercorns are picked January through March when fully ripe, and are either dried or preserved in brine.

WHITE PEPPER

Many cooks either don't care for white pepper or say they only use it in "white" dishes so as not to impart any flecks of color. One of the reasons for these biases is they simply haven't tried properly processed peppercorns and don't know what they're missing. Traditionally, a time-consuming process of soaking almost ripe berries in water and then removing the skins produces white pepper. It also requires proper drying time, but many producers cut it short to get faster results and to retain humidity and weight. After all, more weight means more money. Unfortunately, if it is not done correctly, the spice can develop a fermented scent. As a result, most of what you'll find on the market is anything but white (mainly brown or gray).

The good news is that there is great white pepper out there. In my perspective, the best varieties are Muntok from Indonesia, Penja from Cameroon, and Sarawak from Malaysia. These cream-colored peppercorns have an herbaceous note and are very earthy with a mild, pleasant heat. Unlike what many sources will tell you, white pepper is not a substitute for black pepper. It is an elegant, delicate variety that I love using on raw or cold dishes, or with seafood and dairy. Because it requires more care and labor, it is often more expensive, but I urge you to spend a little more to discover the beauty of it.

HARVEST SEASON White peppercorns are picked January through March when almost ripe with a yellow-red hue. They are then soaked to soften and remove the skins, and then dried.

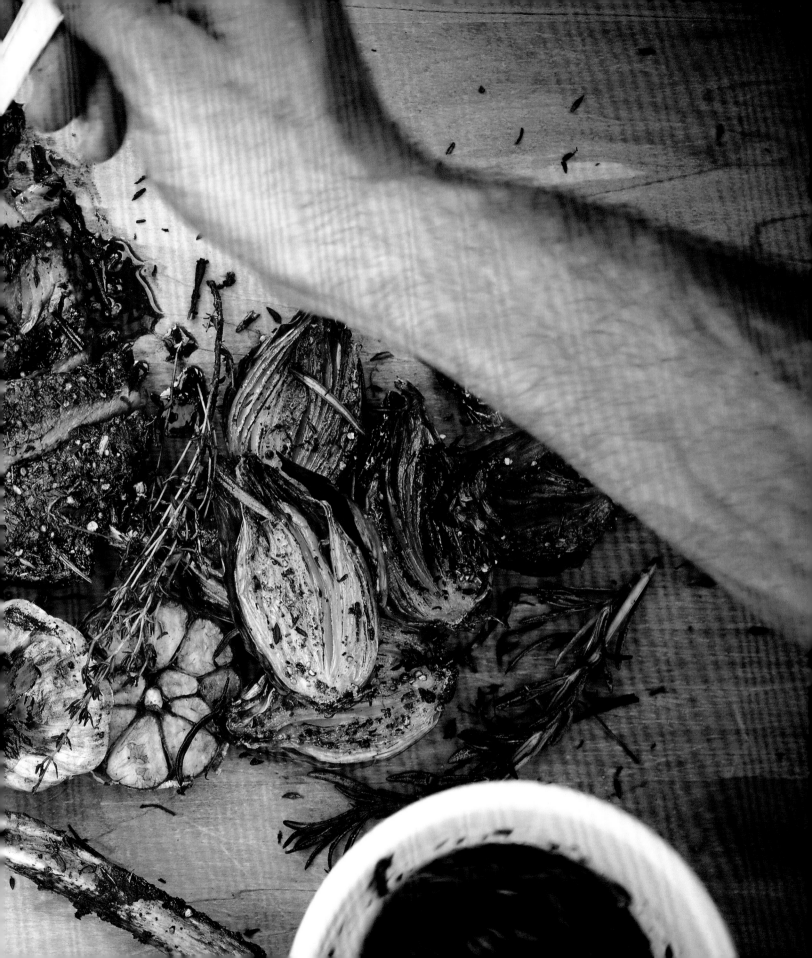

BLACK PEPPER

TRADITIONAL USES

Steak au poivre (pepper steak)—France
Mignonette (condiment for oysters)—France
Cacio e pepe (cheese and pepper pasta)—Italy
Masala Chai (mixed spice tea)—India
Zhoug (herb and chile relish)—Yemen

NOTE

Toasting not recommended

RECOMMENDED PAIRINGS

Salade niçoise
Béarnaise sauce
Roasted venison
Steamed clams
Chocolate brownies

SPICE PAIRINGS

basil, cinnamon, juniper, orange peel, tarragon

RECIPE IDEAS

1. Sprinkle coarsely ground black pepper on sliced fresh peaches, drizzle with balsamic vinegar, and serve with manchego cheese.
2. Combine a pound of softened butter with a handful of coarsely ground black pepper and keep refrigerated for later use as a flavored butter.
3. In a blender, purée black peppercorns with olive oil to make a pepper paste for cooked pasta or grains.

QUICK BLEND
Pilpel

See photograph, pages 210–211.

Season a bone-in rib eye steak with this blend and shallots before roasting. It makes a great condiment for cold meats or crudités when added to mayonnaise.

Makes about ⅓ cup/27 grams

¼ cup/3 grams dried tarragon leaves, crushed
1½ tablespoons/15 grams black peppercorns, coarsely ground
1 tablespoon/3 grams crushed dried mint leaves
½ tablespoon/5 grams mustard seeds
1 pinch/1 gram fleur de sel, or medium-grain sea salt

GREEN PEPPER

TRADITIONAL USES

Stir-fries and curry pastes—Thailand
Mustard—France
Sauce au poivre (pepper sauce)—France
Meat pâté—France
Pickled in brine—Madagascar

NOTE
Toasting not recommended

RECOMMENDED PAIRINGS
Roast pork loin
Caramelized cauliflower
Butter-poached turbot
Duck rillettes
Cherry chutney

SPICE PAIRINGS
dill, ginger, lemon peel, onion, rosemary

RECIPE IDEAS
1. For a sweet, peppery condiment to serve with cheese, add green peppercorns to vermouth and honey and simmer until the mixture reduces and thickens. Let cool.
2. Sprinkle ground green peppercorns on sliced seedless green grapes, and serve with grilled lamb chops.
3. Season diced butternut squash with ground green peppercorns, olive oil, and orange juice, and roast until tender.

QUICK BLEND
Pepe Verde

Season a pork butt with this blend before braising it with white wine, fennel, and tomatoes. It also adds a peppery bite to a spinach frittata.

Makes about ⅓ cup/27 grams

3 tablespoons/15 grams green peppercorns, coarsely ground
½ tablespoon/5 grams green anise seeds, ground
1 teaspoon/3 grams yellow mustard seeds, ground
1 teaspoon/3 grams granulated dried orange peel
1 teaspoon/1 gram celery seeds, ground

RED PEPPER

FAMILIAR USES
Crab stir-fry
Sautéed beef tenderloin
Fish tartare
Coconut curry
Grilled snapper

NOTE
Toasting not recommended

RECOMMENDED PAIRINGS
Baked Camembert
Mignonette sauce for oysters
Grilled short ribs
Squash ravioli
Strawberries and whipped cream

SPICE PAIRINGS
anise seeds, cinnamon, clove, galangal, lemongrass

RECIPE IDEAS
1. Sprinkle coarsely ground red pepper on tomato wedges
before grilling and serving with fresh ricotta.
2. Lightly coat watermelon cubes with extra-virgin olive oil,
season with ground red pepper, and serve with chilled poached shrimp.
3. Season thinly sliced fresh button mushrooms with olive oil, lemon
juice, and cracked red pepper, and serve with an arugula salad.

QUICK BLEND
Kampot

Use this lemon-pepper blend to season
a whole branzino, then wrap in banana
leaves and bake. It also adds a citrus note
to pasta and clams for a fresh, peppery dish.

Makes about ¼ cup/25 grams

1½ tablespoons/15 grams red Kampot, Pondicherry,
or Phú Quốc peppercorns, coarsely ground
1 tablespoon/5 grams ground lemongrass
2 teaspoons/2 grams crushed dried basil leaves
½ tablespoon/3 grams ground galangal

WHITE PEPPER

TRADITIONAL USES

Clam chowder—United States
Potato purée—France
Beurre blanc (white butter sauce)—France
Béchamel sauce (white sauce made with roux
and milk)—France
Gefilte fish (poached ground fish)—Jewish cuisine

NOTE
Toasting not recommended

RECOMMENDED PAIRINGS
Fluke crudo
Baked ziti
Salsify purée
Clams casino
Nectarine tart

SPICE PAIRINGS
amchoor, dill, fenugreek, ginger, orange peel

RECIPE IDEAS
1. Season chilled cooked brown rice with ground white pepper,
lemon juice, hazelnut oil, and diced radish for a fresh salad.
2. Sprinkle ground white pepper on boiled potatoes and
serve with sour cream and smoked haddock.
3. Add coarsely ground white pepper to lemon juice, honey,
and olive oil and drizzle over thinly sliced apples for a crisp, peppery snack.

QUICK BLEND
Penja

Season diver scallops with this blend and then sear them in a
pan with salted butter and garlic. It also adds great texture
and warm, peppery notes to orange-braised endives.

Makes about 3½ tablespoons/26 grams

1½ tablespoons/15 grams white peppercorns, coarsely ground
1½ tablespoons/5 grams crushed dried marjoram leaves
1 teaspoon/3 grams freshly grated nutmeg
1 teaspoon/2 grams dried thyme leaves
½ teaspoon/1 gram ground licorice

PEPPERONCINI
(CALABRIAN CHILE)

CAPSICUM ANNUUM

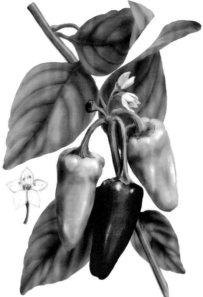

A variety of fiery, fruity chiles from Italy's Calabria region

FLAVOR & AROMA When most people think of pepperoncini, those spicy yellow or green peppers pickled in brine and served in Italian eateries come to mind. But with the growing demand and interest in chiles in the last few years, I am now also able to source fantastic dried peppers from Italy, especially from Calabria in the south. The warm climate of the mountainside offers the perfect conditions for producing a great number of chile varieties. They are, for the most part, narrow and medium in size with a low to medium level of heat and can be ground, coarsely ground or made into a paste with their small round seeds intact.

Dried pepperoncini have a bright citrus and acidic aroma with sweet-and-sour notes followed by mild heat. They are great used as a final seasoning for cooked or raw dishes, or as the heat component in a spice blend. I love a medium-coarse grind, which adds great texture to blends.

ORIGIN ☞ Native to South and Central America, and later Italy ☞ Cultivated in Italy, Greece, and the United States

HARVEST SEASON Traditionally, chiles are allowed to ripen fully on the vine. Once harvested, each variety is individually strung up in a well-ventilated place to dry.

PARTS USED Fresh, pickled, or dried ground peppers

ABOUT When you buy a jar of Calabrian chiles, it actually contains any number of chile varieties (all nightshades in the Solanaceae family) grown in the mountainous region at the toe of Italy's boot, but primarily the Italian cayenne, the *naso di cane* ("dog's nose"), *amando, sigarette,* and *ciliegia.* Just don't confuse them with the mild, tangy pickled Greek pepperoncini.

Calabria's consistently warm sunshine makes it the perfect climate for growing these heat-seeking pepperoncini. Peer onto any of the locals' balconies in late summer and you will find strings (*filas*) of chiles hanging to dry, ready to be used in regional specialties like 'nduja or as a fiery condiment.

In southern Italy's rustic fare, pepperoncini are fried until crisp, preserved in oil, made into hot sauce, and used to punch up vegetable and fish dishes, or pastas and pizzas. They are also great for infusing into vinegars, olive oil, and simple syrups.

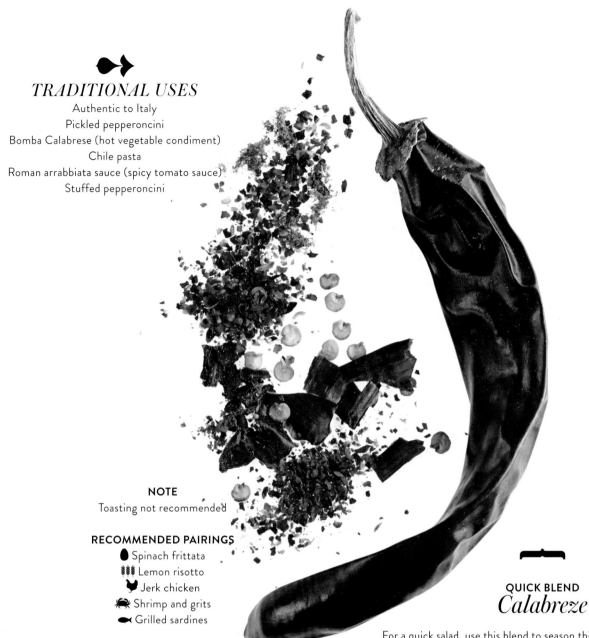

TRADITIONAL USES

Authentic to Italy
Pickled pepperoncini
Bomba Calabrese (hot vegetable condiment)
Chile pasta
Roman arrabbiata sauce (spicy tomato sauce)
Stuffed pepperoncini

NOTE
Toasting not recommended

RECOMMENDED PAIRINGS
Spinach frittata
Lemon risotto
Jerk chicken
Shrimp and grits
Grilled sardines

SPICE PAIRINGS
cumin, fennel pollen, garlic, orange peel, oregano

HEAT INDEX
Light to medium heat

RECIPE IDEAS

1. Season a thinly sliced fresh plum with pepperoncini flakes
and arrange on top of ricotta toasts.

2. Marinate sliced fennel bulb with olive oil, lemon juice, capers, and
pepperoncini flakes before sautéing and serving with roast chicken.

3. In a blender, purée cooked white beans, olive oil,
fresh basil leaves, white balsamic vinegar, and pepperoncini flakes
for a smooth spread or side dish.

QUICK BLEND
Calabreze

For a quick salad, use this blend to season thinly sliced raw artichokes
and radishes and dress with olive oil and lemon juice. Sprinkle the mix on
sautéed porcini mushrooms for a touch of heat.

Makes about ⅓ cup/28 grams

3 tablespoons/15 grams crushed dried pepperoncini
1 tablespoon/3 grams crushed dried oregano leaves
2 teaspoons/2 grams dried rosemary leaves, coarsely ground
1½ heaping teaspoons/5 grams fennel seeds, toasted and ground
1 teaspoon/3 grams granulated dried lemon peel

PIMENTÓN (SPANISH PAPRIKA)

CAPSICUM ANNUUM

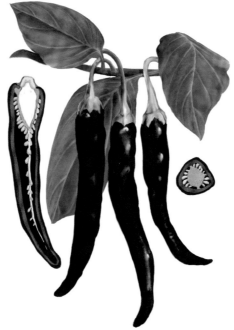

A smoky or not, mild or hot spice made from a number of peppers

FLAVOR & AROMA Pimentón can be produced from a small variety of peppers; no one pepper is to credit for it. If a round, sweeter variety is used, such as the ñora pepper (page 190), it will produce a darker red powder meant for cooking. Longer pepper varieties deliver a lighter red-orange powder typically used as a coloring agent in chorizo, paella, and cured meats. In either case, you can choose the degree of heat you want.

Spain produces great quality unsmoked pimentón (called Spanish paprika), but I love the added depth of smoke, which gives every vegetable or seafood dish the sensation of eating grilled meat. More than just the smoky element, smoked pimentón also has sweet and acidic layers with some pleasantly bitter notes. It adds a great complexity and depth to simple egg dishes, Spanish chorizo, sofrito, and a gamut of slow-cooked stews, soups, fish, vegetable, and meat dishes. It is one of my picks as an essential spice to have in your kitchen.

ORIGIN ☞ Native to the Americas and later Spain ☞ Cultivated in Spain

HARVEST SEASON Peppers are planted in the spring and harvested in the fall when fully ripened. Traditionally, these members of the nightshade (Solanaceae) family are hand-harvested and set out to dry in the sun. For the signature smoky flavor and aroma of Pimentón de la Vera, peppers are smoke-dried with oak wood on large drying racks over the fire and are turned daily for about 2 weeks.

PARTS USED Smoked or unsmoked peppers

ABOUT We can thank Columbus for this particular spice. As a memento of his voyage to the New World, he brought back a variety of peppers to Spain, many of which are used to make pimentón or Spanish paprika. It is there that these red capsicums are hand-harvested, dried and/or smoked, and ground to make the versatile spice we know and love today. These same peppers would also later make their way to new soil in Hungary to be grown and made into a sweeter, unsmoked paprika variety (page 202).

Spanish pimentón mainly comes from La Vera, but also from Murcia. When you buy it, you'll see the denomination of origin on the jar. You'll also find the label delineating between three levels of heat: *dulce* is mild/sweet, *agridulce* is medium, and *picante* is hot. If it is called pimentón, it is smoked; if the label specifies paprika or Spanish paprika, it is not. Just don't call it "smoked paprika" to a Spaniard; it is always pimentón, whether it is smoked or not.

In recent years there has been a shortage of Spanish peppers growing there, so peppers are being brought in from other countries such as Peru and China, and processed locally to keep up with global demand. Also, some manufacturers have been found adding liquid smoke to ground paprika and selling it under the name "Spanish smoked paprika." It smells bad and tastes artificially smoked. For these reasons, the labeling is even more important; you want to purchase authentic, certified pimentón. True pimentón can only be dried (smoked) with oak wood using a ratio of five times more wood than peppers.

TRADITIONAL USES

Authentic to Spain
Gambas al ajillo (shrimp in garlic)
Patatas bravas (fried potatoes)
Beef stew with piquillo peppers
Paella
Chorizo

NOTE

Toasting not recommended

RECOMMENDED PAIRINGS

Corn succotash
Egg salad
Mac and cheese
Clam chowder
Lamb ribs

SPICE PAIRINGS

cinnamon, cumin, fennel, garlic, ginger

RECIPE IDEAS

1. Mix smoked sweet pimentón into Greek yogurt and use as a marinade for chicken thighs before roasting them in the oven.
2. Perk up flaked cooked cod with a few pinches of smoked sweet pimentón, mayonnaise, and lemon juice and serve with garlic bread.
3. Reduce fresh orange juice, smoked hot pimentón, and a couple of garlic cloves by half, strain, let cool, and use as a base for a salad dressing.

QUICK BLEND
La Vera

Marinate a duck breast with this sweet, herbaceous blend before grilling. It also adds vibrant color and texture to tuna kebabs.

Makes about ¼ cup/33 grams

2 tablespoons/15 grams ground sweet pimentón
1½ tablespoons/5 grams crushed dried oregano leaves
1 tablespoon/10 grams yellow mustard seeds
1 teaspoon/3 grams caraway seeds, toasted and ground

PINK PEPPER

SCHINUS TEREBINTHIFOLIUS

*An oily and sweet pink berry—
not a peppercorn*

FLAVOR & AROMA You may have seen more pink pepper adorning branches in floral arrangements than on your food. Although florists will argue that they make an attractive bouquet, in my opinion where they really shine is on the plate.

I use pink pepperberries from Brazil. They are sweet and acidic, reminiscent of citrus with a fruity, resinous aroma. Some claim they have a heat component, but I disagree. Pink peppers are actually a great way to add sweetness to a spice blend or dish without adding sugar.

They are naturally oily and will easily get stuck in your pepper mill. Consider yourself warned. Because of this high degree of moisture, they add a wet aspect to blends that helps to bind the spices. I like to sprinkle them whole into salads or add them to sauces and dressings. They are also popular when crushed and stirred into cocktails or as a garnish for chocolate creations.

ORIGIN ☞ Native to Espirito Santo and Bahia, and other parts of Brazil and South America ☞ Cultivated in Brazil and the French island of Réunion

HARVEST SEASON Tiny white flowers grow in clusters on this small tree or shrub. Each bears a green berry that turns reddish pink when ripe in the fall. Traditionally, they are hand-harvested and sun-dried, or machine dried and cleaned in more modern facilities. When dry, the skin becomes brittle and can be rubbed off easily.

PARTS USED Dried fruits

ABOUT Although often sold alongside black, red, green, and white peppercorns, pink pepper is actually the fruit of the Brazilian pepper tree and part of the sumac (Anacardiaceae) family and not a peppercorn. It only dons the name because of its similar shape and size. To make things more confusing, it is related to the Peruvian pepper tree (*Schinus molle*), which bears a similar fruit and is often sold under the same name.

Pink pepperberries are usually found dried, and less often pickled in brine, where they appear more green than pink. Their colorful exterior and delicate flavor make them a perfect accompaniment to salads, seafood, poultry, pork, and game. They are much too soft to be ground, but can easily be chopped with a knife, sprinkled onto dishes whole, crushed as a garnish, or added to sauces for veal, shellfish, and fatty meats.

FAMILIAR USES

Lobster cream sauce
Pork chops
Pink pepper ice cream
Mango chutney
Goat cheese spread

NOTE
Toasting not recommended

RECOMMENDED PAIRINGS
Orange marmalade
Coconut rice
Apple coleslaw
Sherry vinaigrette
Shrimp dumplings

SPICE PAIRINGS
anise, jasmine flowers, orange peel, vanilla, white pepper

RECIPE IDEAS
1. Sprinkle pink pepperberries into your favorite cereal
or granola for a sweet, slightly acidic flavor.
2. For a refreshing Bellini, stir in ground pink pepperberries.
3. Combine pink pepperberries with melted salted butter and
maple syrup and drizzle over warm waffles or pancakes.

QUICK BLEND
Bahia
See photograph, page 222.

For a light crudo, use this blend to season thinly sliced hamachi
or bass and finish with olive oil and lemon juice. It also adds great
texture when sprinkled over watermelon and feta salad.

Makes about ¼ cup/25 grams

¼ cup/15 grams dried pink pepperberries, coarsely ground
½ tablespoon/5 grams granulated dried orange peel
1 teaspoon/3 grams crushed Aleppo chile, or mild chile flakes
Scant ½ teaspoon/2 grams fleur de sel, or medium-flake finishing salt

PIRI PIRI

CAPSICUM FRUTESCENS

*Tiny but mighty fresh or dried chiles
from Portuguese Angola*

FLAVOR & AROMA During times when peppercorns were not available, these little firecrackers were the main source of heat in Brazil. Although they are pretty hot, they also offer nice acidity and fresh citrus notes. My favorites are chiles that are fully ripe and have a slight purplish hue to them. I like to coarsely grind them or add them whole to dishes. You can easily chop them with a knife or crush them by hand as long as you remember to wash up afterward; accidentally touch your lips or face after handling them, and you'll feel the burn.

ORIGIN ☞ Native to South and Central America and later Brazil and Africa ☞ Cultivated in Africa and wild in jungles of the Sudan

HARVEST SEASON These bushy pepper plants bear some of the smallest chiles in the world (less than an inch long). The fruits are tapered to a blunt end and ripen from green to bright red or even purple. Like other chiles, they are heat loving and are harvested at the end of the summer or early fall and then dried in the sun.

PARTS USED Whole chiles

ABOUT The piri piri chile is also known as African red devil, peri peri, or bird's eye—though it is not the same as another close relative in the nightshade (Solanaceae) family, the Thai bird's eye chile (page 68). It also goes by the name pimenta malagueta in Brazil—not to be confused with grains of paradise (page 136)—or gindungo in Angola.

Originally brought from Brazil to the Portuguese colonies in Angola, Africa, in the early sixteenth century, these chiles have thrived there ever since. It is only fitting that most recipes mentioning piri piri are from the Portuguese, African, or Brazilian cuisines found in Mozambique, Angola, Namibia, and South Africa. You'll find piri piri chiles dried whole, pickled, crushed, and ground. You may also find them made into an aromatic sauce or marinade used as a staple ingredient with citrus peel, onion, pepper, salt, lemon juice, bay leaves, paprika, pimiento, basil, oregano, and tarragon (recipes vary by region). This vibrant red, savory hot sauce adds a welcome kick to grilled chicken or shrimp, pork dishes like *carne de porco à Alentejana*, and even the Portuguese bean stew, feijoada.

TRADITIONAL USES

Piri piri oil—Portugal
Moqueca (fish stew)—Brazil
Piri piri chicken—Africa
African peanut soup—Africa
Piri piri paneer—India

NOTE
Toasting not recommended

RECOMMENDED PAIRINGS
Chilled carrot soup
Hot-and-sour sauce
Sautéed soft shell crab
Pad thai
Pork satay

SPICE PAIRINGS
amchoor, garlic, nutmeg, paprika, pomegranate

HEAT INDEX
High heat

RECIPE IDEAS
1. Soak a handful of whole dried piri piri chiles in
warm water for 30 minutes, then strain and purée with
dried garlic and vinegar for a fiery chile paste.
2. Sprinkle a few pinches of ground piri piri into cane molasses
and use to glaze a whole ham on the bone while cooking.
3. Season a fluke ceviche with a mixture of ground piri piri,
lime juice, and chopped cilantro.

QUICK BLEND
Red Devil

To give fried chicken a kick, use this pungent blend to
marinate the meat before breading it. It is also
great for adding a tart-spicy bite to fish tacos.

Makes about ¼ cup/21 grams

3 tablespoons/10 grams whole dried piri piri, coarsely ground
½ tablespoon/5 grams ground pomegranate seeds
½ tablespoon/3 grams ground ginger
½ teaspoon/1 gram dried garlic slices, ground
Scant ¾ teaspoon/2 grams ground sweet paprika

POMEGRANATE

PUNICA GRANATUM

*The sweet-and-sour fresh or dried seeds
and juice of a pomegranate fruit*

FLAVOR & AROMA Where I lived as a child, we had a few pomegranate trees growing in our yard. We used to go out and pick the fruits, crack them open to enjoy the juicy seeds, and get our clothes completely stained. The flowers blooming in late summer and fruits ripening in early September were signs of the Jewish holidays and the New Year. This mystical fruit plays an essential role in the Jewish tradition, prayers, and holiday dishes.

It's only more recently that pomegranates have crossed borders and become more popular, especially due to their many health attributes. Their only drawbacks, really, are availability, shelf life, and price. A great way to keep the seeds longer is to dry them. Anardana, the Persian word for the dried seeds, have sweet, sour, and tangy notes similar to sumac (page 260) and amchoor (page 46), with a satisfying crunch. Because they are dry, the concentrated flavor and sweetness are more like molasses, contrary to that of the much brighter fresh seeds. Texturally, they can be pliant and soft, or brittle and hard.

I also use pomegranate powder at La Boîte, which is made from dehydrated pomegranate juice. It has a beautiful pinkish color with sour and sweet notes. I like to add it to salad dressings, desserts, and cookie dough.

ORIGIN ☞ Native to regions from Iran to the Himalayas ☞ Cultivated throughout India, parts of Southeast and Western Asia, China, the Middle East (including Israel), and Africa

HARVEST SEASON Pomegranate trees are part of the Lythraceae family of flowering plants and can live a very long time. Reaching 20 to 30 feet high, some are known to live for two centuries. Red, crowned fruits ripen in September and October and need to be harvested by clipping before they split open and spill their seeds. The inside of the fruit is separated by membrane walls, and compartments are filled with hundreds of sacs, each containing a juicy, fleshy red, pink, or white seed. Pomegranate seeds are eaten fresh, or dried in the sun for up to 2 weeks.

PARTS USED Seeds and juice

ABOUT Pomegranates, which thrive in dry landscapes, have graced art and artifacts for centuries. Mesopotamians referred to the trees as sacred during the Neo-Assyrian period, the Romans depicted the fruits in the mosaics of Pompeii, and Buddhists considered pomegranates to be one of the three blessed fruits along with peaches and citrus fruits. Pomegranates are also thought to be one of the first cultivated fruits in the world.

The fruit's rich juice served well for desert caravans, and its dried seeds have long been used in Indian and Persian cuisines. When dried, pomegranate's sticky seeds add depth of flavor to braising liquids, slow-cooked poultry like Persian chicken stew, lamb dishes, *aloo anardana* (potatoes with anardana), and sweetbreads. They bestow a flavorful crunch when sprinkled whole onto salads, or ground and stirred into curries, hummus, Indian sour chutneys, and spice rubs.

TRADITIONAL USES

Muhammara (red pepper and walnut spread)—Iran (Persia)/North Africa
Fesenjān (stew with pomegranate and walnuts)—Iran (Persia)
Güllaç (milk and pomegranate pastry)—Turkey
Grenadine syrup (sweet/tart bar syrup)—Worldwide
Chiles en nogada (stuffed poblano chiles)—Mexico

NOTE
Toasting not recommended

RECOMMENDED PAIRINGS
⬤ Berry lassi
🐑 Braised lamb shank
🧅 Roasted whole shallots
🥄 Barbecue glaze
🥧 Oatmeal cookies

SPICE PAIRINGS
cilantro, fennel, ginger, saffron, sanshō

RECIPE IDEAS

1. Sprinkle dried pomegranate seeds over halved cherry tomatoes before roasting them in the oven.
2. Combine softened butter with pomegranate powder and use as a sweet-sour topping for pancakes.
3. For a tangy beer and lemonade shandy, stir in a few pinches of pomegranate powder.

QUICK BLEND
Rimon

Combine ground lamb, cooked lentils, and this blend to elevate Indian-inspired grilled kebabs. It also gives poached pears a tart, floral element.

Makes about ¼ cup/27 grams

2 tablespoons/15 grams pomegranate powder
1½ heaping teaspoons/5 grams fennel seeds, toasted and ground
½ tablespoon/3 grams cubeb berries, ground
1 tablespoon/2 grams lavender flowers, ground
1 teaspoon/2 grams pepperoncini flakes

POPPY

PAPAVER SOMNIFERUM

The white, brown, or blue-black seeds of the vibrant poppy flower

---

FLAVOR & AROMA Although people regularly eat poppy seeds on top of their bagels, crackers, or cakes, they rarely, if ever, consider cooking with them. Poppy seeds are, however, used regularly in Europe, Turkey, and India. The Middle East and Turkey produce a brown-gray variety destined for baked goods as a pastry filling and as a topping, and India produces a white type found in curries. My favorite kind is the blue-black seed variety that grows in parts of Europe, predominantly in Holland and the Czech Republic. All of these are good; they just grow in different parts of the world.

When shopping for poppy seeds, look for ones with a pleasant scent and a sweet, oily flavor. A uniform size and color are also good signs of quality. Because they are so rich in natural oils, they can oxidize quickly if kept too long, not stored properly, or ground and then stored; this is why I leave them whole in my blends, or grind them just before cooking or baking with them.

They are great on raw dishes and baked goods or salads. If braised or boiled, they will become a paste and lose their crunchy texture, but they still taste good. I like the visual aspect of the poppy seed, the nutty flavor, and the great texture they add to blends and dishes.

ORIGIN ☞ Native to southwestern Asia and parts of the Mediterranean ☞ Cultivated mainly in Turkey, the Czech Republic, Holland, India, and the Middle East

HARVEST SEASON Poppies are an attractive annual in the poppy (Papaveraceae) family that can reach up to 5 feet tall with white, purple, or red flowers. The characteristic crowned seed capsules are harvested mechanically when they turn yellow, after the petals fade. The capsules are cut off, dried, and cracked open to collect the seeds.

PARTS USED Seeds

ABOUT Poppies are known for three things: their tiny, crunchy seeds; beautiful ornamental flowers; and being the source of the drug opium, which comes from the latex of unripe seedpods, not the seeds we eat. So rest easy—your bagels will not alter your mind.

Poppies have been cultivated for centuries for each of these by-products, and the seeds have been used in many ways throughout the years. In North America and Europe, they are commonly found inside or on top of baked goods like hamburger buns, muffins, and pastries, or finely ground and mixed with milk, sugar, and butter for a pastry filling.

In India, the white poppy seed is used instead of the darker European or Turkish varieties to avoid affecting the color of curries or *korma*s, which they help to thicken. They are also sprinkled over naan bread and *khus khus poorie* (fried poppy seed bread), or cooked with jaggery and coconut for flaky *karanji* pastries.

TRADITIONAL USES

Poppy seed bagel—United States
Shukta (vegetables cooked with mustard and
poppy seed)—Bengal
Strudel (filled layered pastry)—Austria
Baklava (filo dough filled with nuts
and honey)—Turkey
Hamantaschen filling (triangular-shaped
pastries)—Israel/Jewish cuisine around the world

NOTE
Toasting not recommended

RECOMMENDED PAIRINGS
Yogurt and berry parfait
Endive-mustard salad
Lemon vinaigrette
Steak tartare
Crepe

SPICE PAIRINGS
basil, celery seeds, mustard, onion, sumac

RECIPE IDEAS
1. Brush rolled-out pizza dough with olive oil and sprinkle
with a few pinches of poppy seeds, coarse salt, and grated pecorino
cheese before baking for a quick, crisp flatbread.
2. Combine canned tuna with lemon juice, diced celery stalk, Dijon
mustard, and a few pinches of poppy seeds and serve on endive leaves.
3. Season diced ripe mango with a few pinches of poppy seeds,
lime juice, and rice wine vinegar for a quick, fresh salsa.

QUICK BLEND
Pereg

Sprinkle this blend on top of a sliced pear and Gorgonzola
cheese crostini and finish under the broiler for a few seconds.
It is also adds a pleasant crunch and a touch of heat to potato salad.

Makes about ¼ cup/26 grams

2 tablespoons/15 grams blue-black poppy seeds
½ tablespoon/5 grams yellow mustard seeds
½ tablespoon/3 grams anise seeds, ground
2 teaspoons/2 grams crushed dried oregano leaves
Scant ½ teaspoon/1 gram cayenne powder

ROSE

ROSA SPECIES

A fragrant, floral spice made from the leaves and buds of roses

——

FLAVOR & AROMA Some people won't consider using roses in food because they think that the flowers are too soapy or candle-like. If used correctly, they add finesse to savory dishes and elevate desserts and drinks. Because of their floral and sweet, slightly acidic notes, the buds and leaves of this ornamental plant are actually a great addition to spice blends and cooked dishes as well as drinks.

I get my pink and red roses from Turkey and India. I like the scent of both but prefer the red buds for their vibrant color. The buds are a bit more pungent than the leaves, but the leaves are drier and better as a fine powder.

You have to be careful when buying dried roses. Many times you find them mixed with rocks or stems if fallen buds or leaves were collected from the ground. They are also sensitive to bugs and sunlight, so it is best to keep them in an airtight container away from the window. If you can't find organic roses, which tends to be difficult, I recommend buying untreated ones.

ORIGIN ☞ Native to the temperate regions of the Northern Hemisphere, most likely China ☞ Cultivated in Iran, Bulgaria, Turkey, Morocco, and India

HARVEST SEASON Rose buds, petals, and leaves are harvested in the cooler mornings of summer and dried, or used to make rose water. They lend their name to their taxonomic family, Rosaceae.

PARTS USED Buds, petals, and leaves

ABOUT As a fragrant, decorative flower, a culinary ingredient, and a historic symbol of love, beauty, and war, roses certainly have made their presence known. Fossils of these flowers dating back to prehistoric times have been discovered, and there are thousands of cultivars in nearly every color and size. Although it would be easy to associate roses primarily with a gift on Valentine's Day, they actually create an incredible spice that is essential to Middle Eastern, Indian, North African, and Persian cuisines.

For sweet dishes, dried buds and petals can be infused into, or coated with, sugar and used to decorate fondant cakes. They can also be ground and stirred into Indian milk-based desserts like *gulab phirni* (rose-flavored rice pudding), Middle Eastern rose ice cream, and honey or jam. Rose water or rose syrup are often used in sweetmeats like marzipan, some Turkish delights, and Indian desserts like sweet lassi (yogurt drink), *kheer* (rice pudding), and *gulab jamun* (milk-based dumplings).

Apart from its sweet uses, rose complements the earthiness of Bahraini *machboos* (spiced chicken and rice) and is essential to spice blends like Moroccan ras el hanout (page 298), North African *bahārāt* (page 296), and Iranian *advieh*.

TRADITIONAL USES

Ash-e mast (chilled yogurt soup)—Iran (Persia)
Advieh (rice spice)—Iran (Persia)
Rose water—Middle East
Rahat loukoum (sweets)—Turkey
Kulfi (ice cream or ice pop)—India

NOTE
Toasting not recommended

RECOMMENDED PAIRINGS
Hot cider
Stuffed onion
Rice with dried fruit
Braised lamb shoulder
Strawberry shortcake

SPICE PAIRINGS
Aleppo, basil, caraway, ginger, pink pepperberries

RECIPE IDEAS
1. Stir rose buds into simmering red wine and use as
a base for fruit punch or sangria.
2. For a floral mousse or cake garnish, incorporate ground rose buds
or leaves into whipped cream and mix with melted white chocolate.
3. Sprinkle ground rose buds or leaves into simmering chicken stock
and use to cook rice or farro.

QUICK BLEND
Vered

See photograph, page 233.

Season diced dried apricots with this sweet and savory blend,
soak in sherry wine, and use a condiment to serve with cheese.
This mix also gives stuffed grape leaves a floral twist.

Makes about ⅓ cup/28 grams

½ cup/15 grams dried rose buds, ground
½ tablespoon/5 grams nigella seeds
½ tablespoon/3 grams ground ginger
1 teaspoon/3 grams caraway seeds, ground
Scant ¾ teaspoon/2 grams black peppercorns, coarsely ground

ROSEMARY

ROSMARINUS OFFICINALIS

A versatile, woody herb with needle-like leaves

FLAVOR & AROMA I have a hard time going shopping for rosemary when I think of the endless quantities still growing on my family's farm in Israel. At La Boîte, I source my rosemary from Israel and Turkey, so I'm still enjoying the benefits of home in some small way.

Rosemary is one of the most versatile herbs, easily cooked or used raw in seemingly endless ways. I love its light resin notes, acidity, and oily scent. When dried, the piney leaves deliver a great crunchy texture to meats and baked goods. The stems, which are often overlooked, can be used as aromatic skewers. You can dry your own rosemary for grilling by leaving a bunch or two on a tray on your kitchen counter for a few days.

ORIGIN ☞ Native to the Mediterranean, Portugal, and northwestern Spain ☞ Cultivated in countries around the Mediterranean Sea; other parts of Europe, including England; as well as the United States and Mexico

HARVEST SEASON Rosemary is a hardy, woody perennial shrub whose sprigs can be cut throughout the year. Edible light blue flowers bloom throughout the warmer seasons, but mostly in early spring and late winter. Leaves are dried in the shade or frozen.

PARTS USED Leaves, sprigs, stems, and flowers

ABOUT A member of the mint (Lamiaceae) family, rosemary is at the heart of a number of legends and superstitions. It is considered the symbol of remembrance—just ask *Hamlet*'s Ophelia. Even in ancient Greece, scholars wore garlands made of rosemary when studying for exams.

But aside from its place in legend, it would be hard to forget this instantly recognizable aromatic herb. It has been an essential flavoring in Mediterranean cuisine since the time of the early Greeks and Romans, particularly in French, Spanish, and Italian dishes (and in some cases Greek). You will find whole sprigs or leaves in the French seasoning bouquet garni, as well as in dishes like mutton, broiled poultry, and pork, or baked goods. It also imparts an herbal element to the liqueurs Bénédictine and older versions of the gold-laced Danziger Goldwasser.

In Mediterranean and American cuisines, it is a popular addition to vegetables, soups, tomato sauce, fish, flavored olive oils and vinegars, marinades, mashed or roasted potatoes, and savory piecrusts. It even makes an indelible impression in sweets like shortbread and sugar cookies.

TRADITIONAL USES
Focaccia bread—Italy
Bistecca Fiorentina (Tuscan steak)—Italy
Herbes de Provence (spice blend)—France
Kotopoulo me dendrolivano (rosemary chicken)—Greece
Meat loaf—United States

NOTE
Toasting not recommended

RECOMMENDED PAIRINGS
Cheese biscuits
Prosecco cocktail
Roasted sunchokes
Fried chicken wings
Carrot cake

SPICE PAIRINGS
black pepper, cayenne, celery seeds, poppy seeds, yellow mustard

RECIPE IDEAS
1. Incorporate ground rosemary into your favorite madeleine cookie recipe and serve with fresh lemon custard.
2. Marinate duck legs with dried rosemary leaves to make a duck confit.
3. Stir ground rosemary into simmering milk and use to cook polenta or potato purée.

QUICK BLEND
Romani

This slightly sweet and acidic blend is great for seasoning diced boneless chicken thighs and bell pepper before threading them on skewers and grilling. It also adds a bit of heat and an herbaceous element to sautéed parsnips.

Makes about ⅓ cup/29 grams

¾ cup/15 grams dried rosemary leaves, coarsely ground
½ tablespoon/5 grams black peppercorns, coarsely ground
½ tablespoon/5 grams yellow mustard seeds, coarsely ground
1 teaspoon/2 grams ground cinnamon
Scant ¾ teaspoon/2 grams ground sumac

SAFFLOWER

CARTHAMUS TINCTORIUS

*A musky, sweet flower often confused
with the pricier saffron*

FLAVOR & AROMA Safflower, or "cheap saffron" as many would call it, has a warm scent, sweet notes, and great color. I mainly source mine from India, and I like it for its floral and slight musky elements. It imparts its dark orange color effectively and without the pungency of saffron (page 238). Plus it costs much less.

ORIGIN ☞ Native to parts of Western Asia and Africa ☞ Cultivated mainly in India, but also in the United States, Canada, Australia, Israel, and Turkey

HARVEST SEASON Safflower is a thistle-like annual in the daisy (Asteraceae) family, with spiny leaves and bracts with yellow to red petals. Flowers are harvested in the late summer, when most of the leaves turn brown and the stems are nearly dry. The petals are then sun-dried and crushed.

PARTS USED Dried flowers

ABOUT What is commonly known as a familiar source of vegetable oil has been used as a flavoring as well as a textile dye for thousands of years. Even King Tut's tomb is said to have been adorned with a crimson safflower garland.

Safflower's spiky yellow-orange flowers so closely resemble the more expensive saffron that it has earned the names false saffron or bastard saffron and is regularly sold deceptively as an imposter. I often meet people who come back from trips around the world all excited about a great deal they made by buying cheap saffron in bulk, only to be disappointed when I tell them they bought safflower. How to know the difference? Safflower petals give soups and broths an orange color, whereas saffron offers a redder hue. Saffron threads are also thinner and not as straight as safflower.

While Western cultures are not as quick to use safflower in cooking, it is an essential ingredient in many other cuisines, including Indian stews and rice dishes, Portuguese fish stews and sauces, as well as a number of dishes in Middle Eastern, Azerbaijani, and Syrian cookery.

TRADITIONAL USES

Safflower-flavored oil—Worldwide
Safflower yellow rice—Worldwide
Piti (lamb stew with chickpeas)—Azerbaijan
Preserved lemons—Middle East
Fish stew—Portugal

NOTE

Toasting not recommended

RECOMMENDED PAIRINGS

 Mango chutney
 Pumpkin soup
 Cheddar cheese sauce
 Chickpea purée
 Boiled potatoes

SPICE PAIRINGS

asafoetida, cardamom, ginger, fennel, lemon peel

RECIPE IDEAS

1. Sprinkle safflower into boiling salted water
and use to cook your favorite pasta.

2. For a poached salmon accompaniment, mix ground
safflower with mayonnaise, lime juice, and tarragon.

3. Combine ground safflower with apple cider vinegar, sugar,
and salt and use to make pickled cauliflower.

QUICK BLEND
Gul Rang

Add this pungent blend to coconut milk and use to cook
an eggplant and mushroom curry or incorporate it into
flatbread dough for a touch of color.

Makes about ½ cup/34 grams

¾ cup/15 grams safflower flowers, ground
1⅓ tablespoons/10 grams dried onion slices, coarsely ground
½ tablespoon/5 grams black mustard seeds, ground
1 teaspoon/3 grams ground amchoor
2 leaves/1 gram fenugreek leaves, ground

SAFFRON

CROCUS SATIVUS

The pricey, but worth it, dried stigma of a crocus flower

FLAVOR & AROMA Although originally believed to be from Greece, most saffron grows in European countries, including Spain, France, and Austria, as well as other parts of the world, such as Kashmir and Iran. Because of political and economic regulations, Iranian saffron is not always available, so I use Spanish and Afghan saffron. The quality is just as great.

For many years, I didn't care much for saffron. I think that's because I didn't grow up with it. It is just too expensive. It takes 150 plants to yield only 1 gram of saffron.

But with its hay-like scent, floral sweet notes, and ability to act as a great coloring agent, saffron has earned my appreciation. At La Boîte, I grind the saffron into powder to add a layer of complexity to my blends. Saffron is best enjoyed when cooking rather than used in cold dishes, and I feel it should be steeped into warm or hot liquid to really develop its flavor and color. When buying saffron, look for a uniform red color (when possible) and whole stamens without powder or broken pieces in the packaging. As great as saffron is, it can be overwhelming if you use too much.

ORIGIN ☞ Native to Western Asia and the Mediterranean ☞ Cultivated in parts of India, Europe, and the Middle East

HARVEST SEASON Crocus bulbs are planted by hand in June, and the three red stigmas of each purple flower are manually harvested in the fall, when the flowers bloom at dawn.

PARTS USED Dried whole flower stigmas

ABOUT Most consider the crocus bloom a sign of spring, but the saffron crocus is a maverick in the crocus (Iridaceae) family, pushing its purple petals up through the turning fall leaves. It is said to be native to Western Asia, but it was originally cultivated in Greece and has a long history in ancient Persia. Saffron stigmas, or threads, have been used for thousands of years to treat illnesses, as a dye, and for weaving into fabrics like the original robes worn by Buddhist and Hindu monks. It has also been used for perfumes, potions, and to impart its reddish-yellow color to food. Alexander the Great, taking his cue from the Persians, would bathe in saffron-colored waters, convinced it would cure his battle wounds during the Asian campaigns. Its rarity and labor-intensive cultivation made it a sought-after treasure for divinities and explorers throughout history.

Today, the backbreaking harvesting methods haven't changed—farmers are literally bent in half from dawn throughout early day picking flowers by hand and later plucking the three stigmas from each. And where there's hard work, there are swindlers trying to make a quick buck. It is not uncommon to find inferior-quality saffron dyed to the vibrant, even color of its high-quality counterparts. And if you think you're getting an amazing price on a large quantity, you might actually be taking home a bag of safflower (page 236).

Not all saffron is created equal: there are different strengths or grades to consider. The strength is determined by age and how much of the yellow style is still attached to the red stigma. Iranian grades are *sargol* (the strongest grade, with only red stigmas), *pushal* (a lower strength, with some of the yellow style), *bunch* (even lower strength, with much more of the yellow style), and *konge* (all yellow style, none of the stigma). Spanish saffron is graded similarly: *coupe* is the strongest, followed by *mancha, río, standard,* and *sierra.* Authentic Spanish Azafrán de la Mancha, which is only grown in La Mancha, has a protected denomination (PDO), so you always know what you are getting.

TRADITIONAL USES

Paella (Valencian rice dish)—Spain
Bouillabaisse (traditional Provençal fish stew)—France
Risotto alla Milanese (creamy rice dish)—Italy
Mughal biryani (aromatic chicken or lamb and
rice dish)—India
Shole zard (saffron rice pudding)—Iran (Persia)

NOTE
Toasting not recommended

RECOMMENDED PAIRINGS
Gin and tonic
Crab bisque
Apple aioli
Fennel purée
Panna cotta

SPICE PAIRINGS
basil, cayenne, mustard, onion, paprika

RECIPE IDEAS
1. Confit salmon fillets in warm olive oil with saffron stamens.
2. Infuse simmering milk with saffron stamens and
a few minced garlic cloves to enrich a potato gratin.
3. In a blender, purée warm sautéed apricots with saffron stamens
and a splash of brandy for a sweet dessert sauce.

QUICK BLEND
Azafrán

Pair this fresh, fennel-scented blend with grated cheddar cheese
and use this mixture to season creamy polenta. It also gives
complexity and color to poached salted cod and potatoes.

Makes about 1 tablespoon/10 grams

½ tablespoon/1 gram saffron stamens, ground
1½ heaping teaspoons/5 grams fennel seeds, toasted and ground
Scant ¾ teaspoon/2 grams ground sweet paprika
½ teaspoon/1 gram ajowan seeds, ground
½ teaspoon/1 gram ground ginger

SAGE

SALVIA OFFICINALIS

A piney, astringent spice from the leaves of the sage plant

FLAVOR & AROMA For some reason, sage is not widely used in the United States except during the holiday season, when it is really put to work on roasted turkeys and in savory stuffing. Sage has a pine scent and herbaceous notes and can even be a bit bitter. It also tends to be very dominant, but if used correctly, it can elevate a simple recipe.

In the Mediterranean, it is often paired with fish, poultry, and even pasta dishes. I love to infuse it in stews and soups, and add it when grilling or searing meat at high heat. It is one of the herbs that is just as interesting dry as it is when fresh. I get my sage from Turkey and Greece, and the leaves are readily available whole or ground.

ORIGIN ☞ Native to the Mediterranean region ☞ Cultivated in Central Europe (mainly Yugoslavia and Albania)

HARVEST SEASON Common sage is a perennial herb in the mint (Lamiaceae) family, with leathery, gray-green pebbled leaves, which are harvested as needed from spring to fall, or year-round in places where winter frosts are more forgiving. Edible blossoms can be picked in late spring.

PARTS USED Leaves and flowers

ABOUT There are a host of sage varieties in varying colors and shapes, each of which offers a slightly different aroma and taste. Mexican, pineapple (you can guess what it smells like), Greek, guava, purple, tricolor, and Peruvian sage are just a few. Common sage, which also goes by garden sage or true sage, has a long history of culinary and medicinal use. Its attractive, aromatic foliage has made it a popular ornamental plant for gardens and landscapes as well.

As a native of the Mediterranean, sage is not surprisingly found mostly in the traditional recipes of the cuisines in and around that region. In Italy, whole sage leaves are placed over veal topped with slices of prosciutto and is often marinated in wine before being cooked to make saltimbocca, which means "jumps in the mouth." Whole leaves are also fried in butter for a luscious gnocchi or pasta sauce, or added fresh or dried to polenta and baked goods.

Its intense notes and ability to cut the flavor of rich meats like pork, duck, and goose also make sage one of the most important ingredients in sausages, specifically the sage-forward pork variety from England's Lincolnshire. It's also credited with giving Sage Derby cheese its signature flavor—though its marbled green color is more of a food coloring special effect in what you find today. Britain and the United States share a common love for sage and onion stuffing. Though less commonly used, fresh edible sage blossoms add a nice visual and flavorful element when used to season salads or softened butter.

FAMILIAR USES

Grilled fish
Meat stuffing
Sage cookies
Roasted poultry
Butter and sage sauce

NOTE

Toasting not recommended

RECOMMENDED PAIRINGS

☞ Red wine–mushroom sauce
🫘 Braised butter beans
🌾 Wheat berry risotto
🍆 Eggplant parmigiana
🐖 Pork ragù

SPICE PAIRINGS

basil, caraway, juniper, lemon peel, nutmeg

RECIPE IDEAS

1. Stir ground sage leaves into cooked rice and ground pork
and use to stuff green cabbage leaves.
2. Elevate diced orange and grapefruit marmalade
by adding dried sage leaves before cooking.
3. Combine mashed baked potatoes with ground sage
leaves and use as a base for gnocchi.

QUICK BLEND
Marva

Season roasted venison tenderloin with this warm, herbaceous
blend and serve it with chestnuts and celery root. It also
offers its pine scent to apple cider–braised red cabbage.

Makes about 3 tablespoons/13 grams

1½ tablespoons/5 grams dried sage leaves, coarsely ground
1 teaspoon/3 grams freshly grated nutmeg
Scant ¾ teaspoon/2 grams dried juniper berries, coarsely ground
Scant ¾ teaspoon/2 grams caraway seeds, ground
½ teaspoon/1 gram ground cinnamon

SALT

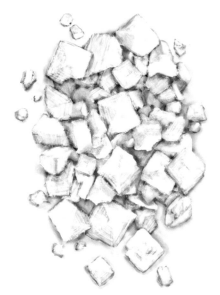

The most ubiquitous mineral, used in kitchens around the world

FLAVOR & AROMA Salt is probably the one spice found in nearly every kitchen in the world. When someone tells me he doesn't use spices, I tell him that if he has salt, he uses spices. Along with heat and acidity, it is one of the basic flavors in a great dish. Salt could be, and has been, the subject of its own book. Here I will cover only what is most important and relevant to home cooks.

The two major salt distinctions I find most helpful to consider—there are others—are mine salt and sea salt. As simple as it sounds, one is dug in a mine on land and the other is harvested from the sea. I like to say the primary difference is that mine salt has a sulfur scent and taste while sea salt has more elements of natural iodine. In the case of black salt, it is actually sea salt mixed with ground lava rock. At La Boîte, I use only sea salt: fine sea salt, gray salt, flaky Maldon salt, kosher salt, and fleur de sel. I always keep a little of each handy and choose one according to the dish I am making.

Not every salt tastes as salty as the next. The process of cleaning the harvested salt and the size of the grain make this distinction. The more salt is washed, the more elements like iodine disappear, bringing the salty flavor to the forefront. Also, smaller grains dissolve faster in your mouth, so that sensation is much more obvious. It is therefore important that you choose the type, or types, of salt that best suit the dish you are making. Maldon and fleur de sel are very delicate, so it would be

a waste to use them to salt water for blanching. On the other hand, they are perfect for a final seasoning, adding texture too. These differences also make it important to use the type of salt specified in a recipe—or to make adjustments accordingly—to make sure you are not over- or undersalting your dish.

ORIGIN ☞ Found worldwide ☞ Harvested mainly in China, the United States, the Mediterranean, and the west coast of France

HARVEST SEASON Year-round

PARTS USED Crystals

ABOUT Salt is a mineral composed mainly of sodium chloride, and it's everywhere. Found in dried-up ancient underground seabeds, lakes, and, most obviously, our vast oceans and seas, it is as prominent in the world as it is important to all living things.

Salt has been around since before recorded history, first consumed by early hunters through their meat. As civilization grew, so did the need for this coveted mineral, giving way to worldwide trading routes—from Morocco to Timbuktu, and the Via Salaria (salt road), which ran between Rome and the salt-rich Adriatic Sea. Because its production was restricted in ancient times, it became a method of trade, currency, and tax; soldiers were paid a salary, a word derived from *sal,* the Latin word for salt. During the times well before modern refrigeration, it was—and still is (think salt cod)—used as a preservation method. Canned and pickled foods as well as some meats and fish rely on it to keep them shelf stable for long periods.

There are three main ways of producing salt: solution mining, deep-shaft mining, or solar evaporation. Most table salt is a product of solution mining, where water is added to salt beds to dissolve the salt into brine and then pumped out to a plant where it is evaporated. Most rock salt, like pink Himalayan salt, comes from the deep-shaft mining of ancient underground sea beds, much like the mining of other minerals. Solar evaporation happens about once a year in the Mediterranean countries, Austria, and other places with similar low-rain, high-sun climates. The wind and sun do all the work, leaving salt behind in shallow pools to be harvested. In the case of fleur de sel, its delicate flakes are hand-harvested for their unmatched ability to finish any dish.

QUICK GUIDE TO SEA SALTS

Fine Sea Salt
Attributes: Small grain
Best for: Everyday use, in every dish

Fleur de sel
Attributes: Delicate flavor; medium grain
Best for: Final touch seasoning

Gray Salt
Attributes: High iodine scent; coarse, large grain
Best for: Roasting, heavy cooking,
blanching water, and dressings

Kosher Salt
Attributes: Low on scent; medium grain
Best for: Everyday use

Maldon
Attributes: Delicate flavor; thin, delicate flakes
Best for: Final touch seasoning

NOTE
Toasting not recommended

RECOMMENDED PAIRINGS
Cured salmon
Salt-baked potatoes
Beef carpaccio
Salted caramel sauce
Chocolate milk shake

SPICE PAIRINGS
cayenne, juniper, orange peel, rosemary, sesame

RECIPE IDEAS
1. Mix medium-grain sea salt with sour cream and
ground cinnamon to serve with waffles.
2. Combine coarse gray salt with egg whites and flour
to form a crust on whole celery root while baking.
3. Blend coarse sea salt with dried thyme leaves and chile flakes
and use to coat whole beets for roasting.

FAMILIAR USES
Caviar—Worldwide
Pretzels—Worldwide
Margarita cocktails—Mexico
Fish in salt crust—France
Prosciutto—Italy

QUICK BLEND
Sal

Sprinkle this coarse blend over thin slices of raw salmon
and serve with shaved radishes and orange segments.
It also adds a peppery, nutty flavor to fresh avocado salad.

Makes about ¼ cup/35 grams

1 tablespoon/15 grams fleur de sel, or medium-grain sea salt
1 tablespoon/10 grams sesame seeds, toasted
1 tablespoon/5 grams Sichuan pepper, coarsely ground
1 teaspoon/3 grams granulated dried orange peel
1 teaspoon/2 grams anise seeds, ground

SANSHŌ

ZANTHOXYLUM PIPERITUM

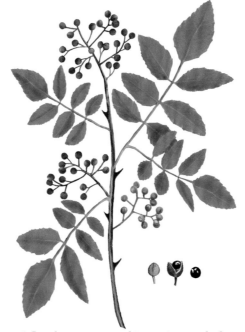

A floral, tongue-numbing spice made from the berries of the Japanese prickly ash tree

---

FLAVOR & AROMA The sanshō pepper is related to Sichuan pepper (page 254), but I find it has more citrus and grassy notes and a floral aroma. After you've eaten it, sanshō creates a light numbness on your tongue (similar to Sichuan), and I find that this effect highlights other flavors, creating a sort of sweet taste even in the absence of any sweet ingredients. It is almost a one-stop-shop spice since it offers heat, acidity, and sweetness all in one.

What also makes the sanshō tree unique is that the leaves are as flavorful as the berries, and they are either sold ground together or separately. Whichever part you use, I think dried sanshō is best when added to raw or finished dishes rather than used for cooking; it tends to lose its aromatic, floral notes when heated.

ORIGIN ☞ Native to Japan ☞ Cultivated in Japan, China, and Korea

HARVEST SEASON Sanshō trees are in the same family as citrus (rue or Rutaceae) and bloom yellow-green flowers in the spring; male flower buds are an edible short-season delicacy known as *hana-sanshō*. Female flowers give way to green berries that can be harvested for fresh use or left on the tree to turn auburn in the fall, when they are harvested, sun-dried, and their bitter black seeds removed. The young tree shoots and leaves, called *kinome*, are harvested in the spring when still soft.

PARTS USED Berries (or seedpods), leaves, male flowers, and young shoots

ABOUT Most of the Japanese prickly ash tree is edible, though these mouth-tingling ingredients are barely used outside of the tree's native home—but that may be about to change. Each ingredient offers up something unique worth exploring. *Kinome,* the 2-inch ends of branches, are a sign of spring used to garnish vegetables like *takenoko* (bamboo

shoots) and *fuki* (Japanese butterbur stalk) and to brighten soups with hints of lemon. When dried or powered, they bring heat to noodle dishes, soups, and various fish dishes and are sometimes mixed with bonito flakes.

In May, tiny, green *hana-sanshō* (sansho flowers) make a short-lived debut, offering even more heat than the leaves, and yet they still do not hold a candle to the fiery berries. *Sanshō no mi* (immature, fresh, bright green berries) are hard to find outside of Japan. If you were there, you would easily see bags of them disappearing from shelves during peak season. Typically, they are simmered in soy sauce or blanched and salted and served with fish over rice.

When dried and ground, sanshō berries offer a sharp, electrifying flavor that lingers long after you eat them. Traditionally, ground sanshō is served alongside unagi (grilled eel) and imparts an essential and distinctive flavor to the Japanese seven-spice blend *shichimi tōgarashi*. In Japan, it is commonly used as a table condiment to sprinkle over rich fatty meats, poultry, and fish.

TRADITIONAL USES
Authentic to Japan
Tako (braised octopus)
Chicken *yakitori* (skewered grilled chicken)
Miso ramen (noodle dish)
Takenoko no kinomeae (bamboo shoots)
Iri-dofu (scrambled tofu)

QUICK BLEND
Kinome

For a fresh take on a corn, avocado, and salmon salad, use this blend to season the chilled flaked fish before serving. It is also a subtle way to add a spicy, citrusy element to shrimp tacos.

Makes about ¼ cup/25 grams

2 tablespoons/10 grams ground sanshō berries
½ tablespoon/5 grams granulated dried orange peel
½ tablespoon/5 grams black sesame seeds, toasted
1 teaspoon/3 grams celery seeds
1 teaspoon/2 grams clove, ground

NOTE
Toasting not recommended

RECOMMENDED PAIRINGS
Avocado toast
Orange vinaigrette
Edamame purée
Hamachi sashimi
Plum tart

SPICE PAIRINGS
clove, ginger, mace, orange peel, sesame

RECIPE IDEAS
1. Combine equal amounts of sugar and ground sanshō and use to cook red fruit jam.
2. Mix ground sanshō with pitted fresh cherries and white balsamic vinegar and serve with mascarpone cheese.
3. Dust freshly baked chocolate chip cookies or brownies with ground sanshō blended with confectioners' sugar.

SASSAFRAS

SASSAFRAS ALBIDUM

The root beer–scented leaves and root of the sassafras tree

FLAVOR & AROMA I only learned of sassafras when I moved to the United States in 2002. In Louisiana, the leaves are still used to make filé powder, the traditional thickening agent in gumbo. Sassafras also imparts some cooling, citrus notes and a touch of bitterness. The root, which is a bit woody with a camphor-like aroma and hints of licorice, can be ground and has more recently become popular in the cocktail domain for the bitterness it brings. A touch of ground leaves or roots can deliver herbaceous elements to soups and stews or grilled meats, and I find that they are best used in long-cooked dishes rather than cold ones. However, fresh young leaves and flowers are an elegant finish for crisp salads.

ORIGIN ☞ Native to and cultivated in eastern North America

HARVEST SEASON Sassafras is a medium-size dioecious tree in the laurel (Lauraceae) family with green aromatic leaves that can have one, two, or three lobes. Leaves are harvested spring through early fall, then dried and ground. Twigs and roots can be harvested at any time.

PARTS USED Dried leaves, roots, and bark or twigs

ABOUT In the sixteenth and seventeenth centuries, early European settlers in the eastern United States were introduced to sassafras by Native Americans, who had long been using the aromatic plant for medicinal purposes and as a flavoring for sassafras tea. The leaves and roots became essential ingredients in two foods native to the United States: gumbo (a thick, spicy shellfish or meat stew) and root beer (the best accompaniment to vanilla ice cream). The blend of French, Spanish, African, and Native American cultures that form the flavor-packed Creole and Cajun cuisines of Louisiana use sassafras as a star ingredient to this day.

People still think sassafras root and its oils are used to make root beer, confectioneries, and pharmaceuticals, but the FDA actually banned its use in mass production in 1960; its high content of safrole was proven to have carcinogenic effects. It is still approved for home cooking in small quantities. Today, root beer gets its familiar taste from artificial flavors, wintergreen oil, or sassafras extracts with the safrole distilled and removed.

TRADITIONAL USES
Authentic to the United States
Filé powder
Sassafras candy
Cured meats
Jelly
Syrup

NOTE
Toasting not recommended

RECOMMENDED PAIRINGS
Cioppino
Root beer glaze
Okra stew
Braised pork shanks
Sorbet

SPICE PAIRINGS
cayenne, ginger, lemongrass, nutmeg, vanilla

RECIPE IDEAS
1. Add ground sassafras to simmering sweet-tart pomegranate juice and use to poach fresh figs.
2. Make an interesting roux with melted warm butter seasoned with sassafras before you add the flour.
3. Combine mayonnaise with ground sassafras, cayenne, and lemon juice for a fried catfish condiment.

QUICK BLEND
New Filé

Season rabbit legs with this blend before braising them with white wine and mustard. It also gives whole roasted turkey breast an entirely new twist.

Makes about ⅓ cup/20 grams

¼ cup/10 grams ground sassafras leaves
½ tablespoon/3 grams ground ginger
½ tablespoon/3 grams sliced dried onions, coarsely ground
1 teaspoon/3 grams ground sweet paprika
Scant ½ teaspoon/1 gram cayenne powder

SAVORY

SUMMER SAVORY (SATUREJA HORTENSIS)
WINTER SAVORY (SATUREJA MONTANA)

*Two peppery, sweet spices that peak
at different seasons*

———

FLAVOR & AROMA Savory is a bit of a forgotten spice. Although you will find it in nearly every farmers' market or supermarket, few recipes call for it and so most cooks are confused as to what to do with it. Its scent is similar to that of thyme (somewhat camphorous), but it has a peppery taste with some oregano and bitter notes akin to those of ajowan (page 40). Summer savory is sweeter and less penetrating than winter savory, and its fresh leaves are softer and not as pointy.

When dried, both complement roasted vegetables, legumes, roasted meat, and fish. Savory holds up well to high heat, which makes it a great grilling spice. It is also a common ingredient in sausages and in some herbes de Provence recipes. It dries quickly and well and can be kept in a jar for many months. I buy Israeli and Turkish savory and use the dried whole or coarsely ground leaves in my blends.

ORIGIN ☞ Native to the Mediterranean region, including southern Europe and North Africa ☞ Cultivated in England, France, Germany, Spain, Kashmir, Yugoslavia, Canada, and the United States

HARVEST SEASON Summer savory is an annual plant that grows up to 2 feet tall and flowers July through September. Leaves can be harvested throughout the growing period, but when used for preserving, they are best picked at their peak, when blooms are just beginning to appear. Winter savory is an evergreen bushy perennial with bright green leaves that should be harvested before the white or soft purple flowers bloom in the spring. Alternatively, young side shoots can be reaped year-round. Older leaves along the woody branches can become tough and leathery.

PARTS USED Leaves, young sprigs, and flowers

ABOUT Savory is a member of the mint family (Lamiaceae) and began its journey in the Mediterranean before the Romans brought it to Britain during the time of Caesar. The Romans were said to have used winter savory in vinegars and sauces, believing it to be an aphrodisiac—as the name, derived from "satyr's herb," suggests. It is still used in vinegars and pickling liquid to this day.

Savory gained popularity in Europe, joining the ranks of other spices like basil, thyme, and marjoram, and even catching the eye of Charlemagne, who planted it in his imperial gardens. It is the early colonists who we can thank for its import to North America, where it thrives today and where it is found perking up the annual holiday stuffing.

This highly aromatic herb is often associated with beans, lentils, and peas, as its German name, *Bohnenkraut,* or "bean herb," suggests; the fact that it has been known to help with digestion makes the name even more sensible. Savory is also often found in the French fines herbes and German versions of bouquet garni and is indispensable in Bulgarian cuisine, where it is one of the country's three table condiments along with salt and paprika; when mixed together, the combo is known as *sharena sol,* or "colorful salt." It is also frequently used in the Acadian comfort foods of Atlantic Canada, including meat pies, grilled meats, and stews. Savory has even been known to make an appearance in cocktails in the form of the flavored herbal liqueurs amaro (winter savory) and vermouth (summer savory).

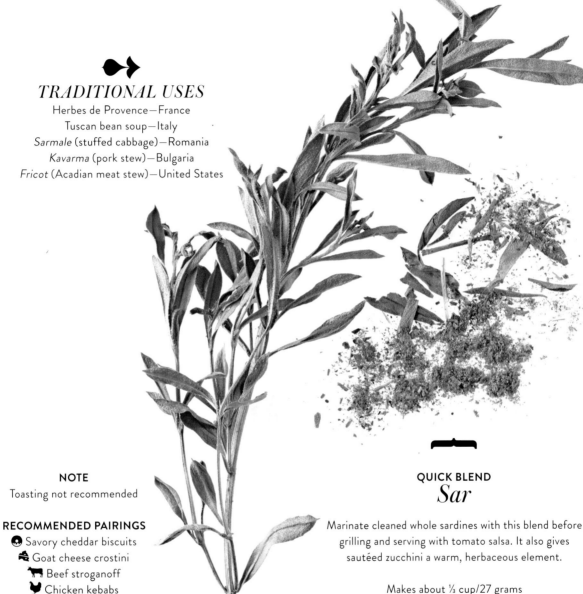

TRADITIONAL USES

Herbes de Provence—France
Tuscan bean soup—Italy
Sarmale (stuffed cabbage)—Romania
Kavarma (pork stew)—Bulgaria
Fricot (Acadian meat stew)—United States

NOTE

Toasting not recommended

RECOMMENDED PAIRINGS

Savory cheddar biscuits
Goat cheese crostini
Beef stroganoff
Chicken kebabs
Baked trout

SPICE PAIRINGS

black pepper, clove, garlic, lavender, mustard

RECIPE IDEAS

1. Season a whole peeled celery root with olive oil, salt, and a handful of dried savory leaves before roasting until tender.
2. Add ground savory leaves to feta cheese and use in a potato and egg frittata.
3. Combine ground turkey with shallots, Dijon mustard, and ground savory leaves for a flavorful turkey burger.

QUICK BLEND
Sar

Marinate cleaned whole sardines with this blend before grilling and serving with tomato salsa. It also gives sautéed zucchini a warm, herbaceous element.

Makes about ⅓ cup/27 grams

Scant ½ cup/15 grams dried savory leaves, ground
1 lime/5 grams black Omani lime, ground
½ tablespoon/3 grams cumin seeds, toasted and ground
½ tablespoon/3 grams coriander seeds, toasted and coarsely ground
Scant ½ teaspoon/1 gram cayenne powder

SESAME

SESAMUM INDICUM

A nutty, oil-rich spice made from tiny tear-shaped seeds

—

FLAVOR & AROMA Sesame seeds are used commonly around the world, but they aren't always thought of as a spice. They are usually sprinkled on breads, bagels, or crackers, and I often think people use them more for their visual appeal than their actual flavor. But sesame seeds shouldn't be overlooked on that front; they are very rich in oil and have a great nutty sweet taste. Of the thousands of varieties in an array of colors like gold, brown, reddish, gray, black, and white, I use the black and white ones.

Seeds can be bought in their natural state with the skin on or hulled with the skin removed, which are whiter in color. I prefer the former since they deliver more taste. There are many varieties, but the two you will find are white (or off-white) and black. The difference to me is more visual than anything else. You can use either as is, but I think sesame seeds are always better when toasted to further develop their nutty flavor. At La Boîte, I often use sesame seeds whole to impart both taste and texture or grind them to use as a thickening agent in blends. Because they are so rich in oil, however, there is a risk of oxidation. Blends with sesame seeds can go rancid if kept too long, especially if the seeds are already ground.

ORIGIN ☞ Native to India ☞ Cultivated mainly in India, Myanmar, and China, but also Africa, Burma, Sudan, the Middle East, the Balkans, Latin America, and the United States

HARVEST SEASON Sesame seeds come from an annual plant in the sesame (Pedaliaceae) family, with white to pale pink flowers. The original scattering varieties open when dry, requiring considerable hand harvesting before fully ripe to prevent loss (hence "open sesame"). These varieties are threshed 2 weeks after harvesting. Scatter-resistant types, which were only developed in the mid-twentieth century, allow for mechanized combine harvesting 90 to 150 days from planting and before the frost. They are then dried and sometimes hulled.

PARTS USED Dried hulled or unhulled seeds

ABOUT Sesame seeds boast the highest oil content of any seed in the world, and they have been cultivated since antiquity. At least four thousand years ago, the seeds were prized as an oil crop in Babylon and Assyria, and ancient Egyptians were said to use ground sesame as grain flour predating Moses.

Sesame seeds are very nutritious and high in protein. They have been a staple ingredient in Middle Eastern, Asian, Indian, and African cuisines for as long as they have been cultivated. These seeds are an essential ingredient in Middle Eastern dishes like tahini, the paste that helps flavor hummus, as well as a sweet confection called halva. The seeds are a main component in the famous za'atar spice blend, Chinese sesame paste and *jian dui* pastries, and Japanese *gomashio* (sesame seed and salt condiment). In Europe and the United States, you'll mostly find them sprinkled over bread, baked into crackers, or made into sesame seed candy.

TRADITIONAL USES

Bagels—United States
Pasteli (sesame candy)—Greece
Dukkah (herbs, nuts, and spices condiment)—Egypt
Til ka ladoo (cardamom and sesame sweets)—India
Shichimi tōgarashi (spice blend)—Japan

NOTE

Toasting recommended

RECOMMENDED PAIRINGS

Granola
Napa cabbage slaw
Korean noodle salad
Crusted tuna steak
Chicken croquettes

SPICE PAIRINGS

ginger, oregano, poppy seeds, sumac, wasabi

RECIPE IDEAS

1. Grind a handful of toasted whole white sesame seeds
with a few pinches of unsweetened cocoa powder and use
to thicken sherry vinaigrette.
2. For a quick batch of cheese straws, brush puff pastry strips
with egg wash, sprinkle with sesame seeds and grated
Parmesan cheese, and bake until crisp.
3. Combine toasted white and black sesame seeds
with freshly grated carrots and season with lime juice
and hot sauce to serve with roasted chicken.

QUICK BLEND
Soom Soom

Sprinkle this nutty, whole spice blend on top of beef
or salmon tartare and serve with flatbread. It also
adds a great crunch to whipped feta cheese.

Makes about 3 tablespoons/34 grams

1 tablespoon/10 grams black sesame seeds, toasted
½ tablespoon/15 grams white sesame seeds, toasted
½ tablespoon/5 grams ground sumac
1 teaspoon/3 grams caraway seeds, toasted and coarsely ground
Scant ½ teaspoon/1 gram Urfa or ancho chile flakes

SICHUAN PEPPER

ZANTHOXYLUM SIMULANS

The tongue-numbing, citrus-scented berry of a Chinese prickly ash tree

FLAVOR & AROMA Sichuan, or Szechuan, pepper is obtained from several local species in its genus throughout Asia. It is a staple of Chinese cuisine, the name of a province, and a style of cooking associated with its use. The Japanese sanshō (page 246) is a near relative of this spice and is often used interchangeably, but they impart very different flavors and aromas.

Sichuan pepper is not related to regular pepper (*Piper nigrum*; page 208), nor does it carry the same heat. When you eat Sichuan pepper, you initially get a pleasant, floral, warm, and citrusy aroma. The heat surprises your taste buds a bit later on, accompanied by a strange numbness on your tongue. It is one of the secret spices I use to deliver floral notes with a kick.

For the most part, only the berry's outer shell—where the pungency and aroma come from—is used, and the shiny black, often bitter and grainy seed is discarded, though I personally don't mind it. Typically, these peppers are toasted and crushed before being incorporated into a dish, usually just before serving. Sichuan pepper pairs well with citrus, ginger, and anything in the anise family. I also really enjoy how it plays with cinnamon.

ORIGIN ☞ Native to Sichuan province of China ☞ Cultivated throughout Asia

HARVEST SEASON Harvesting is done in early fall when the reddish-brown berries' shells begin to open, exposing the black seeds. The berries are sun-dried and the seeds are typically removed.

PARTS USED Dried berries

ABOUT Sichuan pepper comes from one of many varieties of prickly ash tree, all in the rue (Rutaceae) family, native to the Chinese province of the same name. Until recently, the USDA and the FDA had a ban on the importation of this mouth-tingling spice because of a virus it brought with it, ready to harm citrus crops wherever it landed. Thankfully, with a little heating (to 160°F) before shipping, it is now safe to import.

Now the world enjoys access to one of the key elements in Sichuan cuisine, which is made up of what is called *ma-la*. *La* is the inclusion of fiery red chiles that add a kick to the already tingly sensation the pepper (*ma*) imparts. The two flavors together work in symphony with other elements that add salty, smoky, sweet, bitter, and sour notes to create authentic Sichuan cuisine. It is so much more than just heat.

Sichuan pepper is essential to Chinese five-spice powder (page 296) and is often used as a table condiment in *hua joa yan* (a flavored salt) or on its own. It is also found in homemade *doubanjiang* (broad bean paste) and *shui zhu niu rou* or *shui zhu yu* (water-cooked beef or fish, respectively). It can be used to perk up stir-fried vegetables and grilled or roasted meats as well.

TRADITIONAL USES

Wuhan noodles—China
Hua jiao yan (pepper-salt condiment)—China
Saksang (spicy pork stew)—Indonesia
Momo (meat or cheese dumplings)—Tibet
Thukpa (noodle soup)—Tibet

NOTE
Toasting not recommended

RECOMMENDED PAIRINGS
Berry smoothie
Sweet potato casserole
Pork tacos
Battered fried shrimp
Pots de crème

SPICE PAIRINGS
cinnamon, ginger, mace, orange peel, pink pepperberries

RECIPE IDEAS
1. Mix ground Sichuan pepper with light brown sugar and use to make granola.
2. Combine ground Sichuan pepper with melted butter and maple syrup and drizzle over hot popcorn.
3. Season thinly sliced avocado with ground Sichuan pepper to serve with smoked salmon and toasted bread.

QUICK BLEND
Z-Pepper

Sprinkle this aromatic coarse blend over diced ripe pineapple, pulled cooked chicken, and lime juice for a salad. It also gives a little heat to fresh strawberries and yogurt sorbet.

Makes about ¼ cup/32 grams

3 tablespoons/15 grams Sichuan pepper, coarsely ground
1 tablespoon/5 grams ground ginger
½ tablespoon/5 grams granulated dried orange peel
½ tablespoon/5 grams white sesame seeds, toasted
2 teaspoons/2 grams dried pink pepperberries, coarsely ground

STAR ANISE

ILLICIUM VERUM

A sweet, licorice-scented spice made from distinct eight-pointed fruits

FLAVOR & AROMA If there were ever a spice competition based on looks, star anise might win it. Though it shares the same anethole component as anise or fennel seeds—the element that gives them their familiar licorice aroma and flavor—this flower- or star-shaped spice is much warmer and sweeter in taste. It also has floral notes with a touch of acidity that make it great when used whole in stews, soups, or roasts, or when ground and added to desserts, purées, and sauces. I like the fact that this spice works equally well in sweet and savory dishes. Use star anise sparingly—a little goes a long way.

ORIGIN ☞ Native to China and Vietnam ☞ Cultivated in the tropical areas of East Asia and Southeast Asia

HARVEST SEASON Star anise fruits grow on an evergreen tree in the schisandra (Schisandraceae) family that can live for many years, typically along streams or in damp areas. Fragrant yellowish-green or pink-red flowers give way to star-shaped fruits with about eight pointed sections, each of which is a seedpod. Fruits are harvested before they ripen (March to May and August to October) and are sun-dried until they become hard and woody.

PARTS USED Whole star anise (fruits)

ABOUT Star anise has been cultivated for thousands of years and used widely in the cuisines of India, China, Malaysia, and Indonesia. It has long been coveted for its rich, intense flavor, scent, and general good looks, and is used for cooking, in perfume, and for crafts. In fact, its Latin genus, *Illicium,* means "alluring." Star anise should not be confused with the similarly scented anise seed (*Pimpinella anisum,* page 54) or the highly toxic Japanese star anise (*Illicium anisatum*)—also alluring, but regretfully so. They are nearly impossible to tell apart, so be sure to buy from a reputable source.

Star anise is one of the main ingredients in Chinese five-spice powder (page 296), along with cloves, cinnamon, Sichuan pepper, and fennel seeds and is often used with poultry and pork dishes or chewed after meals to freshen breath. It is also found in Chinese red cooking (meat simmered for long periods in soy sauce and spices) and in the Lunar New Year's staple, Chinese marbled eggs, as well as in soups and Peking duck.

In Vietnamese cuisine, it is one of the main components in phở (rice noodle soup), and in India it is found in biryani (rice dish) and masala chai (spiced tea). Star anise also makes an appearance in alcoholic and nonalcoholic beverages and liqueurs, including *vin chaud* (French hot mulled wine), sambuca (Italian anise-flavored liqueur), pastis (French spirit), Thai iced tea, and some absinthe.

In the West, where you may only find star anise adorning a potpourri basket, it is underutilized as a spice. Occasionally, you may be lucky enough to see its iconic shape decorating fruit jams and compotes.

TRADITIONAL USES

Ouzo (aperitif)—Greece
Pastis (spirit)—France
Galliano (sweet herbal liqueur)—Italy
Garam masala (spice blend)—South India
Condensed sweet iced tea—Thailand

NOTE
Toasting not recommended

RECOMMENDED PAIRINGS
Rum punch
Chicken consommé
Roasted parsnips
Braised brisket
Poached pears

SPICE PAIRINGS
black pepper, cardamom, cinnamon, clove, pink pepperberries

RECIPE IDEAS
1. Season grated carrots with ground star anise,
fresh orange juice, and chopped cilantro for a fresh salad.
2. Infuse star anise in simple syrup and use to make
a cranberry cosmopolitan cocktail.
3. For a licorice-scented beet borscht, add ground
star anise while cooking.

QUICK BLEND
Badiane
See photograph, page 258.

Use this blend to season a whole duck before roasting it with
dried fruits and white wine. Add it to cranberry chutney
with orange zest for a sweetly spiced surprise.

Makes about ¼ cup/36 grams

12 pieces/24 grams whole star anise, ground
1 tablespoon/5 grams ground cinnamon, preferably Vietnamese
1 teaspoon/3 grams ground amchoor
1 teaspoon/2 grams coriander seeds, toasted and coarsely ground
Scant ¾ teaspoon/2 grams black peppercorns, coarsely ground

SUMAC

RHUS CORIARIA

An astringent, sour spice made from the red berries of a nonpoisonous plant

FLAVOR & AROMA I like to think of sumac as the Middle Eastern lemon powder or dry vinegar. In a time when citrus and lemon actually had a season—unlike today, when everything is available year-round—there was a need for a readily available acidic ingredient to brighten food. Also, because lemon juice is a liquid that can fade when cooked, sumac berries offer a more versatile souring agent that holds up better when heated. Sumac has acidic notes both in scent and taste, with a floral element and a dry, nearly tannic finish. It is great on raw dishes, meats, and fish, and the za'atar blend (page 290) would not exist without it.

As with paprika (page 202), there is a lot of importance placed on sumac's hue. Consumers expect sumac to be a deep burgundy color, but not every season delivers that—though the scent and taste remain constant, no matter the color. Along the way some "genius" came up with the idea that incorporating beet powder would fix the occasional color deficiency. The same guy probably suggested adding salt to help prevent clumps, because sumac is fairly humid. The result is that a majority of the product on the market

has a fair amount of coloring and salt added to it.

I work with a few companies in Turkey that sell us pure ground sumac, and it is still hard to buy whole berries in the quantities I use on a yearly basis. Also, because the dried berries are so hard to grind, they are usually ground at the source. I always look forward to visiting my family in Israel, where I can find whole berries at the spice market.

ORIGIN ☞ Native to the Mediterranean (particularly Italy and Sicily) and the Middle East (mainly Iran) and parts of Asia ☞ Cultivated and growing wild in the mountains of Sicily and Italy, as well as parts of Western Asia

HARVEST SEASON In the fall, white flowers give way to small, hairy, rust-colored berries that swell into dense clusters of drupes called sumac bobs. They are harvested before they ripen, dried in the sun, and left whole or ground into a russet-colored powder.

PARTS USED Dried berries

ABOUT Every time I mention sumac in the United States, someone asks me if it's poisonous. There are actually many varieties in the sumac (Anacardiaceae) family growing in the United States, most of which are not edible but are also not dangerous. What you want to stay far away from is poison sumac (*Toxicodendron vernix*).

It is said that the Romans cooked sumac down in a manner similar to how tamarind (page 262) is prepared in Indian cuisine. It was used as a souring agent for meat before the introduction of lemons. Sumac is predominantly found in Middle Eastern cuisine. In Iranian and Turkish cookery, it is rubbed on kebabs or stirred into rice dishes to add both color and acidity. It garnishes Arabic dishes like hummus and tahini and is used to season grilled fish in Syria. Berries can also be macerated in hot water to extract the liquid for recipes where lemon juice is called for, such as salad dressings, drinks, or marinades.

TRADITIONAL USES
Fattoush (bread salad)—Lebanon
Za'atar (spice blend)—Middle East
Rice pilaf—Iran (Persia)
Adana kebabs—Turkey
Sumac oil—Greece

NOTE
Toasting not recommended

RECOMMENDED PAIRINGS
Shallot vinaigrette
Crab and watermelon salad
Roasted artichokes
Shepherd's pie
Pear sorbet

SPICE PAIRINGS
caraway, cardamom, marjoram, poppy seeds, sesame seeds

RECIPE IDEAS
1. Season mascarpone cheese with ground sumac, honey, and olive oil and serve with waffles and fresh figs for breakfast.
2. Stir ground sumac into simmering water with sliced strawberries and thyme sprigs and serve chilled as a refreshing beverage.
3. Sprinkle steamed green beans with ground sumac and finish with olive oil and coarse sea salt.

QUICK BLEND
0g

See photograph, page 94.

Make a sardine or tuna escabeche with this blend, red pearl onions, and preserved lemons. It also adds an astringent element to halved radicchio heads when grilled.

Makes about 3 tablespoons/24 grams

1½ tablespoons/15 grams ground sumac
2 teaspoons/2 grams dried rosemary leaves, ground
½ tablespoon/3 grams cumin seeds, toasted and ground
1 teaspoon/3 grams fennel seeds, toasted and ground
Scant ¾ teaspoon/1 gram crushed Aleppo chile, or other mild chile flakes

TAMARIND

TAMARINDUS INDICA

The tart, acidic fruits of a tropical shade-giving tree

FLAVOR & AROMA You have probably walked pass the Asian aisle of your local store and noticed brown tamarind fruit or a jar of tamarind paste but never known what to make of either. Although tamarind is very popular in other parts of the world, it doesn't get much attention in the United States, outside of ethnic cuisine.

Originally from Africa, tamarind's dark-colored pulp has sour, tart notes. Most tamarind consumed is from ripe fruits—the less ripe it is, the more sour it will taste. The leaves are used as well, but mainly in countries where it grows. It can be sold whole, in a paste form, or as tamarind water. I use tamarind powder, which is made from the dried pulp. It keeps its scent and taste in long-cooked dishes but also imparts a great dark color and works as a natural thickener.

ORIGIN ☞ Native to tropical Africa ☞ Cultivated in most tropical areas of the world, including the East Indies and the islands of the Pacific

HARVEST SEASON Long, brown, bulging pods of acidic pulp surrounding seeds grow along the new branches of massive trees. As they ripen—from April to June or late summer to fall, depending on the area of cultivation—the pods swell, the pulp turns into a reddish-brown sticky paste, and the skin becomes brittle. Harvesters often shake branches to cause the mature fruits to fall and either preserve them by shelling and covering in sugar and/or syrup, forming them into balls, or by steaming and sun-drying them.

PARTS USED Pulp of ripe pods, leaves, flowers, and seeds

ABOUT The edible, tart tamarind fruit comes from an evergreen shade tree in the pea (Fabaceae) family native to Africa but is often falsely considered to be indigenous to India. The Persians and Arabs who came across it in Africa compared its appearance to another familiar fruit, giving it the name *tamar hindi* ("Indian date"). Wherever the tamarind tree first put down its roots, word of its sticky, delicious pulp spread far and wide, finding its way into many cuisines. Its natural sourness makes it an essential ingredient in pickles (like the Indian tamarind fish), fermented drinks, chutneys, and sauces. The young leaves and flowers are also eaten as greens or stirred into curries, particularly in India, and the seeds can be eaten raw or cooked.

Unripe pods are used in Indian rice, fish, and meat dishes, or in Thai or Vietnamese soups (like *tom yum* or *canh chua*) and stews. It is often combined with sugar to make a sweet treat, as is done in Cuba, Jamaica, Thailand, Vietnam, the Philippines, and the Dominican Republic. In tropical regions it is also made into a popular carbonated drink known as tamarind ade, or frozen into flavored ice pops.

TRADITIONAL USES

Worcestershire sauce—United Kingdom
Rice stew—Jamaica
Vindaloo (curry dish)—Goa
Rasam (tamarind and spice broth)—India
Bisi bele bhath (hot lentil rice dish)—India

NOTE

Toasting not recommended

RECOMMENDED PAIRINGS

🍸 Daiquiri
🥣 Coconut chicken noodle soup
🍆 Eggplant curry
🐖 Sweet-and-sour pork loin
🥄 Satay sauce

SPICE PAIRINGS

basil, cardamom, clove, ginger, lemongrass

RECIPE IDEAS

1. Coat the rim of a margarita glass with a little honey and ground tamarind for a sour garnish.
2. For a ravioli filling, combine ground tamarind, squash purée, and ricotta cheese.
3. Sprinkle ground tamarind on thin slices of hamachi or tuna, and drizzle with mustard oil for a quick Asian-inspired crudo.

QUICK BLEND
Tambali

See photograph, pages 264–265.

Use this acidic, mildly hot blend to marinate cubed swordfish and then thread on skewers with diced onions and bell peppers before grilling. It also enlivens braised octopus.

Makes about ¼ cup/27 grams

2 tablespoons/15 grams ground tamarind
½ tablespoon/5 grams yellow mustard seeds, ground
½ tablespoon/3 grams dried garlic slices, ground
1 teaspoon/2 grams cubeb berries, ground
Scant ¾ teaspoon/2 grams ground ancho chile

TARRAGON

ARTEMISIA DRACUNCULUS VAR. SATIVA

*A fennel- or anise-scented
leafy herb*

FLAVOR & AROMA I do not remember hearing much about tarragon when I was growing up. It just wasn't used that often in the Middle East. But as soon as I ventured into Persian, Armenian, or French cuisine, it became a bit of a VIP.

Tarragon has star anise–like notes, with a hint of licorice and some floral elements. It is great fresh when added to salads or dried in sauces. In France, it is the star ingredient in béarnaise sauce, and it is mostly recognized in the United States for its part in the tartar sauce used for dipping crab cakes and other seafoods. Because it is a delicate herb and can wilt and brown very easily, you can substitute the fresh leaves for the dried leaves in nearly any dish.

I get fantastic dried green tarragon leaves from France. This spice allows me to create blends with those anise notes without actually adding any anise seed. It also brings a lot of sweet and herbaceous elements to my blends. Over the years I have met a number of people who do not care for any of the licorice-tasting spices but still enjoy tarragon. It gave me the idea of substituting fennel seeds and the like with tarragon when needed.

ORIGIN 🖘 Native to temperate Europe and Asia in the areas around the Caspian Sea 🖘 Cultivated in southern Europe, particularly France and Spain, and the United States

HARVEST SEASON Tarragon is a perennial herb in the daisy (Asteraceae) family with long, narrow leaves that can be harvested as needed or for drying in batches during the summer and early fall. When drying, it is best to do so in partial shade to preserve the bright green color.

PARTS USED Leaves and sprigs

ABOUT French tarragon has arguably the best flavor when pitted against Russian or wild varieties. Its recorded history goes back to the Greeks around 500 BC and, much later, was apparently cultivated by Charlemagne. After the Arabs (or Mongolians—there is some debate here) introduced it to Spain in the mid-1100s, tarragon eventually made its way to England in the early sixteenth century, and finally to North America in the mid-1600s. Even Thomas Jefferson was said to favor its fresh scent in his garden.

While it has mostly made its mark on French cooking—it is essential to fines herbes—it is also widely used in the cuisines found in the areas surrounding the Mediterranean Sea. Fresh or dried leaves and even flowers can be added to soups, salads, pickles (salty Persian *khiar shoor*, in particular), and meat dishes, or it can be steeped in vinegar to impart its essential oils. Its concentrated, aromatic oils are often used in mustard and in tartar sauce. Both fresh and dried leaves work well in chicken dishes, including Hungarian chicken ragout soup. Tarragon is also used to flavor the dyed green soft drink originating in the country of Georgia called Tarhun and found across parts of Central Asia and Eastern Europe.

In Armenia, fresh, abundant tarragon is often served in heaping plates as a green vegetable during the spring and summer months. During breakfast, it is not uncommon to find tarragon sprigs paired with boiled egg and wrapped in fresh lavash. The Persians have a special appreciation for herbs like this when they are in peak season; *sabzhi khordan* is a side dish that can include tarragon, basil, chives, mint, summery savory, and watercress and that marks the time of year in a refreshing way.

TRADITIONAL USES

Tartar sauce—United States
Fines herbes—France
Sauce béarnaise—France
Chicken with tarragon—France
Chakapuli (lamb stew)—Georgia

NOTE

Toasting not recommended

RECOMMENDED PAIRINGS

- Egg salad
- Mushroom cream sauce
- Endive and orange salad
- Salmon gravlax
- Duck rillettes

SPICE PAIRINGS

black pepper, mint, mustard, onion, orange peel

RECIPE IDEAS

1. Mix ground tarragon with mayonnaise, lemon juice, and a splash of Tabasco sauce and serve with poached shrimp.

2. Brush freshly baked biscuits with a mixture of melted butter, honey, and ground tarragon.

3. Combine dried tarragon leaves with warm cooked potatoes, salted butter, and grated horseradish and whip into a pungent purée.

QUICK BLEND
Estrago

Make a compound butter with this blend and serve with grilled meats or fish. It also adds a fennel scent to sautéed shrimp and fettuccine pasta.

Makes about ⅓ cup/23 grams

¾ cup/15 grams dried tarragon leaves, ground
1 tablespoon/3 grams crushed dried basil leaves
2 teaspoons/2 grams dried dill, ground
Scant ¾ teaspoon/2 grams granulated dried lemon peel
Scant ½ teaspoon/1 gram black peppercorns, coarsely chopped

TASMANIAN PEPPER

TASMANNIA LANCEOLATA

Pungent, tongue-numbing pepperberries and leaves

FLAVOR & AROMA While it is also known as mountain pepper, at La Boîte I simply call it Tasmanian pepper. I love the piney, resin-like scent it gives off when you first open the jar, and then the floral and sweet notes it reveals later. After you take a little bite, it starts with a very pleasant sweetness and acidity, but a few seconds later the heat and numbness hits you (a bit like Sichuan pepper). It is not overwhelmingly hot and allows you to discover sweet and fruity elements when paired with vegetables and fruits. It may not be used by many outside of Australia, but try it in place of your regular pepper and you may change your mind.

Because they are still a bit soft and larger than regular black pepper, Tasmanian pepperberries can be chopped with a knife and then sprinkled over raw or cooked dishes. One of my favorite pairings is with foie gras, whether a chilled terrine or sautéed slice. The leaves are also pungent and flavorful and can be dried and ground into larger flakes or a fine powder. When used whole and added to longer-cooking dishes as you would a bay leaf (page 66), the leaves will lose their pungency but still impart fruity, acidic notes. The leaves

lack the sweet element of the berries but certainly aren't missing any of the numbing heat, and the dried leaves tend to pack more punch than fresh.

ORIGIN 🖝 Native to and cultivated in southeastern parts of Australia (Victoria, New South Wales, and Tasmania)

HARVEST SEASON The evergreen Tasmanian pepper shrub is part of the winter's bark (Winteraceae) family and can reach 15 feet tall and 10 feet wide. The plant's edible leaves are dark green and oval shaped and set along vibrant red stems. In the summer, aromatic cream-colored flowers bloom, giving way to black, two-lobed berries that ripen in the fall.

PARTS USED Leaves and berries

ABOUT Tasmanian pepper is found growing in the mountainous regions of southeastern Australia, where aboriginals and

early colonists harvested its berries for the indigenous cuisine. Colonists found that the dried berries were a more accessible substitute for black pepper and still use them as a condiment along with other bush spices like wattleseed and lemon myrtle (page 164).

Tasmanian pepperberries are commonly crushed and used to marinate meats such as emu hamburgers before grilling them. Whole berries are added to beans or meat stews, often toward the end of cooking. Ground leaves also make a peppery dry rub for lamb, especially when brightened by ground lemon myrtle.

TRADITIONAL USES

Authentic to Australia
Kangaroo steaks
Fish marinade
Beef stew
Grilled vegetables
Salad dressing

NOTE
Toasting not recommended

RECOMMENDED PAIRINGS
Sweet potato casserole
Roasted monkfish
Cold soba noodles
Veal saltimbocca
Pineapple upside-down cake

SPICE PAIRINGS
basil, cumin, ginger, paprika, verbena

RECIPE IDEAS
1. Sprinkle coarsely ground Tasmanian pepperberries
on thinly sliced ripe avocado, drizzle with lemon juice,
and salt to taste for an avocado carpaccio.
2. For a spicy cocktail, add coarsely ground Tasmanian pepperberries
to pineapple juice mixed with dark rum and serve over ice.
3. Infuse Tasmanian pepperberries into warm olive oil
and use to poach arctic char or salmon.

QUICK BLEND
Tasman

Slow-roasted pork shoulder gets a peppery punch when
massaged with this blend before cooking. It also adds
pleasantly hot and acidic notes to duck ragout.

Makes about 3 tablespoons/24 grams

1½ tablespoons/15 grams Tasmanian pepperberries, coarsely ground
½ tablespoon/5 grams unsweetened cocoa powder
½ tablespoon/3 grams ground ginger
½ teaspoon/1 gram ground mace

THYME & LEMON THYME

THYMUS VULGARIS; THYMUS CITRIODORUS

The dried or fresh sweet and slightly bitter spice made from small leaves

FLAVOR & AROMA Thyme is one of the most used and versatile herbs found in cuisines around the world. With its slight citrus notes (particularly the lemon variety) and warm, somewhat pungent hints, thyme lends itself nicely to savory dishes as well as sweet desserts. Both stems and leaves are great fresh and dried, and I like to keep the leaves whole in blends for texture and flavor. Thyme really develops best when cooked or infused into liquids, and since it dries very quickly, it is easy to dry your own at home.

ORIGIN ☞ Native to the Mediterranean, Central Europe, Asia Minor, and North Africa ☞ Cultivated in Europe, Canada, the United States, and North Africa

HARVEST SEASON Thyme is a small but dense, mat-like plant in the mint (Lamiaceae) family with tiny, heart-shaped leaves. In temperate growing areas, thyme can be picked throughout the year or during the warmer months where winters are harsher. The flavor, particularly if drying, is best just before the pink or lavender flowers bloom toward the end of summer.

PARTS USED Leaves, sprigs, and flowers

ABOUT Before thyme lent its floral notes to bouqet garni, it was used for thousands of years as a protector and a sign of courage. In the Roman era, it was believed that if thyme were if eaten or added to bathwater, it could protect one from poison. Soldiers would exchange sprigs as a sign of respect, tucking them into their armor as a badge of honor. Of course, thyme isn't some magic healer, but they weren't completely off base; one of thyme's key chemical compounds is the strong antiseptic thymol, which is found along with alcohol in modern-day hand sanitizer.

But apart from its mystical ability to ward off ancient evil, this vigorous little herb is cultivated today for the essential elements it adds to cuisines, especially those of the Middle East, France, and the United States. Aside from imparting its flavor to French stocks and soups, it is indispensable in pot-au-feu, cassoulet, and herbes de Provence. In the United States, thyme is key to clam chowder and gumbo, and the lemon variety works well in seafood dishes, marinades, or any recipe that calls for citrus. Those bright, fresh notes also help to cut the taste of fatty or strong-tasting meats like pork and game. It's a natural match for roasted chicken, salad dressings, and stuffing, and it is one of the major players in the Middle Eastern blend of herbs known as za'atar.

TRADITIONAL USES

Bouquet garni (herb bundle)—France
Herbes de Provence (spice blend)—France
Jerk spice—Jamaica
Za'atar (spice blend)—Middle East
Dukkah (herbs, nuts, and spices condiment)—Egypt

NOTE
Toasting not recommended

RECOMMENDED PAIRINGS
- Honey vinaigrette
- Broiled goat cheese
- Tomato barley soup
- Stuffed tomatoes
- Herb-crusted rack of veal

SPICE PAIRINGS
ancho, annatto, lavender, paprika, sumac

RECIPE IDEAS
1. Combine dried thyme leaves with melted butter and chopped garlic and use to brush a freshly baked croissant before serving.
2. For a flavorful baked salmon fillet, spread a mixture of Dijon mustard and dried thyme leaves over the fish before putting it in the oven.
3. Season halved fresh figs with olive oil, balsamic vinegar, and dried thyme leaves before roasting.

QUICK BLEND
Timin

Season a whole rack of lamb with this blend before roasting it with garlic and new potatoes. It also gives pork chops a fragrant, herbaceous flavor.

Makes about ½ cup/37 grams

¼ cup/15 grams dried thyme leaves
¼ cup/10 grams crushed dried oregano leaves
½ tablespoon/5 grams yellow mustard seeds, coarsely ground
½ tablespoon/5 grams ground sweet paprika
Scant ¾ teaspoon/2 grams black peppercorns, coarsely ground

TOMATO POWDER

SOLANUM LYCOPERSICUM

A dry, richly flavored powder made from ripe, sweet tomatoes

FLAVOR & AROMA Tomato is not the first thing you think of when the word *spice* comes to mind, but since my approach to spices is a little different, I consider it a worthy member of the group. While fresh tomatoes are fantastic for cooking or eating raw, tomato powder, which really captures the essence of the fruit, offers a few advantages. For one, you can season with it as you would any dry spice. If you added fresh tomatoes to a salad, the wet aspect of the fruit would affect the crispness of your lettuce. But if you sprinkle dried tomato powder on instead, you will still get the sweet taste and keep the crunch. This shelf-stable powder will easily turn any liquid into an instant tomato sauce. For that reason alone, it's a convenient spice to have on hand.

Tomato powder is also a great coloring agent. Because it is so concentrated, its red hue remains unaffected when cooking—unlike fresh tomatoes, which can sometimes fade. It is, however, sensitive to humidity, so I recommend storing it in an airtight container. If it ever forms lumps over time, you can run it through a coffee grinder to obtain a powder again.

ORIGIN ☞ Native to South America ☞ Cultivated worldwide

HARVEST SEASON The tomato is a member of the nightshade (Solanaceae) family, harvested when the fruits fully ripen and turn red during the mid- to late summer. Once picked, they are dried and sold whole as sun-dried tomatoes or ground into a fine powder.

PARTS USED Dried fruits

ABOUT Tomatoes originated in the Andean region of South America and began their journey as a culinary ingredient in Mexico. The Spanish are said to have brought seeds to Europe in the early sixteenth century, but upon discovering its familial connection to its cousins belladonna and deadly nightshade, tomatoes were grown mostly as ornamentals. Tomatoes earned the name "poison apple" from European aristocrats who, after eating them on pewter plates, died

of lead poisoning; they never put two and two together that the acid from the tomatoes caused a deadly reaction with that type of metal. But when people realized that not only was the fruit safe to eat, but unbelievably delicious, tomatoes solidified their starring role in Spanish and Italian cuisines. We can thank the early Spanish colonizers for bringing the crop back to their side of the ocean.

Fresh, cooked, and as a powder, tomatoes have a recognizable flavor that complements a variety of dishes, both sweet and savory, as well as drinks like the Bloody Mary. Its seasonality, which peaks in the summer months, makes the ground spice an even more attractive option during cold winter months when the best fresh options are pulpy, hardly ripe imports. Tomato powder can be used to add rich color and strong tomato taste to soups, gumbos, and stews. When added to liquid, it can easily be turned into tomato sauce or paste. It also makes quick work of perking up salad dressings, bread doughs, and dips.

TRADITIONAL USES

Shakshuka (eggs in tomato and chile
sauce)—Middle East
Bouillabaisse (fish stew)—France
Tomato Provençal—France
Marinara sauce—Italy
Bolognese (meat sauce)—Italy

NOTE
Toasting not recommended

RECOMMENDED PAIRINGS
Huevos rancheros
Tomato vinaigrette
Risotto
Meat loaf
Sorbet

SPICE PAIRINGS
basil, cayenne, cumin, garlic, oregano

RECIPE IDEAS
1. Stir tomato powder into orange juice and use as
a base for a vinaigrette with honey and olive oil.
2. Brush thin strips of puff pastry dough with egg wash
and sprinkle with tomato powder, grated Parmesan cheese,
and oregano to bake into pizza sticks.
3. Cook white butter beans in simmering chicken stock
seasoned with tomato powder for a side dish.

QUICK BLEND
Bandora

Use this rich, sweet blend to season braised pork butt.
Shred the cooked meat, and serve with cavatelli pasta, tomato sauce,
and a few more pinches of the blend. It also gives a
vodka Bloody Mary a fresh, smoky twist.

Makes about ¼ cup/27 grams

1½ tablespoons/15 grams ground tomato powder
1 tablespoon/3 grams crushed dried oregano leaves
½ tablespoon/5 grams granulated dried orange peel
Scant ¾ teaspoon/2 grams celery seeds, ground
Scant ¾ teaspoon/2 grams ground sweet pimentón

TURMERIC

CURCUMA LONGA

The yellow-orange spice that delivers color and a warm, somewhat bitter flavor

FLAVOR & AROMA Turmeric, which also goes by the Latin *curcuma,* is a great spice both in flavor and color. Though often used for its ability to impart a golden hue to foods, including mustard, cheeses, and sauces, it really offers so much more than its natural good looks. I love the bright scent and floral notes with the sweet, slightly bitter taste.

In my early years as a chef, I was confused about spice blending—there is, after all, no school for spices. Sometimes I would get bags of bright yellow turmeric powder and other times that same powder would have a deep orange hue. Later I learned that there are actually two kinds of turmeric, each named for its place of origin in India: Madras (the lighter colored and warmer, sweeter tasting of the two) and Alleppey. I like to mix them to get a nice color and flavor in my blends.

The reason turmeric is found in most curry powders is not only for its coloring, flavoring, and aromatic properties; it also helps to thicken sauces, stews, and traditional dishes. Turmeric has a starchy quality that replaces cornstarch or flour.

ORIGIN ☞ Native to South or Southeast Asia ☞ Cultivated mainly in India, but also parts of Southeast Asia and China

HARVEST SEASON Turmeric rhizomes are harvested about 8 months after planting, when the lower leaves turn yellow. The plant is dug up, the leafy tops and roots are removed, and the rhizomes are washed and boiled before being dried for up to 2 weeks. Dried rhizomes are polished and sold whole or ground.

PARTS USED Rhizomes

ABOUT A member of the ginger (Zingiberaceae) family, turmeric rhizomes are grown almost entirely in India for use as a spice and as a yellow dye—even Marco Polo wrote about turmeric's ability to imbue color like saffron (page 238). Its recorded history goes as far back as AD 700 in China, and then later in Africa, but has been a vital part of Indian culture for the last few thousand years.

Though most people are only familiar with its role in curry powder (not actually from India, by the way), it has a long history of use in medicinal applications. As far back as 250 BC the *Suśrutasamhitā* suggested using an ointment made with turmeric to mitigate the effects of poisoned food. Its curcumin compound has been considered Indian gold for its anti-inflammatory properties, said to be the reason so few indigenous elders have Alzheimer's.

It delivers its yellow-orange color to a number of traditional Indian dishes like curry (and Thai yellow curry), pickles, rice, and dhals. The Vietnamese use it in the savory mini pancakes, *bánh khọt,* and to tint the rice noodles found in *mì quảng* soup. In North Africa, turmeric has a starring role in the Moroccan ras el hanout spice blend and flavors a number of meat and vegetable stews, as well as tagines. In Persian cuisine, it is often used to start many dishes; in Iranian *khoresh,* for example, it seasons caramelized onions and oil to be used as a base for other ingredients. It is also used in a number of processed foods and sauces like English piccalilli relish, popcorn coloring, gelatin, and baked goods.

While mostly used in its dried and ground forms, fresh turmeric can be used like ginger in recipes like Cambodian *amok* (steam-cooked seafood served in banana leaves) and *kroeung* (curry paste).

TRADITIONAL USES

Mustard—Worldwide
Hawayej (soup spice)—Yemen
Harira (soup)—Morocco
Yellow rice pilaf—Malaysia and Indonesia
Masalas (spices blends) and curry powders—India

NOTE
Toasting not recommended

RECOMMENDED PAIRINGS
Butternut squash velouté
Split pea purée
Braised veal shoulder
Roasted cauliflower
Blondies

SPICE PAIRINGS
clove, ginger, onion, wasabi, yellow mustard

RECIPE IDEAS

1. For a refreshing smoothie, blend ground turmeric,
ripe melon, yogurt, and honey.
2. Sprinkle ground turmeric into simmering chicken stock
and use to cook whole new potatoes.
3. Whisk lemon juice with olive oil and ground turmeric
for a colorful citrus dressing.

QUICK BLEND
Curcuma
See photographs, pages 245 and 277.

Use this blend to season a cod fillet before poaching it in coconut milk
with bok choy and diced eggplant, or sprinkle it on sliced puff pastry with
shredded cheddar and bake for a batch of crispy cheese sticks.

Makes about 3½ tablespoons/26 grams

1½ tablespoons/15 grams ground turmeric
1 tablespoon/5 grams ground ginger
½ tablespoon/3 grams ground cinnamon
1 teaspoon/2 grams cumin seeds, toasted and ground
Scant ½ teaspoon/1 gram cayenne powder

URFA

CAPSICUM ANNUUM

A smoky-sweet, mildly hot chile with an unusual drying process

FLAVOR & AROMA The first scent you get from an Urfa chile is just captivating. It smells like chocolate and wine tannins, oily with a slightly bitter orange note. The taste is sweet and acidic at first, and then a mild heat comes through. I would include it on the short list of "everything spices," meaning it could be added to literally everything, whether raw, cooked, sweet, or savory. You might become addicted.

ORIGIN ☞ Native to South and Central America and later the Turkish town of Urfa ☞ Cultivated in Turkey

HARVEST SEASON This fairly large pepper is harvested when ripe and dark red. What makes Urfa chiles unique is their drying process: After being picked, they are set out in the sun to dry during the day, which gives them a dark red, nearly burgundy color. Then at night, they are covered with fabric to sweat so they retain their essential oils. So, while they are basically dry, they still have a bit of their natural humidity. They are later coarsely ground—finely ground chiles become a humid powder—and occasionally mixed with a touch of salt to prevent lumps or big chunks.

PARTS USED Dried, sweated ground peppers

ABOUT This Turkish chile, also known as Urfa biber or isot pepper is in the nightshade (Solanaceae) family and grows in the southern part of the country, not far from the Syrian border. It is often paired with or used in the same way as the Aleppo chile (page 42), which seems only fitting—they are grown only a mountain range apart. Though traditionally used in Turkish and sometimes Kurdish cuisines, it is gaining popularity among chefs in the West due to its unusual complexity, raisin notes, and signature smokiness. Together, these elements make it a perfect match for both sweet and savory recipes.

In Turkey, they use chiles in the same way we use black pepper, so you'll typically find Urfa chiles imparting their tangy heat to pickles, cured meats, and lamb dishes. Now that this chile is breaking into mainstream kitchens outside of its native region, you may find it coarsely ground and sprinkled over roasted vegetables and meats, rich stews, rice pilafs, and even pizza. And because those sweet, smoky chocolate notes are ever-present, you might be surprised that the subtle heat you can't seem to place in a bite of brownie or vanilla ice cream is the result of a little Urfa.

TRADITIONAL USES
Authentic to Turkey
Smoky eggplant dip
Lamb kebabs
Roasted vegetables
Lahmacun (flatbread)
Çiğ köfte (raw meatballs)

NOTE
Toasting not recommended

RECOMMENDED PAIRINGS
Fried eggs
Carbonara
Orange barbecue sauce
Hummus
Chocolate mousse

SPICE PAIRINGS
garlic, onion, orange peel, oregano, rose

HEAT INDEX
Light to medium

RECIPE IDEAS
1. Sprinkle crushed Urfa chile on thinly sliced fresh sea scallops and finish with a drizzle of olive oil and lemon juice for a quick carpaccio.
2. For a different take on fritters, add crushed Urfa chile to sautéed kale or collard greens and add bread crumbs, eggs, and ricotta cheese before frying.
3. Combine crushed Urfa chile with melted dark chocolate and drizzle over vanilla ice cream, then top with Urfa-spiced nuts.

QUICK BLEND
Pasha
See photograph, page 280.

Use this blend to season grilled lamb *kofte* (ground meat patty) and add tahini and chopped cilantro to make grilled kebabs.
Brush it over grilled pita bread with olive oil for a touch of heat.

Makes about ¼ cup/28 grams

1½ tablespoons/15 grams crushed Urfa chile
½ tablespoon/5 grams ground sumac
2 teaspoons/2 grams crushed dried oregano
½ tablespoon/3 grams dried onion slices, coarsely ground
1 teaspoon/3 grams nigella seeds

VANILLA

VANILLA PLANIFOLIA

The sweet aromatic seeds and fruit pod of the hand-pollinated vanilla orchid

FLAVOR & AROMA Many cooks have never experienced real vanilla beans, which are actually fruits, and have only used extracts. There is nothing wrong with extracts, but the beans are far superior. I love their sweet, floral scent with hints of chocolate and cocoa. The seeds inside offer a heady aroma as well as a wonderful texture and flavor. But to me, vanilla is more about the scent than the taste. Our minds naturally translate that scent into the flavor we perceive—try tasting something while pinching your nose to see what I mean.

For years, vanilla was only used for desserts and baked goods, but luckily more chefs and home cooks are starting to see the potential in adding it to savory dishes as well. I love blending it with herbs and strong savory spices such as cumin and caraway; it really balances them. Just be sure to use it moderately so it does not overpower everything else. Since most dessert recipes specifically call for the inner seeds, you are left with the scraped vanilla bean for another use. This can easily be dried and ground or chopped and then added to spice blends.

Good-quality vanilla beans can be aged for a few months in cellars to enhance their flavors. My mentor and friend, Olivier Roellinger, has such a cellar in Paris where he ages more than ten kinds of vanilla. Tahitian is the most fragrant and expensive and thus is used a lot in the perfume industry. It is also the thickest of all of them. Madagascar has creamy, fruity notes that pair perfectly with desserts. Mexican vanilla has deeper sweet notes but also has smoky and savory hints that complement both desserts and seafood dishes—probably because it's also very buttery. Another variety, Bourbon, is named for the original domain of its native island,

Réunion, and is considered by professionals to be the best. It offers a great buttery characteristic with fruity scents. Some Madagascar vanilla is mistakenly labeled Bourbon.

ORIGIN ☞ Native to Mexico and Central America ☞ Cultivated in Madagascar, Mexico, Central America, Tahiti, Réunion, Indonesia, and the Comoros Islands

HARVEST SEASON Part of the orchid (Orchidaceae) family, vanilla flowers only bloom for one day if not pollinated, and can be naturally pollinated only by the Melipona bee, found in Central America. Flowers grown everywhere else are hand-pollinated, traditionally with a small wooden needle. If not pollinated, the flower will drop the very next day. The fruits are long, green pods resembling green beans. They take months to ripen, develop, and turn yellow-green, at which point they are harvested and cured to retain their essential oils and develop their recognizable dark color and sweet aroma.

PARTS USED Fruits (beans), inner seeds, and extract

ABOUT Vanilla is probably one of the most recognized and used spices around the world. Because of the labor-intensive process of growing and harvesting vanilla, it is no wonder the spice is so expensive.

The first to discover and cultivate this beloved spice were the Totonec people of Mexico. The Aztecs, having conquered the region in the fifteenth century, came to love what they called *tlilxochitl*, or "black flower," named for the appearance of its shriveled fruit pods. This reign was brought to an end by Spanish conquistador Hernán Cortés, who forced his way into a meeting with the Aztec ruler in 1519 only to lead the expedition that would bring down the entire empire a few years later. Cortés's parting gifts from the Aztecs? Vanilla *and* chocolate.

Because of the delicate and specific nature of vanilla orchid pollination, it wasn't really cultivated outside of Mexico until the nineteenth century. The turning point came when Edmond Albius, a twelve-year-old slave on the French island of Réunion, discovered how to hand-pollinate the flowers. Today, vanilla is still produced in much the same way. In recent years, production has dropped due to the increase of synthetic vanilla substitutes. For the purists who understand there is simply no replacement for the real thing, only natural vanilla will do to flavor and add a sweet fragrance to puddings, milk-based beverages, soufflés, custards, cakes, liqueurs such as crème de cacao and Galliano, and, of course, ice cream.

TRADITIONAL USES

Mayan chocolate—Mexico
Pastry cream—France
Crème brûlée—France
Strudel—Germany
Vanilla rum—Madagascar

NOTE
Toasting not recommended

RECOMMENDED PAIRINGS
Hazelnut vinaigrette
Rice pudding
Cauliflower purée
Chestnut ravioli
Meringue-topped cream pie

SPICE PAIRINGS
clove, ginger, jasmine, nutmeg, pink pepperberries

RECIPE IDEAS
1. Split a vanilla bean lengthwise and tie it onto a pork loin with twine before roasting the meat.
2. Coarsely chop a vanilla bean and add it to a green tomato-and-orange chutney for a sweet, fragrant condiment.
3. Infuse a quart of simmering milk with a split vanilla bean and then chill to use in cereals, coffee drinks, and smoothies.

QUICK BLEND
Albius

See photograph, page 285.

Mix this blend with honey and rum and use to coat whole pears before roasting with butter. Or stir it into whipped cream and lemon custard for a spiced dessert.

Makes about ⅓ cup/30 grams

7 beans/15 grams vanilla beans, cut and ground
1½ tablespoons/5 grams pink pepperberries, ground
1 tablespoon/5 grams ground ginger
½ tablespoon/3 grams mace blades, ground
Scant ¾ teaspoon/2 grams black peppercorns, coarsely ground

WASABI

EUTREMA WASABI

A green, pungent root often served alongside sushi

FLAVOR & AROMA Thanks to a global interest in Japanese cuisine and a sushi restaurant in nearly every city, we have all experienced the sinus-opening wasabi root. Or so we thought. Most sushi places actually serve a green paste made from horseradish, mustard, and food coloring. The challenges that come with growing the fresh root make it very expensive, so it is more often than not replaced with the imposter.

Traditionally, and because the flavor dissipates so quickly, the root is grated only as needed. In Japan, a *samegawa oroshigane,* or sharkskin grater, is used to turn it into a fine paste. To me, this fantastic root is a cross between horseradish and mustard. It has a sharp, acidic scent with a strong heat level, but not at all like what you'll find with chiles. It is more like Dijon mustard, only multiplied five times over. Even people who do not like the heat of peppers and chiles will often like wasabi. I think it is because of the approachable bright green notes and grassy scent. Also, it doesn't create that burning sensation chiles do. The dried powder is a great substitute for chiles in blends and offers complex notes to boot.

ORIGIN ☞ Native to Japan ☞ Cultivated in Japan, China, Taiwan, New Zealand, and North America

HARVEST SEASON The wasabi plant is very challenging to grow and only thrives in clean, flowing water. Traditionally, it is found growing along the cold, rocky streambeds of Japan's mountain river valleys. Roots are harvested when the temperatures are relatively cool, in spring or fall.

PARTS USED Roots and leaves

ABOUT Cultivation of wasabi dates back to about the tenth century in Japan—the only producer for centuries (small amounts are now produced in the United States). Though it remains one of the hardest crops to grow in the world, its cultivation has spread. The two main cultivars are daruma wasabi and the hotter mazuma wasabi.

This hot, edible root is a member of the cabbage (Brassicaceae) family along with horseradish, though it's a different plant altogether. You'll actually be hard pressed to find real wasabi in most places unless you seek it out in specialty stores or high-end restaurants. Even then, it is usually reserved for the select few who would fully appreciate it. Wasabi is typically paired with sashimi and sushi and served as a condiment along with soy sauce for mixing. The powder (mixed with water) or freshly grated green root is made into a paste and the leaves can be eaten fresh as a leafy salad green, or pickled.

TRADITIONAL USES

Authentic to Japan
Wasabi paste
Wasabi-zuke (pickle)
Crackers
Wasabi ale or beer
Nuts

NOTE

Toasting not recommended

RECOMMENDED PAIRINGS

Whitefish salad
Beet carpaccio
Shrimp cocktail
Cold soba noodles
Prime rib roast

SPICE PAIRINGS

amchoor, caraway, fennel, ginger, star anise

RECIPE IDEAS

1. Blend ground wasabi with ponzu sauce and
sesame oil and use to dress a spinach and radish salad.
2. Season cream cheese with ground wasabi and use as a spread
for bagels served with smoked salmon and pickled ginger.
3. Add ground wasabi to rice wine vinegar and oil
and use as a dressing for grilled mushroom salad.

QUICK BLEND
Daruma-Mazuma

Season a parcooked lobster tail with this blend before roasting
it with butter and sake. Or try sprinkling it over thinly sliced
avocado to serve on toasted brioche.

Makes about ⅓ cup/27 grams

3 tablespoons/3 grams dried tarragon leaves, ground
1½ tablespoons/15 grams wasabi powder
2½ teaspoons/5 grams anise seeds, ground
½ tablespoon/3 grams dried onion slices, ground
½ teaspoon/1 gram ground ancho chile

WATERCRESS

NASTURTIUM OFFICINALE

*A pungent, peppery leafy herb loaded
with vitamins and nutrients*

FLAVOR & AROMA Watercress, which we call *rashad* in Hebrew and Arabic, is a popular herb or salad green that can be found fresh in most supermarkets year-round. Sadly, once picked, it does not last very long, quickly turning brown and losing its great taste and scent.

At La Boîte, I use freeze-dried watercress leaves as well as the seeds of the plant. Because it is hard to dry at home, I rely on buying it already prepared this way. The dried leaves perk up various dishes with their greenish color and pleasant bitterness, while the seeds deliver more peppery notes with a slight nutty flavor. I love adding the dried leaves to soups and stews, and using the seeds to give a peppery bite to salads, dressing, and breads.

ORIGIN ☞ Native to Europe and Asia ☞ Cultivated in Europe, Asia, China, and the United States

HARVEST SEASON Watercress is a hardy perennial that thrives in the wild along running streams and banks but is also commercially cultivated for its fresh and dry uses year-round. Typically, the aerial parts of the plants are harvested before flowering in the summer when the flavor becomes very pungent.

PARTS USED Leaves, stems, and seeds

ABOUT Watercress is an aquatic plant belonging to the Brassicaceae, or cabbage, family. While its botanical name may resemble that of the flowering annual nasturtium, they aren't actually in the same family. Where they do share some similarities are in a common piquant flavor and pungent smell, as implied by the Latin expression *nasus tortus,* meaning "twisted nose."

Though commonly used as a fresh salad green, watercress works equally well as a cooked vegetable, much like a more peppery spinach, and when dried works wonders in soups like Chinese wonton, stews, and hot tea.

And as much as it piques the palate, it is also incredibly healthy. Watercress is a source of those coveted omega-3 fatty acids, as well as a great way to get more vitamins A, B_6, C, and K into your diet. What's more, it is also a one-stop shop for calcium, iron, manganese, iodine, and folic acid.

TRADITIONAL USES

Potage au cresson (soup)—France
Sichuan stir-fry—China
Tea sandwiches—England
Salt meat watercress soup—Hawaii
Egg salad sandwich—United States

NOTE
Toasting not recommended

RECOMMENDED PAIRINGS
● Scrambled eggs
🌾 Tabbouleh
🥄 Leek velouté
🍝 Pasta primavera
🌱 Stuffed zucchini

SPICE PAIRINGS
bay leaves, celery seeds, fennel, nutmeg, turmeric

RECIPE IDEAS
1. Sprinkle watercress seeds on thinly sliced green zucchini
and finish with olive oil and vinegar for a salad.
2. Mix softened salted butter with watercress seeds and serve
with fresh young radishes and raw thin asparagus.
3. Stir crushed dried watercress leaves into simmering chicken stock
and use to cook fragrant jasmine rice.

QUICK BLEND
Rashad

Add this peppery blend to cooked white beans before puréeing
them with olive oil and garlic for a smooth dip or side dish.
It also gives a pungent kick to kohlrabi salad.

Makes about ⅓ cup/22 grams

¼ cup/5 grams crushed dried watercress leaves
1 tablespoon/10 grams watercress seeds
1 teaspoon/3 grams celery seeds
Scant ¾ teaspoon/2 grams ground turmeric
Scant ¾ teaspoon/2 grams fennel seeds, toasted and ground

ZA'ATAR

ORIGANUM SYRIACUM

An oregano variety with hints of thyme and savory

———

FLAVOR & AROMA Before there was a za'atar spice blend, there was an herb of the same name. It is kind of a cross between oregano, thyme, savory, and hyssop and is often confused with all these. Arab thyme, wild thyme, Bible hyssop, conehead thyme, and Lebanese oregano all take credit for the za'atar domain. The one I am covering here, which also goes by Syrian oregano, has a nice savory, herbaceous, and warm scent. The taste is sweet, bitter, and slightly salty.

Not surprising, it is the main component in the Middle Eastern za'atar spice blend—along with sesame, sumac, thyme, and other spices that vary by country. I love to sprinkle it on salads, grilled meats, and fish, or simply add it to oil to serve with bread.

ORIGIN ☞ Native to the Middle East ☞ Grows wild in the Syrian-Lebanese mountains, and cultivated in Lebanon

HARVEST SEASON Za'atar is traditionally harvested out in the wild, but with growing demand it is now being commercially cultivated. It is a perennial in the mint family (Lamiaceae), with hairy stems and aromatic gray-green leaves that are best when harvested before its white or pale pink flowers bloom in the summer. After harvesting, leaves (and sometimes flowers) are dried and crushed.

PARTS USED Leaves and flowers

ABOUT Za'atar is called *ezov* in Hebrew, which translates to "hyssop" in English. It is often credited as the one referenced in the Old Testament, hence the often used Bible hyssop moniker, but hyssop (page 144) is an entirely different plant altogether.

This variety of oregano is popular in the Middle East and Mediterranean for adding an herbaceous element to sauces, soups, roasted meats and vegetables, stews, and, most commonly, breads. It is often baked into pita bread doughs and is a main component in Lebanese *man'ousheh,* in which za'atar is mixed with oil and brushed over disk-shaped flatbread dough before being baked. Za'atar is also used to season the pizza-like *manakish,* a Levantine Arabic baked flatbread topped with cheese and meat. In the Middle East, street vendors dole out za'atar mixed with olive oil as a dip to accompany the soft sesame bread *ka'ak.*

TRADITIONAL USES

Za'atar (spice blend)—Middle East
Marinated olives—Middle East
Tomato salad—Middle East
Shanklish cheese—Lebanon
Herbal tea—Oman

NOTE

Toasting not recommended

RECOMMENDED PAIRINGS

- Shakshuka
- Meatball soup
- Arancini
- Grilled mackerel
- Honey-lemon chicken

SPICE PAIRINGS

black pepper, caraway, coriander, lemon peel, mint

RECIPE IDEAS

1. Add crushed dried za'atar leaves to your favorite
cheese biscuit dough before baking.

2. Whisk crushed dried za'atar leaves with honey, lemon juice,
and olive oil and use for basting a whole Cornish hen while roasting.

3. Mix dried za'atar leaves with toasted sunflower seeds, raisins,
sliced almonds, and olive oil and use as a salad topping.

QUICK BLEND
Vadi

Season cooked chopped Swiss chard with
this blend and combine with ricotta cheese, bread crumbs,
and salt to make small, herbaceous fritters.
It also elevates a cold pasta and shrimp salad.

Makes about 1 cup/29 grams

¾ cup/15 grams crushed dried za'atar leaves
1½ tablespoons/5 grams crushed dried mint
½ tablespoon/5 grams nigella seeds
½ tablespoon/3 grams dried sliced onions, ground
1 teaspoon/1 gram crushed dried rose petals

ZEDOARY

CURCUMA ZEDOARIA

*The bitter, mango-flavored
cousin of ginger*

FLAVOR & AROMA Zedoary is basically white turmeric. Its notes and flavors are similar to those of ginger but have more of a pleasant bitterness, unless the rhizome is very young and fresh—and therefore less bitter. Because of these bitter notes, many disregard zedoary—but I love it for that reason. I also enjoy the light mango elements it brings to cold and hot dishes. I rarely use zedoary on its own, but rather add it to blends in which bitterness is an important element. If you are lucky to live in Indonesia or Thailand, you might have access to the fresh rhizome leaves and shoots, which work great in salads.

In Indian markets, you may come across two types of zedoary: the small, round *Curcuma zedoaria,* which I use, and the longer, skinnier *Curcuma zerumbet,* which is a bit less bitter and looks more like turmeric.

ORIGIN ☞ Native to Southeast Asia and Indonesia ☞ Cultivated in India, Southeast Asia, and China

HARVEST SEASON Zedoary is an orange-yellow hard rhizome with thin brown skin and is an aromatic aboveground plant that bears yellow flowers and long leaf shoots. This tropical plant is left to mature for about 2 years before being harvested. Once unearthed, it is either sold fresh as is or boiled and then sun-dried.

PARTS USED Rhizome, young shoots, flower buds, and leaves

ABOUT Zedoary is a member of the Zingiberaceae, or ginger, family and was very popular through the medieval period. From that point until now, there has been a strong decline of its appearance in recipes, particularly in Western countries, where the less bitter ginger is preferred.

But while it may have lost its appeal here, it is still very much a popular spice in and around its native regions. In Thai cuisine, it is commonly used raw. You may find thinly sliced strips of it in salads. In India, it is called *amb halad—amb* means "mango"—and is typically used in hot-and-sour pickles, in soups, or is used raw. In Indonesia, stems are eaten raw, leaves are added to seafood dishes, and the rhizome is ground and used to season curry.

Zedoary is also perhaps more commonly used for its medicinal properties. On the Indian subcontinent, it has been lauded for centuries for its anti-inflammatory properties and even believed to offer an anti-aging solution for wrinkles. But before you apply it under your eyes, know that its staining orange hue earned it the Arabic name for saffron, *kurkum.* The only thing these spices have in common is their ability to leave a literal mark.

TRADITIONAL USES

Thai chile paste—Thailand
Curries—Indonesia
Achar pickles—India
Amb halad ka shorba (zedoary vegetable soup)—India
Chickpeas/lentils—India

NOTE

Toasting not recommended

RECOMMENDED PAIRINGS

Green papaya slaw
Clam chowder
Lamb curry
Pickled turnips
Green curry

SPICE PAIRINGS

fennel, mustard, poppy seed, turmeric, white pepper

RECIPE IDEAS

1. Stir ground zedoary into a classic gin and tonic
for a touch of bitterness.

2. Sprinkle ground zedoary on fresh-sliced apricots with
olive oil and balsamic vinegar and serve with sliced ham.

3. Season fresh orange segments with ground zedoary
and add to an endive and blue cheese salad.

QUICK BLEND
Cedvar

Add this blend to flavor pickle brine for whole green tomatoes or okra. It
also gives corn chowder with sautéed calamari a nice hint of bitterness.

Makes about 3 tablespoons/22 grams

1 tablespoon/10 grams ground zedoary
1½ heaping teaspoons/5 grams fennel seeds, toasted and ground
1 teaspoon/3 grams white peppercorns, ground
1 teaspoon/3 grams ground turmeric
½ teaspoon/1 gram cayenne powder

ZUTA

MICROMERIA FRUTICOSA

*A sweet, minty herb known for its floral
aroma and curative properties*

FLAVOR & AROMA My father grows zuta in his olive and fig orchard in the Galilee. He planted it between the trees because he believes it keeps the bugs away. It also make delicious tea infusions and fantastic tooth-picks. Zuta has a sharp menthol aroma and flavor and delivers a fresh, bright taste after eating it. It reminds me of a combination of mint (page 184) and lemon balm (page 158). The dried leaves and stems, which are equally good, dry quickly and keep for a long time. They can be ground or used whole for roasting and infusing. When I smell it, I am reminded of being back in the orchard, where every morning and evening the wind delivers its sweet floral scent.

ORIGIN ☞ Native to Israel and the Eastern Mediterranean ☞ Cultivated in the Mediterranean region

HARVEST SEASON Zuta is a perennial herb that thrives on the wild cliffs of the Mediterranean, the Balkan Peninsula in particular. It grows as a small shrub with thin stems and bright gray-green leaves that can be harvested from spring to late summer. White to soft pink flowers bloom late summer through fall.

PARTS USED Leaves and stems

ABOUT Part of the mint (Lamiaceae) family, zuta, or zuta levana, is closely related to winter and summer savories, though it is most often confused with pennyroyal. Zuta is a member of the Lamiaceae, or mint, family and is used as a spice and for its medicinal benefits, specifically in the Eastern Mediterranean and Middle East. Outside of these regions, you'll be hard pressed to find it. As an edible, it is often mixed with salt and olive oil for a fragrant bread dip, or used as one of a group of herbs found in the za'atar blend.

Also called tea hyssop, zuta is known for its ability to clear sinus congestion, aid digestion, and alleviate stomach pain. Back home we call it "sleepy tea." Women who are, or may be, pregnant should avoid zuta due to its level of pulegone.

FAMILIAR USES

Tea infusions
Bulgur wheat salad
Grilled fish
Roasted chicken
Sorbet

NOTE

Toasting not recommended

RECOMMENDED PAIRINGS

Almond vinaigrette
Salmon escabeche
Chicken dumpling soup
Carrot cake
Prune flan

SPICE PAIRINGS

cardamom, cinnamon, clove, rosemary, vanilla

RECIPE IDEAS

1. Sprinkle a halibut fillet with a few pinches of dried zuta leaves, drizzle it with olive oil, and bake wrapped in parchment.

2. Mix ground zuta leaves into gnocchi dough before poaching and serve with sautéed bay scallops.

3. Give your favorite mint julep recipe a twist by stirring in ground zuta leaves.

QUICK BLEND
Bustan

Sprinkle this blend over grape and red onion salad topped with fresh cilantro leaves and crumbled goat cheese. It also adds a fresh, spiced element to chocolate pound cake.

Makes about ⅓ cup/23 grams

¾ cup/15 grams zuta leaves, coarsely ground
1 teaspoon/3 grams green cardamom, coarsely ground
1 teaspoon/2 grams cloves, ground
Scant ¾ teaspoon/2 grams black peppercorns, coarsely ground
½ teaspoon/1 gram ground ginger

CLASSIC SPICE BLENDS

These are just a few of the classic blends that have been used for centuries as the foundational, authentic flavors of world cuisines. They are easily made and can be used on a daily basis at home. While they are inspired by traditional recipes and remain true to their native origins, I have added a few personal touches to make them my own. Try them in sweet, savory, or even drink recipes and feel free to modify them as you like. They will allow you to explore the essence of global cuisines while preparing your favorite everyday recipes.

BAHĀRĀT

Bahārāt, the Arabic word for "spices," can be found in many places, including Yemen, Turkey, Egypt, and North Africa. It is usually finely ground, and the mixture is dependent on whether it is intended for meat, fish, or vegetables. The version below has Vietnamese cinnamon, which is sweet and floral, along with unexpected savory notes from caraway seeds. My recipe works great with lamb, beef, sauces, and roasted vegetables.

MAKES ABOUT ½ CUP/46 GRAMS

2½ tablespoons/15 grams allspice berries, toasted and ground
2 tablespoons/10 grams ground ginger
2 tablespoons/10 grams ground cinnamon, preferably Vietnamese
2 tablespoons/5 grams rose buds, ground
1 teaspoon/3 grams black peppercorns, ground
1 teaspoon/3 grams caraway seeds, toasted and ground

BERBERE

This blend is based on the fiery, aromatic berbere found in North African cuisine that enhances simply prepared corn or lamb, honey, and cereals. My version does not include garlic, which is typical of berbere, but rather highlights ginger and caraway for a more acidic, floral blend. The depth and complexity it delivers to dishes comes from the seafaring early conquerors whose ships sailed past, brimming with the spices of their journeys to new lands.

MAKES ABOUT ⅓ CUP/33 GRAMS

2½ tablespoons/5 grams cumin, toasted and ground
2 tablespoons/10 grams ground ginger
1½ heaping teaspoons/5 grams caraway seeds, toasted and ground
1½ tablespoons/10 grams ground sweet paprika
1 teaspoon/3 grams crushed dried chile flakes

CAJUN

Honoring the great culinary traditions of Louisiana, this robust blend pays homage to Cajun cuisine. I made a very small but important change: I replaced the classic recipe's paprika with pimentón to give vegetarian dishes a smoky depth. Whether you are preparing a crab boil, crawfish, or gumbo, this blend will take it to another level.

MAKES ABOUT 1 CUP/54 GRAMS

Scant ½ cup/15 grams crushed dried oregano, ground
2 tablespoons/10 grams dried garlic slices, coarsely ground
1⅓ tablespoons/10 grams dried onion slices, coarsely ground
1 tablespoon/10 grams ground sweet pimentón
½ tablespoon/3 grams dried thyme leaves, ground
1 teaspoon/3 grams cayenne powder
½ teaspoon/3 grams fine sea salt

CHAI

Traditionally made to enhance the popular Indian milk-based spiced black tea, this version of the blend, which is made without cloves or fennel seeds, takes on a whole new life when used to season meat and vegetable dishes, or even desserts.

MAKES ABOUT ⅓ CUP/27 GRAMS

1½ tablespoons/10 grams green cardamom, toasted and ground
½ tablespoon/5 grams black peppercorns, ground
½ tablespoon/3 grams dried black tea leaves, ground
½ tablespoon/3 grams ground cinnamon, preferably cassia
½ tablespoon/3 grams ground ginger
1 teaspoon/3 grams fennel seeds, toasted and ground

CHINESE FIVE-SPICE POWDER

Traditionally used for pork, duck, chicken, and seafood, my take on the blend substitutes fennel seeds with sweeter green anise seeds. It is also great for baking and stirring into soups for a warm, floral taste. You'll notice there are six spices instead of five; I added a bit of chamomile to give desserts a floral element.

MAKES ABOUT ½ CUP/36 GRAMS

3 tablespoons/10 grams star anise, ground
2½ tablespoons/15 grams green anise seeds, ground
2 tablespoons/2 grams dried chamomile flowers, ground
½ tablespoon/3 grams ground cinnamon, preferably cassia
½ tablespoon/3 grams cloves, ground
½ tablespoon/3 grams Sichuan pepper, ground

DUKKAH

This lighter version of the Egyptian spice blend or condiment is made without paprika, with fewer nuts, and with the addition of dry mint. Although traditionally used for dips and spreads, it works just as well with roasted fish, pasta dishes, and salads. Because it contains ground nuts, it should be used quickly to avoid oxidation.

MAKES ABOUT ⅔ CUP/63 GRAMS

2 tablespoons/15 grams whole hazelnuts, toasted and coarsely ground
3 tablespoons/15 grams dried coriander seeds, toasted and coarsely ground
1½ tablespoons/15 grams white sesame seeds, toasted and coarsely ground
1½ tablespoons/10 grams cumin, toasted and ground
1½ tablespoons/5 grams crushed dried mint
½ tablespoon/3 grams dried thyme leaves, ground

GARAM MASALA

Its name, meaning "hot spice blend," is not only a tribute to its quantity of black pepper, but also speaks to the collection of warm spices that meld together for an unmistakable flavor. Traditionally used in both northern and southern India, this floral and savory blend pairs well with vegetables, soups, stews, and grilled meats. I've replaced sweet cinnamon with fragrant ginger for a twist on this classic.

MAKES ABOUT ¼ CUP/33 GRAMS

1 tablespoon/10 grams black peppercorns, ground
1 tablespoon/5 grams ground ginger
½ tablespoon/5 grams ground mace
2½ teaspoons/5 grams cloves, ground
½ tablespoon/3 grams cumin seeds, toasted and ground
3 pods/3 grams black cardamom pods and seeds, ground
10 leaves/2 grams dried bay leaves, ground

JERK

The main components of this traditional tropical Jamaican blend are allspice and fiery Scotch bonnet peppers. This dry version of the recipe calls for ground chipotle to give it the heat component with a light smoky note. It is known for its use as a fragrant rub or marinade for slow cooking or smoking pork or chicken, but it would also work wonders on seafood and vegetables.

MAKES ABOUT 1 CUP/55 GRAMS

Scant ½ cup/5 grams light brown sugar
3½ tablespoons/20 grams allspice berries, ground
1 tablespoon/5 grams dried garlic slices, ground ◗➤

½ tablespoon/5 grams ground chipotle
2½ teaspoons/5 grams clove, ground
½ tablespoon/3 grams ground ginger
1 teaspoon/2 grams dried thyme leaves, coarsely ground

MADRAS CURRY

English merchants named this dark orange-red curry blend for the south Indian town of the same name. Its savory notes and balanced heat pair well with fish, meat, seafood, or vegetable dishes. I added curry leaves for their fresh, herbaceous flavors to cut an otherwise heavy blend. A bit of Vietnamese cinnamon makes it more floral and sweet scented as well.

MAKES ABOUT ¾ CUP/36 GRAMS

½ cup/2 grams dried curry leaves, ground
2½ tablespoons/5 grams cumin seeds, toasted and ground
2 tablespoons/10 grams coriander seeds, toasted and ground
1 tablespoon/10 grams ground turmeric
1⅓ teaspoons/4 grams green cardamom pods, toasted and ground
1 teaspoon/3 grams fenugreek seeds, toasted and ground
1 teaspoon/2 grams ground cinnamon, preferably Vietnamese

MULLED WINE SPICE

Typically infused in warm wine or other spirits and served hot during the winter and holiday seasons, this iteration, with sharp, floral cardamom and vanilla notes from long pepper, is also nice in braised meats, roasted root vegetables, and desserts.

MAKES ABOUT ⅓ CUP/44 GRAMS

2 sticks/10 grams cinnamon sticks, preferably Sri Lanka soft stick, coarsely ground
3 whole/3 grams long pepper, ground
1½ tablespoons/10 grams cloves, coarsely ground
1 tablespoon/5 grams allspice berries, coarsely ground
½ tablespoon/5 grams granulated dried orange peel
1½ heaping teaspoons/5 grams green cardamom pods and seeds, toasted and ground
½ tablespoon/3 grams ground ginger
1 teaspoon/3 grams freshly grated nutmeg

PICKLING SPICE

While most pickling recipes call for whole spices, I find it interesting to grind them so that you can eat the spices along with what is being pickled. I added pine-scented juniper berries, which are not usually found in brines, and amchoor, which gives this blend an acidity that expands its usage beyond pickling. Try adding this to the brine for quick pickled carrots, cucumbers, or cauliflower or use it to perk up fish and seafood.

MAKES ABOUT ½ CUP/51 GRAMS

¼ cup/3 grams dried bay leaves, ground
2 tablespoons/20 grams yellow mustard seeds, coarsely ground
1½ tablespoons/10 grams fennel seeds, toasted and coarsely ground
1 tablespoon/5 grams green peppercorns, coarsely ground
1 tablespoon/5 grams dried sliced garlic, ground
½ tablespoon/5 grams ground amchoor
1 teaspoon/3 grams juniper berries, ground

QUATRE ÉPICES

Traditionally used to season terrines, sausages, and charcuterie, this French blend enhances dairy products and roasted vegetables with a complex, peppery heat. In my version of the blend, I use white and green peppercorns instead of black for a sour note, citrusy mace in place of nutmeg, and replace ginger with galangal for a floral, sharp scent.

MAKES ABOUT ¼ CUP/17 GRAMS

½ tablespoon/5 grams white peppercorns, ground
1 tablespoon/5 grams green peppercorns, ground
½ tablespoon/3 grams cloves, ground
1 teaspoon/2 grams freshly grated nutmeg or ground mace
1 teaspoon/2 grams ground galangal or ginger

RAS EL HANOUT

The traditional Moroccan or North African blend, its name meaning "head of the shop," is a collection of spices that are the pride and glory of the store. This simplified version, made without paprika and turmeric, gets its complexity from cubeb's pine notes, which offset the sweetness of cinnamon and the savory notes of cumin. There are endless variations, but this recipe works particularly well with poultry, vegetables, grains, and even salads.

MAKES ABOUT ½ CUP/42 GRAMS ◆➤

2 sticks/10 grams ground cinnamon, preferably soft stick
1½ tablespoons/10 grams cumin seeds, toasted and ground
1½ tablespoons/4 grams rose buds or leaves, ground
1 tablespoon/5 grams cubeb berries, ground
1 tablespoon/5 grams allspice berries, ground
2½ teaspoons/5 grams clove, ground
½ tablespoon/3 grams dried thyme leaves, ground

SATÉ

Saté, or satay, usually refers to marinated meat or seafood skewers that are grilled and served with a peanut sauce or other spices. You can use this variation, which has a lot of lemongrass and only a bit of cumin, both for the marinade and the sauce—just add coconut, peanut butter, and lime juice—as well as for grilled vegetables or noodle dishes.

MAKES ABOUT ½ CUP/37 GRAMS

2 tablespoons/10 grams ground lemongrass
1 tablespoon/8 grams ground turmeric
1 tablespoon/5 grams ground ginger
1 tablespoon/5 grams dried sliced garlic, ground
1 tablespoon/5 grams coriander seeds, toasted and ground
½ tablespoon/3 grams cumin seeds, toasted and ground
Scant ½ teaspoon/1 gram cayenne powder

TANDOORI

This blend has long been used for marinating (together with yogurt) or seasoning dishes, particularly chicken, to be cooked at high heat in a tandoor clay oven. You can enjoy this iteration with meat roasts, whole fish, soups, and stews with or without the traditional oven.

MAKES ABOUT ½ CUP/48 GRAMS

2½ tablespoons/5 grams cumin seeds, toasted and ground
2 tablespoons/15 grams ground sweet paprika
1 tablespoon/5 grams coriander seeds, toasted and ground
1 tablespoon/5 grams ground ginger
1 tablespoon/5 grams dried sliced garlic, ground
½ tablespoon/5 grams dried sliced onion, ground
½ tablespoon/3 grams ground cinnamon, preferably Vietnamese
1 teaspoon/3 grams black peppercorns, ground
Scant ¾ teaspoon/2 grams cayenne powder

ACKNOWLEDGMENTS

This book is one of many milestones in my long journey of food discovery, spice hunting, and life exploration. This is not one man's adventure, but rather one that is shared with family, friends, and partners who all partake in a passion for everything tasty, exciting, and inspirational. It is the result of more than thirty years of travels, encounters, stories, and long hours in front of the stove. It is a summary of thousands of meals—both good and bad—many bottles of wine, and, beyond that, priceless moments with loved ones. I want to thank all of those who believe in this mission and for the good and bad advice that allows me to be better at what I do.

Thank you to my parents for their free spirits without boundaries. To my wife, Lisa, for her ongoing support in my crazy lifestyle. My sons, Luca and Lennon, for the joy they bring. My sisters, Shelly and Iris. Susan and Gary Fisher, for their help and support. The whole team at La Boîte, for the long hours of work. The magical photography of Thomas Schauer. The inspirational writing of Jaime Gottlieb. Christine Fischer, for the design. Nadine Westcott, for the fantastic illustrations. Rica Allannic, Aaron Wehner, Marysarah Quinn, Terry Deal, Kim Tyner, and Doris Cooper, at Clarkson Potter, for creating this beautiful book. Michael Solomonov, for the friendship; Ana Sortun, Marc Forgione, David Malbequi, Cyrille Allannic, Justin Smillie, Paul Kahan, Jim Meehan, Garret Oliver, Laurent Tourendel, Helen Park, Gil Frank, Apollonia Poilane, Michelle Bernstein, Gail Simmons, Brad Farmerie. Olivier Roellinger, for the foreword. Eric Ripert, for his friendship and inspiration. Daniel Boulud, for his mentorship. Amanda Zaslow and Joe Moseley, for opening their home to us for the photo shoots. Eitan Shapira, for the recipe testing. Kate Krader and Dana Cowin from *Food & Wine,* for their ongoing love. To Jeremy Flowers, all our spice partners and clients, Marco Polo, Vasco da Gama, and all of the explorers who sailed the seas. Pierre Poivre and everyone I did not forget but just did not mention. I am eternally grateful.

For the love of spices,

Lior

INDEX

A

achiote (annatto), 56–57
African flavors, 186–87, 224–25
    see also North African flavors; West African flavors
ajowan, 40–41
Albius blend, 283
Aleppo, 42–43
allspice, 44–45
Anardana (pomegranate), 226
amchoor, 46–47
ancho, 50–51
anise, 54–55
Anisette blend, 55
annatto (achiote), 56–57
Apium blend, 87
Apollo blend, 67
apples, 99, 101, 111, 214
apricots, 89, 169, 231, 239, 293
Ar-Ar blend, 153
arctic char, 159, 269
artichokes, 69, 139, 217
arugula pesto, 29
asafoetida, 58–59
asparagus, 71, 289
avocado, 205, 243, 247, 255, 269, 287
    dips and spreads, 47, 147
Azafran blend, 239

B

bacon slices, glazing, 83
Badiane blend, 257
Bahārāt blend, 296
Bahar blend, 45
Bahia blend, 221
banana bread, 137
Bandora blend, 273
barberry, 60–61
barley risotto, 175
basil, 62–63
Basilicum blend, 63
Basque blend, 123
bass, 67, 173, 221
bay, 66–67
béarnaise sauce, 159
béchamel sauce, 105
beef, 143, 253

broth, 69, 175
    roast, 109, 129, 175
    short ribs, 171
    steak, 57, 212
beets, 77, 119, 145, 243
    borscht, 143, 257
Bellini cocktail, 221
Bengali flavors, 186–89
Berbere blend, 296
Biber blend, 43
bird's eye chile, 68–69
biscuits, 267, 291
Black & Yellow blend, 111
blending spices, 16–17, 29–32
Bloody Mary, 273
bok choy, 69
borscht, 143, 257
branzino, 63, 137, 169, 213
bread:
    crumbs, seasoned, 205
    cubes or croutons, 145, 191
    pita, grilled, 279
    see also flatbreads
broccoli, 97
broccoli rabe, 167, 189
Brussels sprouts, 73, 99, 139, 173, 185
bulgur, 199
Bustan blend, 295
butters, compound, 212, 267
buying spices, 26–27, 33

C

cabbage, 101
    leaves, stuffed, 241
    red, 81, 153, 203, 241
Cajun blend, 296
Calabreze blend, 217
Calabrian chile (pepperoncini), 216–17
calamari, 43, 293
calamint, 70–71
Canela blend, 99
cantaloupe, 69, 165
caraway, 72–73
cardamom:
    black, 72–73
    green and white, 76–77
carrot(s):
    pickled, 298
    puréed, 123, 171
    roasted, 109, 153
    salad, 73, 111, 187, 197, 253, 257

cascabel, 80–81
cassia, 98–99
catfish, fried, condiment for, 249
cauliflower:
    pickled, 237, 298
    roasted, 61, 83, 121, 171
cayenne pepper, 82–83
Cedvar blend, 293
celery (seeds), 86–87
celery root:
    puréed, 87, 119
    roasted, 169, 195, 243, 251
Central American flavors, 42–45, 120–21, 140–41
Cepa blend, 93
cereals, 221, 283
Chai blend, 296
chamomile, 88–89
cheddar cheese, 119, 239, 275
cheese biscuits, 291
cheese sticks or straws, 119, 253, 275
cherries, 129, 179, 247
chicken:
    cutlets, breading for, 125, 133
    fried, 91, 133, 225
    grilled or roasted, 81, 115, 133, 219, 235
    salad, 119, 143, 255
    sliders, 161
    soup, 47
    stock, seasoned, 73, 89, 141, 183, 195, 231, 273, 275, 289
chickpeas, 97, 123, 203
Chihuahua blend, 91
chiles:
    Aleppo, 42–43
    ancho, 50–51
    bird's eye, 68–69
    cascabel, 80–81
    cayenne pepper, 82–83
    chipotle, 90–91
    espelette, 122–23
    guajillo, 138–39
    jalapeño, 146–47
    pepperoncini (Calabrian chile), 216–17
    piri piri, 224–25
    see also pepper(s)
Chinese Five-Spice Powder blend, 296

Chinese flavors, 150–51, 254–57
chipotle, 90–91
chives, 92–93
chocolate, 179, 247, 279, 295, 297
    mousse or pudding, 45
    white, garnishes, 231
chutneys, 59, 257, 283
cilantro, 96–97
Cilantro Verde blend, 97
cinnamon, soft stick, cassia, or Vietnamese, 98–99
Citron blend, 167
clams, 175, 213
cloves, 100–101
cocktails, 83, 101, 123, 131, 141, 155, 221, 227, 257, 269, 273, 293, 295
    coating glass rims, 147, 263
cocktail sauce, 83
cod, 219, 239, 275
coffee drinks, 283
coleslaw, 135
collard greens, 139, 279
Combava blend, 155
cookies, 183, 235, 247
coriander, 102–3
corn, 41, 91, 247
    chowder, 121, 293
Cornish hens, roast, 291
Cousbara blend, 103
couscous, 89, 109
crab, 147, 195
cranberry chutney, 257
cream cheese, seasoning, 55, 287
crepes, 173
croissants, 271
croutons, 145
crudité dips, 87, 109, 147, 189, 212
cubeb, 104–5
cucumber(s), 169
    grilled, and goat cheese salad, 205
    pickled, 41, 298
cumin, 108–9
    black (kala jeera), 110–11
Curcuma blend, 275
curry leaves, 114–15

D

daikon radish, 141
Daisy blend, 89
Daruma-Mazuma blend, 287
dessert sauces and toppings, 89, 151, 171, 231, 239, 279
Dhania (coriander), 102
dill, 118–19
dressings, 45, 57, 61, 97, 111, 139, 151, 153, 159, 167, 185, 191, 199, 205, 219, 275, 287
    vinaigrettes, 51, 115, 253, 273
drying your own herbs, 33
duck, 219, 269
    breast, sliced, 103, 105, 129
    confit, 235
    roast, 135, 155, 185, 203, 257
Dukkah blend, 297

E

egg(s):
    deviled, 51
    French toast, 135
    frittatas, 215, 251
    omelets, 67, 111
    salad, 175
    shakshuka, 91
eggplant, 41, 97, 237, 275
    braised in coconut milk, 115
    soup, 155
endive, 214, 229, 293
epazote, 120–21
espelette, 122–23
Estrago blend, 267
Ethiopian flavors, 172–73

F

farro, 231
fava beans, 147, 189
fennel (seeds), 124–25
fennel bulb, sautéed, 217
fenugreek, 128–29
Ferula blend, 59, 125
feta cheese, 59, 93, 111, 119, 183, 199, 251
    spread, 63

watermelon and, 147, 221
    whipped, 41, 189, 253
figs, 157, 181, 193, 249, 261, 271
flatbreads, 199, 229, 237
    see also pizza
flounder, 165
fluke ceviche, 225
French flavors, 122–23, 156–57, 266–67, 270–71, 298
French toast, 135
frittatas, 215, 251
fritters, 59, 279, 291

G

Gala blend, 131
galangal, 130–31
Garam Masala blend, 297
garlic, 41, 132–33
ginger, 134–35
gnocchi, 171, 203, 241, 295
goat cheese, 71, 103, 181, 205, 295
Gorgonzola cheese, 229
grains of paradise, 136–37
granola, 221, 255
grape leaves, stuffed, 231
grapes, 215, 295
Gravlax blend, 77
Greek flavors, 178–79, 182–83, 184–85, 198–99
green beans, 77, 155, 261
green goddess dressing, 205
Green to Red blend, 47
grilled cheese sandwiches, 191
grinding spices, 31
ground vs. whole spices, 27
guajillo, 138–39
Guiana blend, 83
guinea hens, 185, 191
Gujarat blend, 41
Gul Rang blend, 237

H

haddock rillettes, 93
halibut, 61, 75, 295
halloumi cheese, 199
ham, 225, 293
hamachi crudo, 183, 221, 263

hibiscus blossom, 140–41
horseradish, 142–43
hummus, 97, 203
Hungarian flavors, 202–3
hyssop, 144–45

I

ice cubes, flavored, 83
Indian flavors, 40–41, 46–47, 58–59, 74–75, 108–11, 114–15, 128–29, 172–73, 186–89, 262–63, 274–75, 297, 298
Indonesian flavors, 100–101, 104–5, 172–73
Italian flavors, 70–71, 216–17

J

jalapeño, 146–47
    dried, smoked (chipotle), 90–91
Japanese flavors, 246–47, 286–87
jasmine flower, 150–51
Java blend, 103
Jerk blend, 297
jicama, 87
Joon blend, 195
juniper, 152–53

K

kaffir lime, 154–55
kala jeera (black cumin), 110–11
kale fritters, 279
Kampot blend, 213
Ketazh blend, 189
Kinome blend, 247
kohlrabi salad, 289
Komino blend, 109

L

lamb, 75, 169, 215
    kebabs, 43, 227, 279
    marinades and rubs for, 59, 101, 109, 121, 133, 167, 197, 271
    meatballs, 99, 183
Latin American flavors, 108–9, 224–25
    see also Central American

flavors; Mexican flavors
latkes, potato, 145
Lavandou blend, 157
lavender, 156–57
La Vera blend, 219
leeks, 59, 167
lemonade, 43
lemon balm, 158–59
lemon desserts, 151, 283
lemongrass, 160–61
lemon myrtle, 164–65
lemon peel, 166–67
lemon thyme, 270–71
lemon verbena, 168–69
lentils, 55, 187, 195, 227
licorice, 170–71
lime:
    kaffir, 154–55
    Omani, 194–95
    Limon Omani (Omani Lime), 195
Limonit blend, 161
Little Bell blend, 81
Little Bird blend, 69
Little Gourd blend, 139
Liveche blend, 175
lobster, 89, 151, 287
long pepper, 172–73
Louisa blend, 169
lovage, 174–75
Lucknow, 124–25

M

macaroni and cheese, 143
mace, 192–93
Madras Curry blend, 297
mahlab, 178–79
Malguetta blend, 137
Maluku blend, 101
mangoes, 43, 77, 161, 229
mango powder (amchoor), 46–47
maple syrup, flavored, 83, 221, 255
Marjolaine blend, 181
marjoram, 180–81
marmalade, 131, 241
martini, 131
Marva blend, 241
mascarpone cheese, 183, 247, 261
Mashia blend, 193
mastic, 182–83
measuring spices, 30

medicinal uses, 21, 40, 76, 108, 110, 128, 132, 152, 156, 158, 170, 172, 196, 274, 292, 294

Mediterranean flavors, 52–53, 66–67, 70–71, 124–25, 128–29, 180–83, 198–99, 234–35, 238–39, 260–61, 294–95

Melissa blend, 159

Methi blend, 129

Mexican flavors, 50–51, 56–57, 80–81, 90–91, 108–9, 120–21, 138–39, 146–47, 198–99

Middle Eastern flavors, 42–43, 108–9, 128–29, 134–37, 178–79, 184–85, 188–89, 194–95, 290–91

milk shakes, spiced, 173

mimosas, 155

mint, 184–85

mole sauce, 75

Mulled Wine Spice blend, 297

Muntok (white pepper), 209

Muraya blend, 115

mushrooms, 139, 213, 237, 287

    porcini, 71, 217

    portobello, 63, 75, 159

    sautéed, 93, 125, 133, 217

mussel and clam stew, 175

mustard, 186–87

N

Na'ana blend, 185

Nanglo blend, 75

New Filé blend, 249

nigella, 188–89

ñora pepper, 190–91

North African flavors, 72–73, 104–5, 128–29, 136–37, 172–73, 182–83, 184–85, 274–75, 296, 298

nutmeg, 192–93

O

oats and oatmeal, 179, 197

octopus, 263

Og blend, 261

okra, 293

Omani lime, 194–95

omelets, 67, 111

onions, 67, 75, 187, 193, 295

orange peel, 196–97

oranges, 71, 105, 129, 131, 137, 155

oregano, 198–99

    za'atar, 290–91

organic spices, 33

P

Paico blend, 121

pancakes, 41

    condiments for, 151, 221, 227

    potato, 59, 145

paprika, 202–3

    Spanish (pimentón), 218–19

Paprikash blend, 203

parsley, 204–5

parsnips, 93, 135, 235

Pasha blend, 279

pasta, 69, 71, 93, 133, 147, 181, 185, 197, 212, 213, 273

    cooking in seasoned water, 67, 237

    fettuccine, 71, 193, 267

    fresh, seasoning dough for, 167

    gnocchi, 171, 203, 241, 295

    penne, 93, 99, 199

    ravioli, 139, 263

    salad, 87, 291

peaches, 75, 212

peanuts, spicy, 81

pears, 131, 141, 171, 227, 283

peas, puréed, 73

Penja blend, 214

Pepe Verde blend, 215

pepper(berries):

    pink, 220–21

    Sichuan, 254–55

    Tasmanian, 268–69

pepper(corns), 208–15

    black, 212

    green, 209, 213

    red, 209, 214

    white, 209, 215

pepper(s):

    cubeb, 104–5

    long, 172–73

    ñora, 190–91

    see also chiles

pepperoncini (Calabrian chile), 216–17

Pereg blend, 229

Persian flavors, 60–61, 194–95, 226–27, 238–39

Petruzilia blend, 205

Pickling Spice blend, 298

piecrust dough, 55

Pilpel blend, 212

pimentón (Spanish paprika), 218–19

pineapple, 59, 131, 161, 255, 269

pink pepper, 220–21

Pippali blend, 173

piri piri, 224–25

pizza, 133, 181, 198, 229

    sticks, 273

plums, ricotta toasts with, 217

Poivre, Pierre, 18, 100

Poivre d'Ane blend, 145

polenta, 199, 235, 239

pomegranate, 226–27

popcorn, 255

poppy, 228–29

pork, 125, 161, 193

    butt, 215, 273

    chops, 61, 73, 101, 195, 271

    condiments for, 51, 61, 73, 101, 131

    cutlets, breading for, 133, 197

    ground, 91, 97, 241

    loin, 131, 161, 283

    meatballs, 97

    shoulder, 45, 269

Portuguese flavors, 108–9, 224–25

potato(es):

    boiled, 87, 214, 275

    frittata, 251

    gnocchi, 171, 203, 241, 295

    gratin, 239

    pancakes, 59, 145

    patties, 41

    puréed, 63, 235, 267

    roast, 135, 137

    salad, 61, 229

    salted cod and, 239

    samosas, 205

pound cake, 157, 295

Puebla blend, 51

puff pastry, 119, 253, 275

Pumpernickel blend, 73

Q

Quatre Épices blend, 298

R

rabbit legs, braised, 249

radicchio, grilled, 261

radishes, 55, 111, 141, 214, 217, 287, 289

Raifort blend, 143

Ras el Hanout blend, 298

Rashad blend, 289

ratatouille, 91

ravioli, 139, 263

red bean purée, 51

Red Devil blend, 225

red wine, 45, 231

    mulling spice for, 297

rice, 185, 191, 195, 231, 241, 289

    salad, 197, 214

ricotta cheese, 71, 157, 159, 179, 213, 217, 263

    fritters, 59, 279, 291

Rigani blend, 199

Rimon blend, 227

roasting spices, 30–31

Rojo blend, 57

Romani blend, 235

rose, 230–31

Rose Mallow blend, 141

rosemary, 234–35

roux, seasoned, 249

S

safflower, 236–37

saffron, 238–39

sage, 240–41

salad dressings, *see* dressings

salad toppings, 103, 191, 291

Sal blend, 243

salmon, 169, 247, 271

    confit, 239

    gravlax-style cured, 77

    poached, 237, 269

    raw, 243, 253

    rillettes, 93

    smoked, or lox, 55, 255, 287

salsas, 51, 229

salt, 242–43

samosas, potato, 205

sanitizing spices, 24, 25

sanshō, 246–47

Sar blend, 251
sardines, 205, 251, 261
Sarso blend, 187
sassafras, 248–49
satay sauce, 173, 298
Saté blend, 298
savory, 250–51
scallop(s):
    carpaccio, 279
    seared, 105, 155, 159, 161,
      214, 295
scones, 101, 157
sesame, 252–53
Shamir blend, 119
shandy, beer and lemonade,
    227
Shoum blend, 133
shrimp, 119
    grilled or sautéed, 111, 267
    poached, 77, 151, 213, 267
    salad, 161, 175, 291
    tacos, 247
Sichuan pepper, 254–55
Siena blend, 71
smoothies, 275, 283
snapper, 115, 131, 161
soba noodle salad, 105
Soom Soom blend, 253
sourcing spices, 23–27
South Asian flavors, 74–75,
    114–15
    see also Indian flavors
Southeast Asian flavors, 68–69,
    114–15, 130–31, 154–55,
    160–61, 256–57, 274–75,
    292–93, 298
Spanish flavors, 108–9, 190–91,
    218–19
**Spanish paprika (pimentón),
    218–19**
spinach, 59, 67, 121, 215
    salad, 103, 187, 287
squash, 171, 193
    butternut, 193, 215
    kabocha, 51, 99
    ravioli, 263
    soup, 47
star anise, 256–57
storing spices, 35–36
strawberries, 103, 111, 123,
    141, 255, 261
sumac, 260–61
sweet potatoes, 121, 129, 137,
    141, 165
Sweet Smoky Root blend, 171

Sweet Verbena blend, 165
Swiss chard, 291
swordfish skewers, 263

T

tacos:
    fish or shrimp, 121, 225, 247
    pork, 91
tamarind, 262–63
Tambali blend, 263
Tandoori blend, 298
tapenade, 181
Tapuz blend, 197
tarragon, 266–67
Tasman blend, 269
Tasmanian pepper, 268–69
Tears of Chios blend, 183
teas, 45, 129, 145
    Chai blend, 296
    iced, 75, 111
Tellicherry (black Pepper), 208
Thai flavors, 184–85
thyme, 270–71
Timin blend, 271
toasting spices, 30–31
toffee pudding, 115
tomato(es), 147, 199
    condiments, 51, 99, 181,
      283
    green, 283, 293
    grilled or roasted, 145, 213,
      227
    sauces, seasoned, 91, 197
tomato powder, 272–73
trail mix, 137
trout, 169
tuna, 125, 175, 189, 219, 261
    crudo, 183, 189, 263
    salad, 55, 189, 229
turkey, 153, 249, 251
Turkish flavors, 42–43, 128–29,
    178–79, 182–83, 260–61,
    278–79
turmeric, 274–75
turnip salad, 137, 181

U

Urfa, 278–79

V

Vadi blend, 291
Valencia blend, 191

vanilla, 282–83
veal stew, 143, 157, 193
venison, 241
Vered blend, 231
vinaigrettes, 51, 115, 253, 273
vodka, hibiscus-infused, 141

W

waffles, 45, 133, 183, 221, 243,
    261
Waldorf salad, 179
wasabi, 286–87
watercress, 288–89
watermelon, 184, 213
    and feta cheese, 147, 221
West African flavors, 136–37,
    140–41
wheat berries, 185, 195
white beans, 123, 217, 273, 289
whitefish salad, 73
White Flower blend, 151
whole vs. ground spices, 27
Wild Cherry blend, 179

Y

yogurt, 109, 169, 189, 255, 275
    dressings, 61, 111, 205
    flavorings for, 157, 179
    marinades, 59, 133, 185, 219

Z

za'atar, 290–91
Zangvil blend, 135
zedoary, 292–93
Zereshk blend, 61
Z-Pepper blend, 255
zucchini, 63, 125, 251, 289
zuta, 294–95

ICON KEY

 Beef

 Fruits

 Breakfast

 Grains

 Cheese

Lamb

Chicken

Legumes

 Cocktails

Mollusks

 Crustaceans

 Pasta

Deer

Pork

 Desserts

 Salad

Dressings

Sauces

 Drinks

Soup

 Duck

Veal

 Eggs

 Vegetables

Fish

CHRISTINE FISCHER

Christine Fischer is an art director, based in Zurich, Switzerland.
Growing up in Germany's Black Forest, she graduated from the University
of Design Schwäbisch Gmünd, Germany, one of the top design schools
in Germany. Her passion and sensibility for typography take part in
many book and editorial designs for German, Austrian, and Swiss clients.

JAIME GOTTLIEB

Jaime Gottlieb is an established food and travel writer and brand copywriter,
and the principal of Mighty Specs, a written communications company. She received
her bachelor of arts degree in creative writing at Florida State University and spent
the next several years as a journalist and copywriter. To further explore her passion and
elevate her experience in cooking and world cuisines, Gottlieb completed the Culinary
Techniques course at the French Culinary Institute in New York City. For ten years, she
has written for a number of notable brands across the food, spirits, entertainment, and
hospitality genres. Her projects have included works for Jim Beam Global, Tormaresca
Wines, Vera Bradley, American Express, FHM Online, Kimpton, the James Hotels,
Marriot, and Starwood Hotels and Resorts. In 2012, she had the pleasure of working
with Lior Lev Sercarz on his first book, *The Art of Blending*. Gottlieb currently
resides in Portland, Oregon, where, when she's not writing, her wife, son, dogs,
cat, and vegetable garden happily rule her life.

THOMAS SCHAUER

With more than twenty years in the business, Thomas Schauer is a world-renowned
and talented commercial director and food photographer. His passion for capturing
moments on film began at an early age. Growing up in his native Austria, Thomas
cultivated an artistic sensibility inspired by the aesthetics of European culture that
surrounded him. After obtaining his master's certificate in photography at the most
prestigious photography school in Austria, he opened a studio in Vienna and a second
in New York City. His commercial culinary work includes projects with Nespresso,
Uncle Ben's, Wegmans, and Papa John's. Chefs Dominique Ansel, Daniel Boulud,
David Bouley, and José Andrés have all had Thomas work on various cookbook projects,
and, just recently, Thomas won Best Photography (USA) for *Dominique Ansel:
The Secret Recipes*, by Dominique Ansel, at the prestigious Gourmand Awards (2015).

NADINE BERNARD WESTCOTT

Nadine Bernard Westcott is an internationally known illustrator and
author of more than one hundred children's books, including *Silly Milly*,
Peanut Butter and Jelly, and *I Know an Old Lady Who Swallowed a Fly*.
Her illustrations also appeared in a monthly column in *Gourmet* magazine for
several years. Nadine lives on Nantucket Island in Massachusetts and divides
her time among illustrating, painting, and designing her own line of fabrics.

FOR
THE
LOVE
OF
SPICES

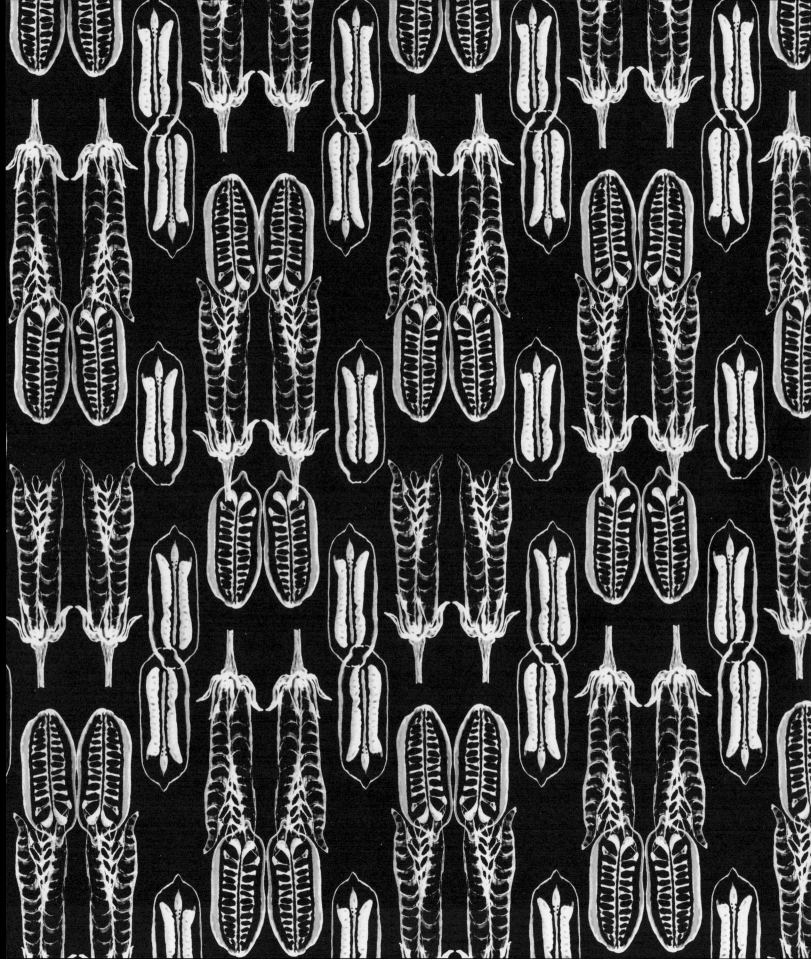